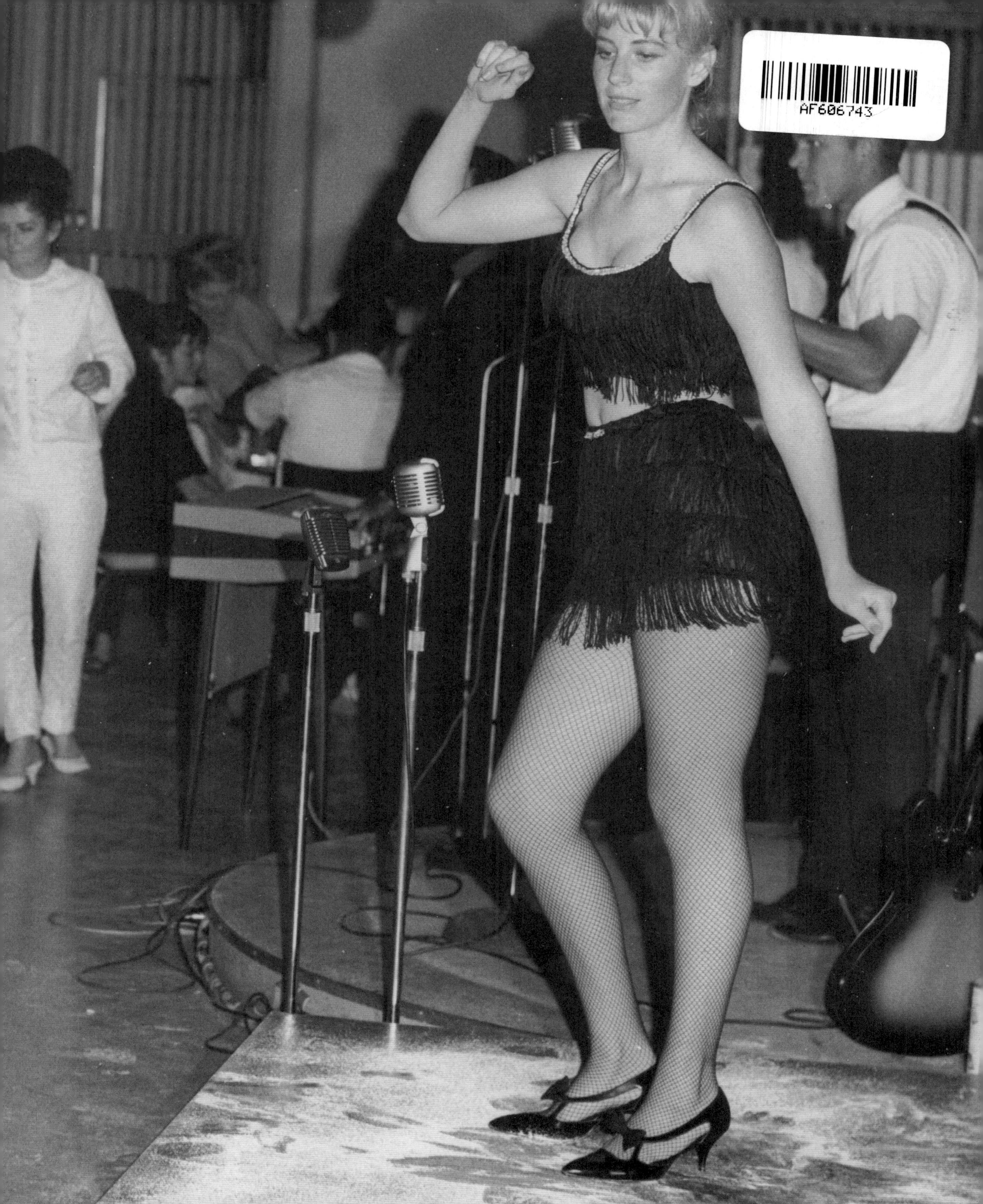

THE BIRTH of ROCK and ROLL

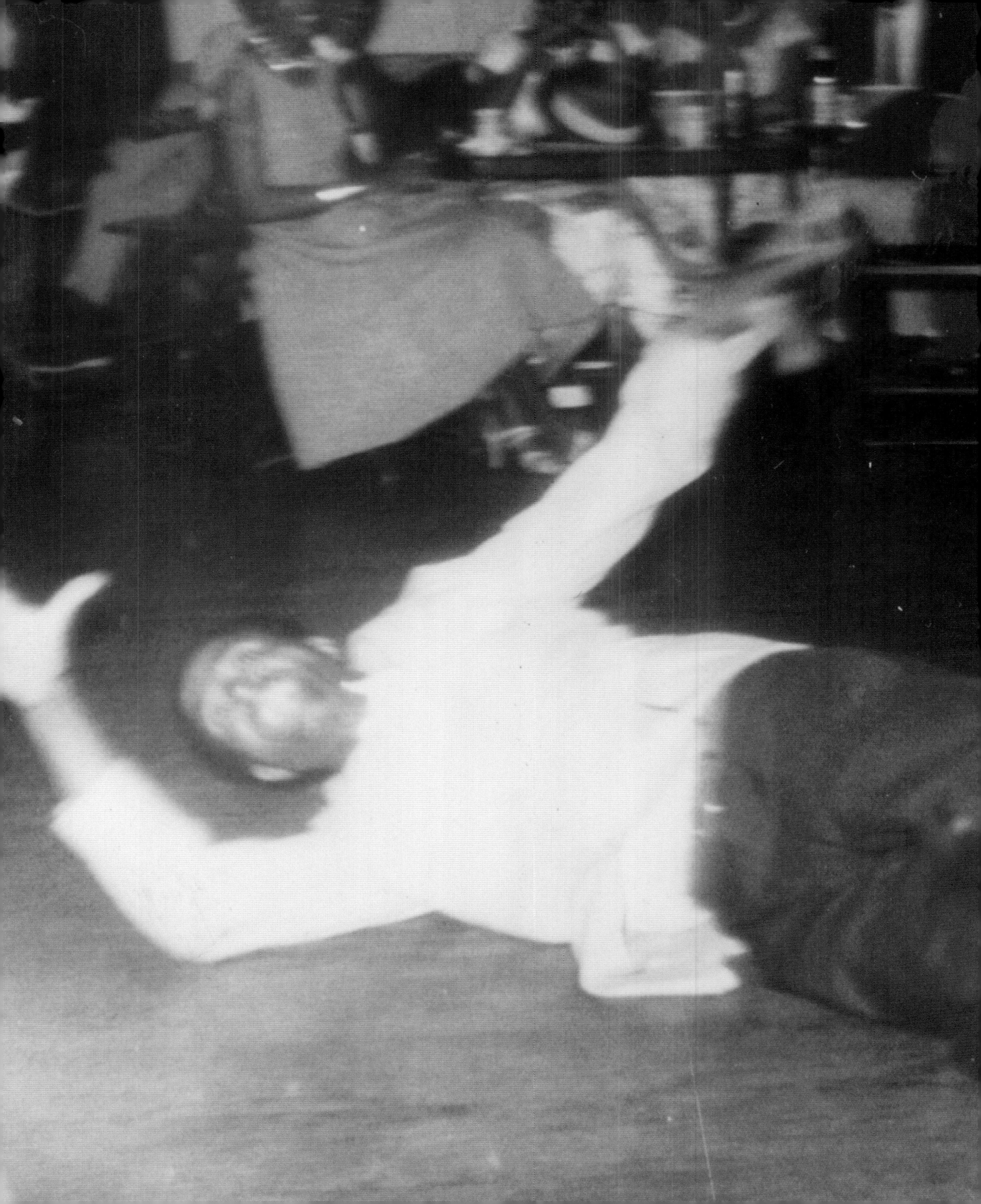

THE BIRTH of ROCK and ROLL

Photographs from the collection of Jim Linderman plus a conversation with Joe Bonomo

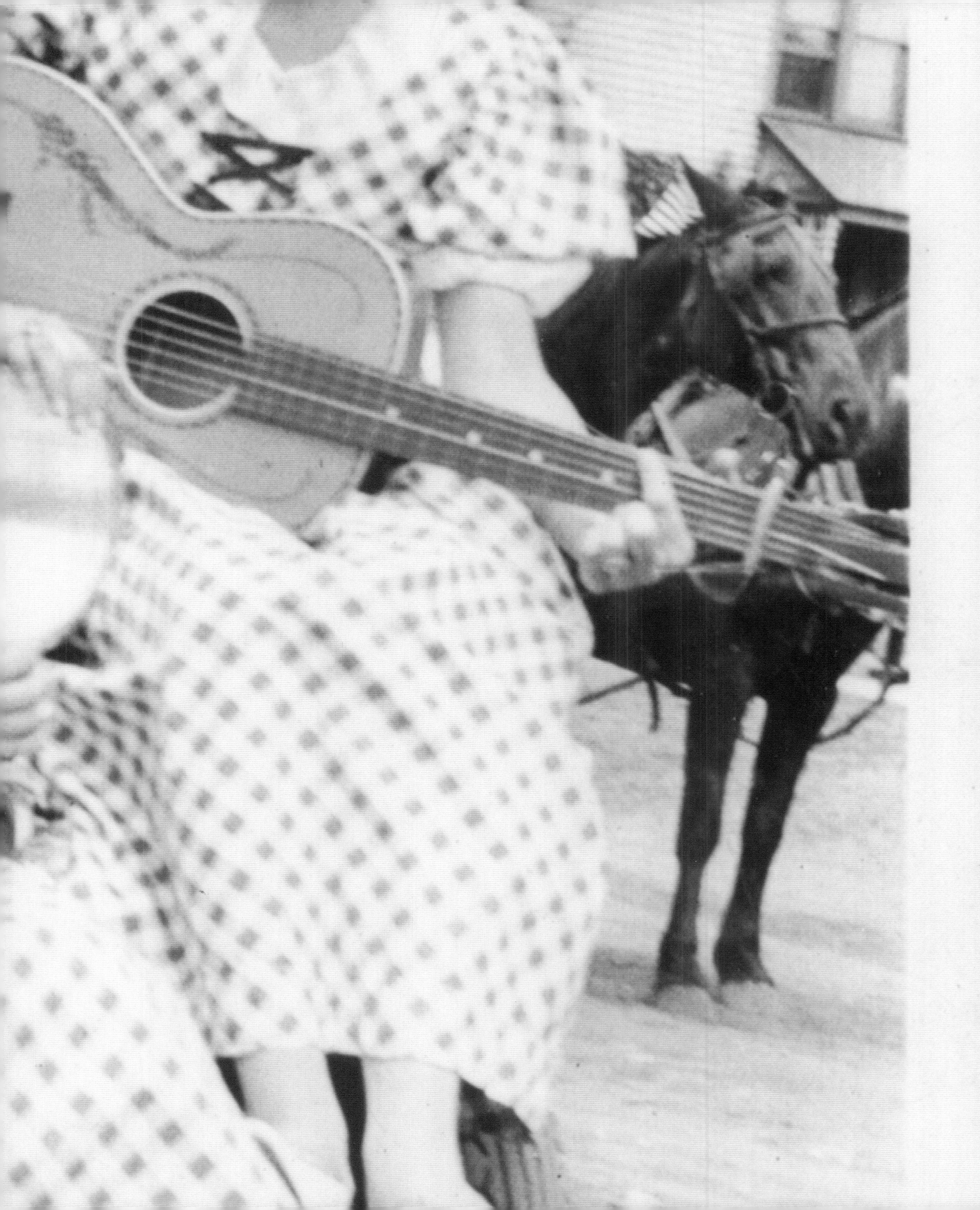

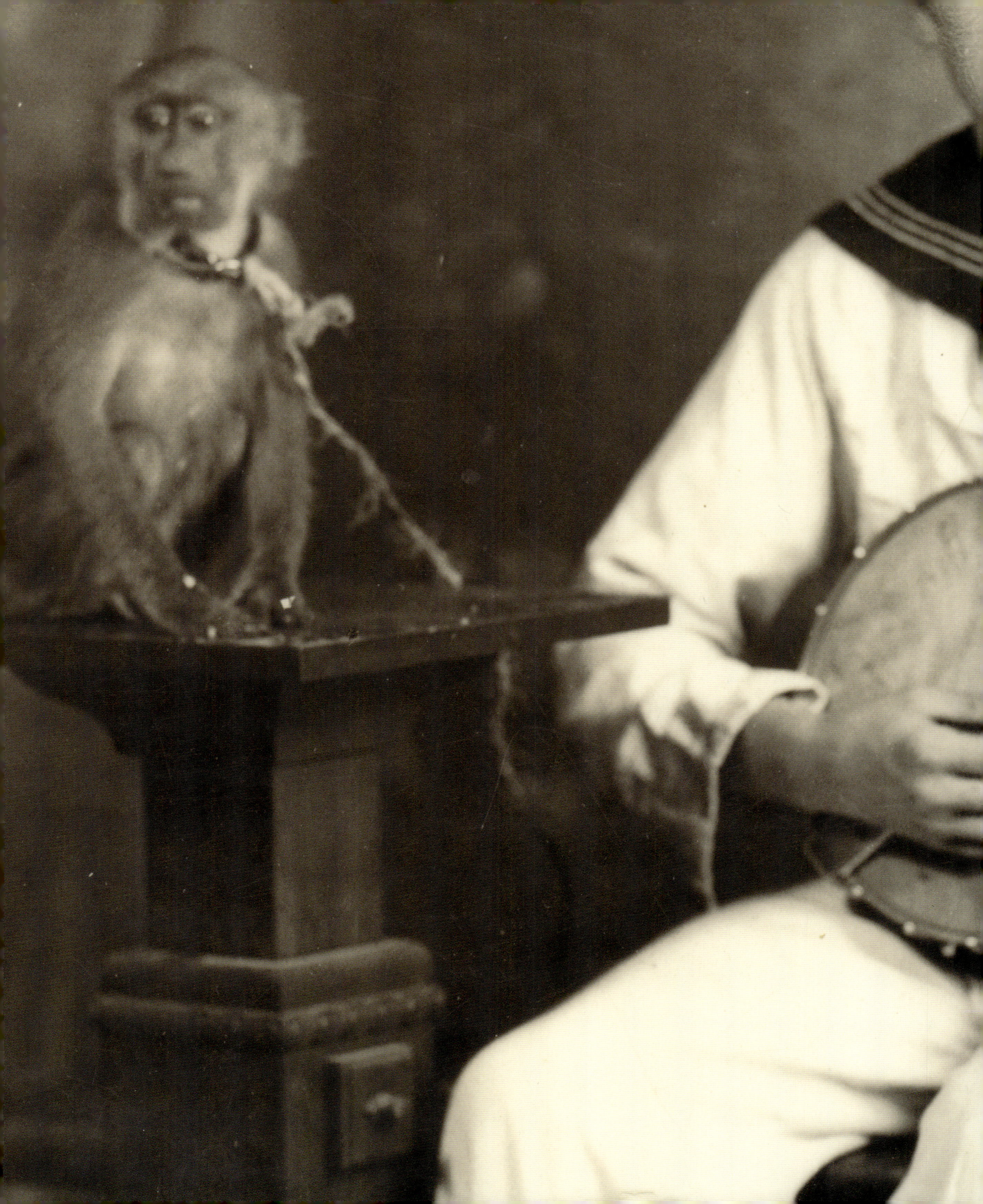

**We
think
our
lifetimes
last
a
long
time.**

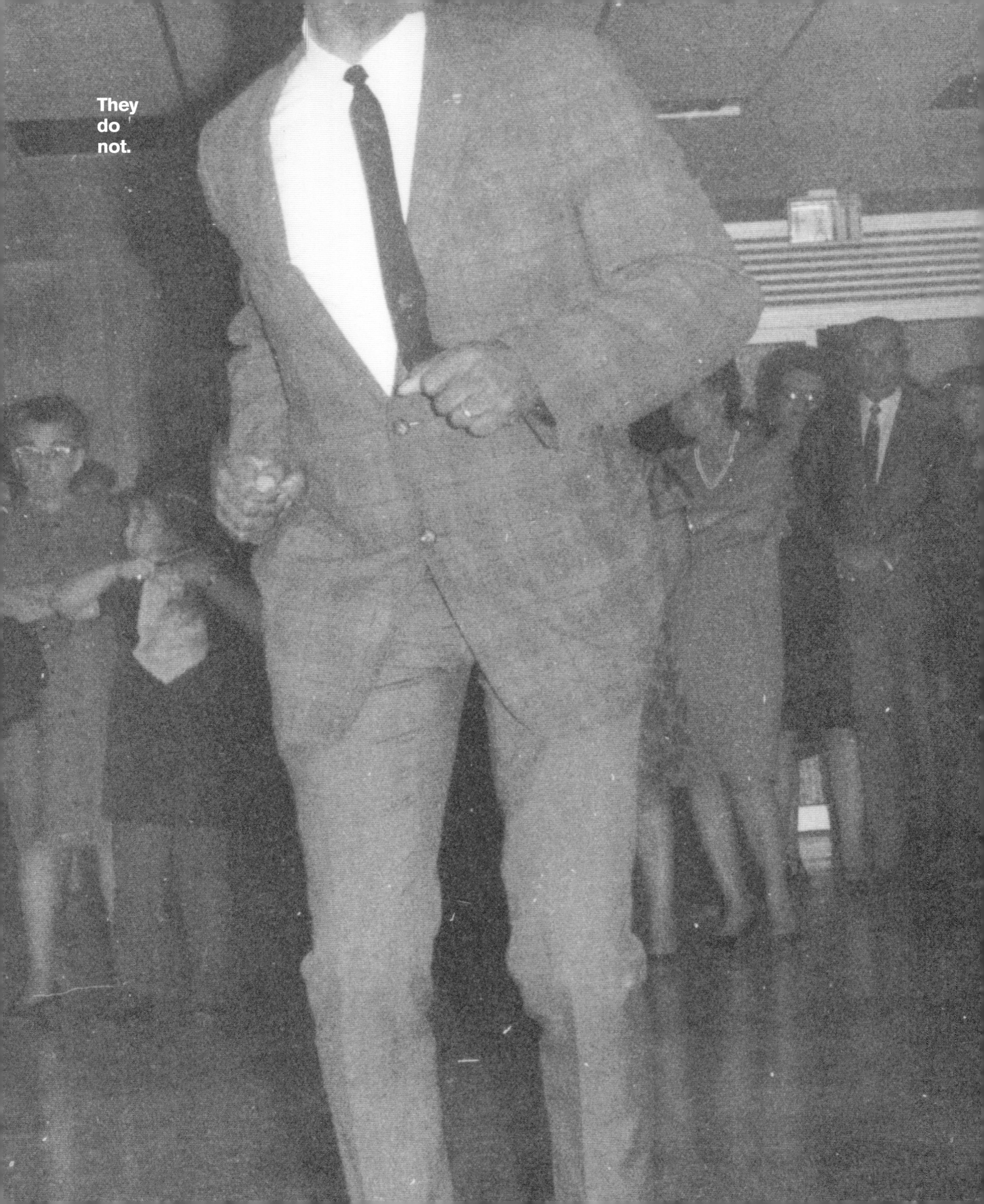

They
do
not.

We
think
our
lifetimes
last
a
long
time.

They
do
not.

We
think
what
has
happened
in
our
lifetime
is
significant
too,
but not really. On the contrary, we and the events we live through are brief blips. We celebrate the 50th anniversary of an event as though it was forever. Nope. The Beatles appeared on the Ed Sullivan Show 50 years ago? It is nothing in time really, though it must seem considerable to Sir Paul and Ringo.

An introduction
by
Jim Linderman

The entire span of Rock and Roll occurred in just one century out of millions of centuries, and it is now over. A tiny and brief stirring, a mere bump we passed on the road now well behind us. Royalties remain, songs change hands like soybean futures and a museum in Cleveland attempts to recreate the era like a sacred archeological dig. To kids, Rock and Roll is but the fundraiser week on PBS.

Hank Williams died the year I was born, and Elvis Presley made his first recordings a year later. The Beatles, the Rolling Stones, James Brown, you name one . . . they all were alive when ol' Hank propped his boots up on the back of his driver's front seat and died. Today, the Beatles and Rolling Stones are into their seventies, and James Brown is dead. Rock and Roll award shows scramble to find contemporary performers for reaction shots.

If you were also lucky enough to share my fortunate accident of being here when Rock and Roll came together . . . you will be able to name your own heroes.

When Keith Richards remembers the creators who influenced him, they were not only still alive, his band five years later opened for them. When the prized blues records from the United States arrived in England (those Keith wanted to nick from Mick) they were not reissues. They were N E W. The day Keith was born, Muddy Waters' only recordings were those laid down on a porch and then into a chunky disc recorder in Alan Lomax's automobile trunk. When Muddy (a man who would have been a Chief if his ancestors hadn't been enslaved) offhandedly referred to the Rolling Stones as his children, he literally could have sired them and made a young father. A mannish boy.

Recording techniques? Think how many times you have changed formats at home. They all came and went as fast as an advertising campaign, and today they are gone. The product is now back in a cloud . . . where it started. Notes heard and plucked from ether.

Michael Bloomfield played electric guitar at that mythic gig when Bob Dylan went electric, "way back when" but not long before Mike had traveled and gotten drunk with Big Joe Williams. Big Joe "went electric" in his own way ten years before Bob. He hung beer cans and a pie plate over the grill of his amplifier to invent the fuzz tone while Bloomfield watched. Scholars might call that a kind of distorted "masking" of sorts. A technique going back to Africa, but to Big Joe it just sounded cool and made people dance. A few years after that, Dylan's first recordings were B A C K I N G Big Joe Williams and Victoria Spivey, another ancient blues phantom and innovator who was still alive when we were. Bob put his photo of them on the back of an LP once to prove it. Big Joe Williams. Minstrel musician, work camp performer, Jug band member and rock and roll innovator lived until 1982.

Roots music has very short roots, and they all "went electric" because they could. Simply to be heard over the din of a Juke. So few could talk and hear, but all could dance. Which in turn sold drinks and led to back seat rumblings of another sort.

Several forces combined in one century to create Rock and Roll. Loosely in order of their importance? Racism and subsequent integration, gospel, blues (racism again . . . I am afraid) hillbillies, minstrels in blackface, cheap Silvertone guitars from Sears, the Hawaiian music craze, burlesque, booze, weed, vaudeville, the circus, some showtime razzle-dazzle and the spoiled generation following World War Two. That pretty much sums up the whole damn fad which many of us have lived entirely through. Those forces, and of course the necessity to procreate the species. Rock and Roll was more than anything else about sex. Not romance at all. Romance was pop chart pre-rock.

When a bar band had to play one for slow dance (romance) they did it with apology. Ladies Choice. We're going to take a break now. They couldn't wait to rock again. Rock and Roll was sexual attraction, hot passion and down-dirty rutting . . . even when it was being created in the church. They tried to cover it up with holy gospel, but there was a back door in every church. Lord knows they worshiped the flesh too, and it helped fill the pews. Rock and Roll was not love songs.

The couplings resulting from rock and roll created a few consumers who purchased records along the way, and that was fine. Records lasted a century. Just about as long as Rock and Roll.

There were basically two types of music. African, with no scale but sliding notes, and European which had precise dots on a scale and slid little. Fortunately, the twain did meet and what resulted was good times. As soon as the musicians figured out they could learn from each other, any racism among musicians was gone. Hank Williams, who could not read music, learned to play guitar from a Black fellow named Rufus Payne. Ol' Hank was a fortunate and remarkable by-product of the great musical realization that there is but one race, the human race. Thank the Lord it happened. It has made our lives, brief as they are, considerably more interesting and far more exciting.

If you doubt my thesis that Rock and Roll was about sex, think of one of the great Rock and Roll songs "Farmer John" and you will agree. Every garage band learned it. The premise? Doing the farmer's daughter. That's the whole song. It is a story as old as farming itself, but again in the scope of time? Not so long. Even the change from "hunt and gather" to agrarian didn't take long really. Longer than Rock and Roll, of course, but that is still not as old as the rocks under your feet.

When Rock and Roll started, a juke-joint with fifty patrons was a big show. A church with fifty congregants was a full house. The annual square dance at the town hall, a rent party, a fish-fry, the honky-tonk piano in the whore house, the union meeting . . . there was no real money in it. A performer was lucky to be fed, get drunk and get laid. If he didn't, he would busk for lunch the next day and try again that night. There were no tickets, no reserved seats, no website to get the good seats into the hands of the wealthy. No wealth involved at all. For a time, Rock and Roll was a small industry indeed, but now it is just part of one of the few exports left in this country. That being the selling of our popular culture to the rest of the world as a product and a lifestyle choice. Whether they want it or not.

These original photographs were collected with the intention to tell a one hundred year story.

Jim Linderman 2014

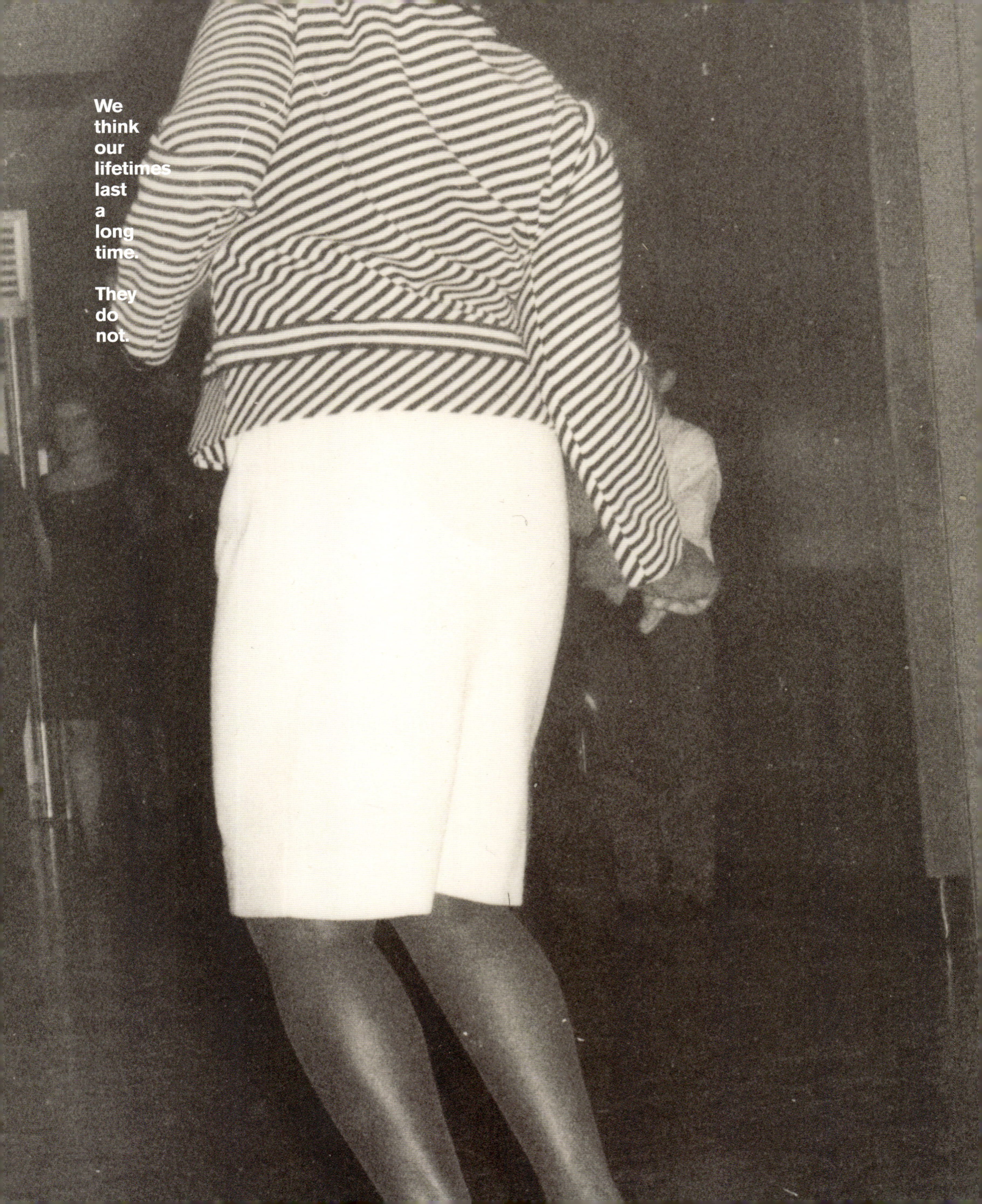

We
think
our
lifetimes
last
a
long
time.

They
do
not.

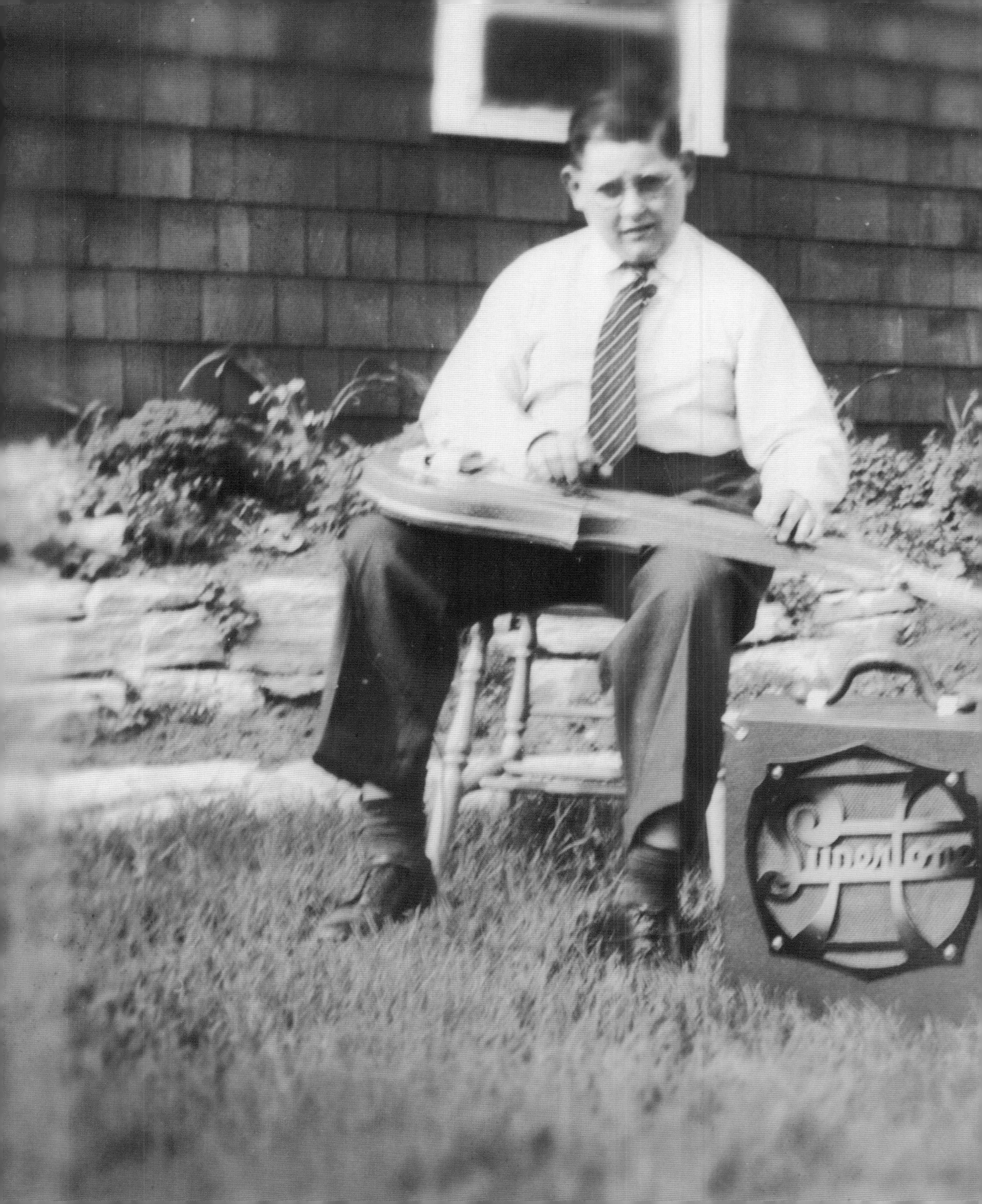

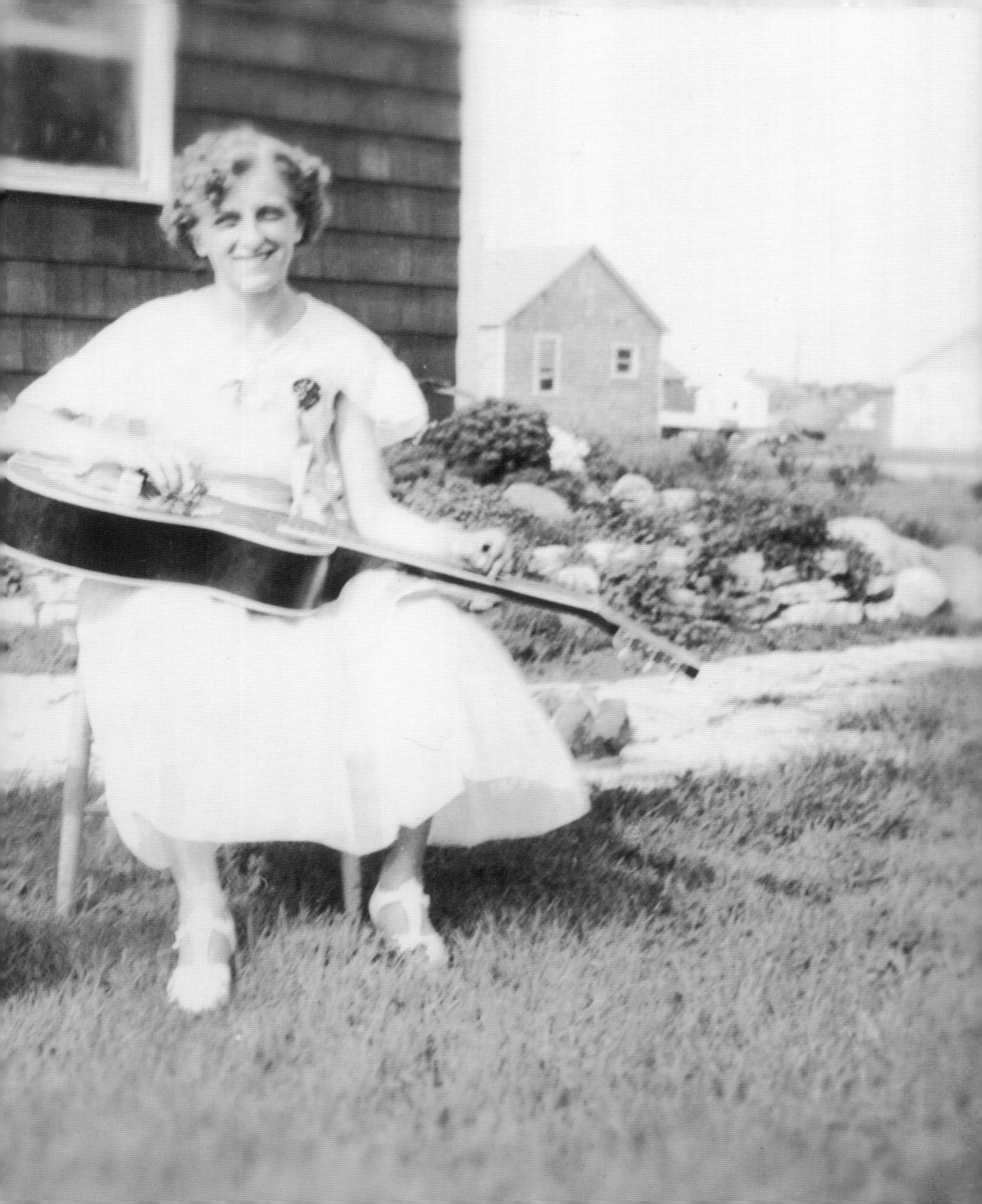

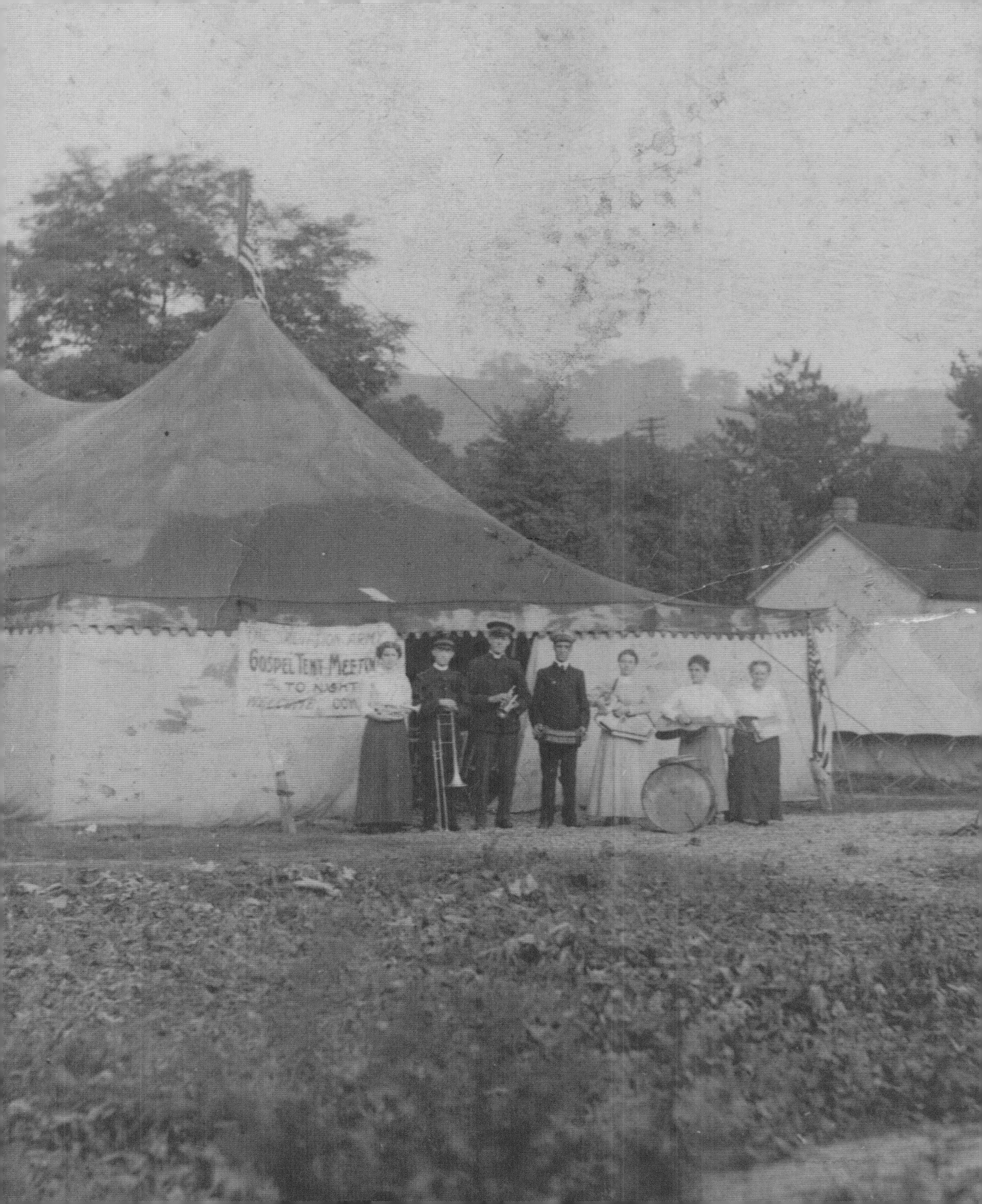
GOSPEL TENT MEETIN
TO NIGHT

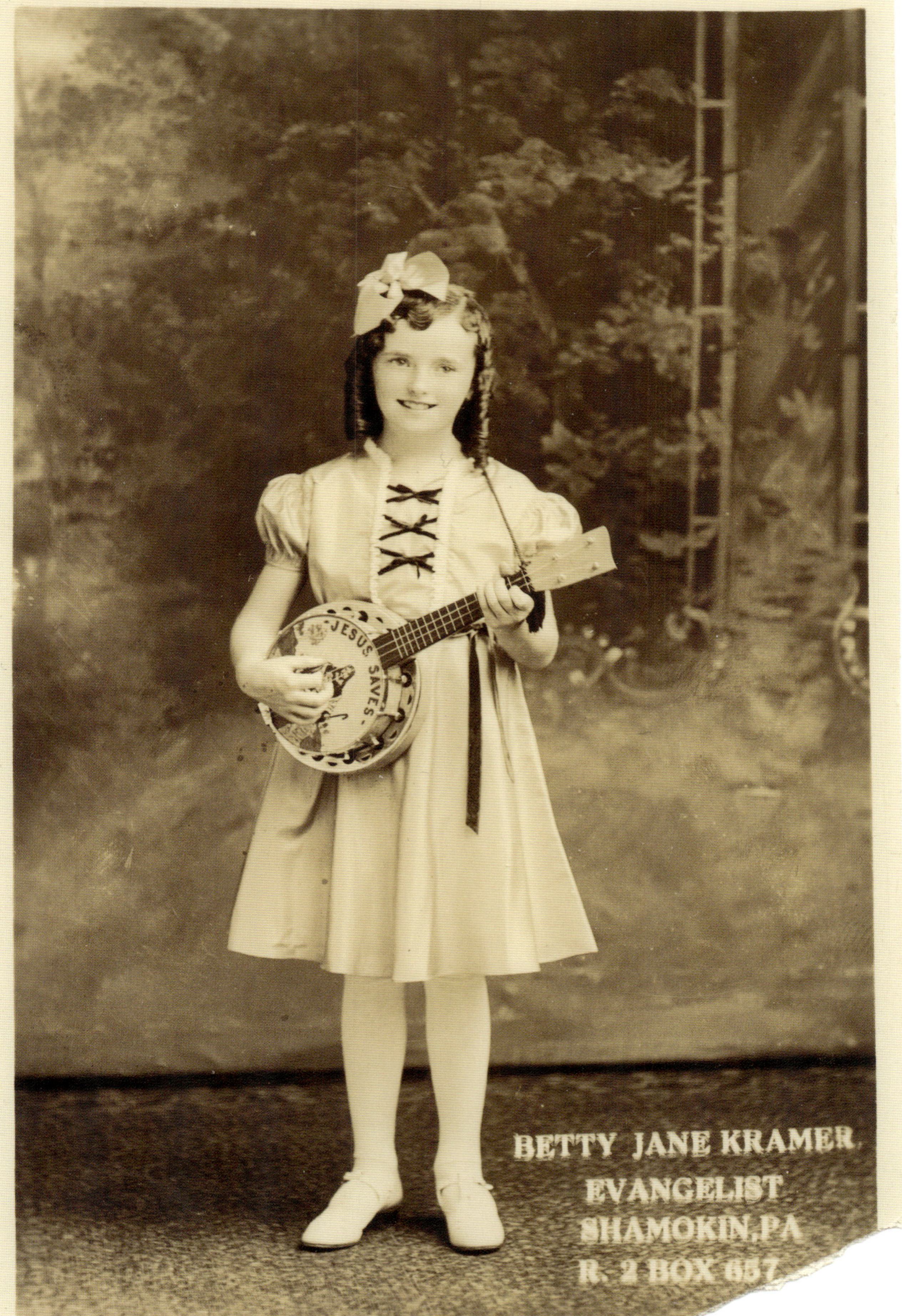
JESUS SAVES
BETTY JANE KRAMER
EVANGELIST
SHAMOKIN, PA
R. 2 BOX 657

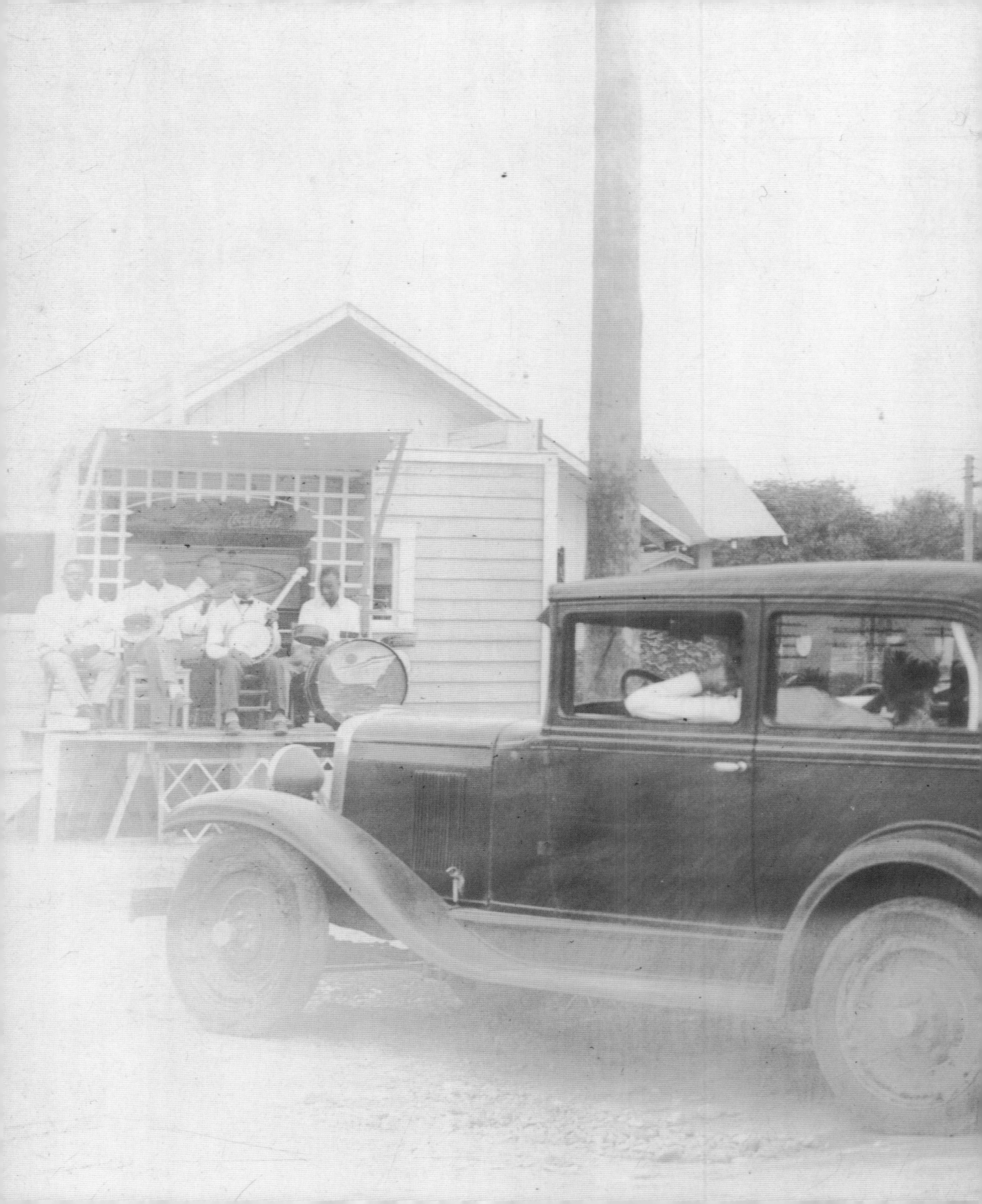

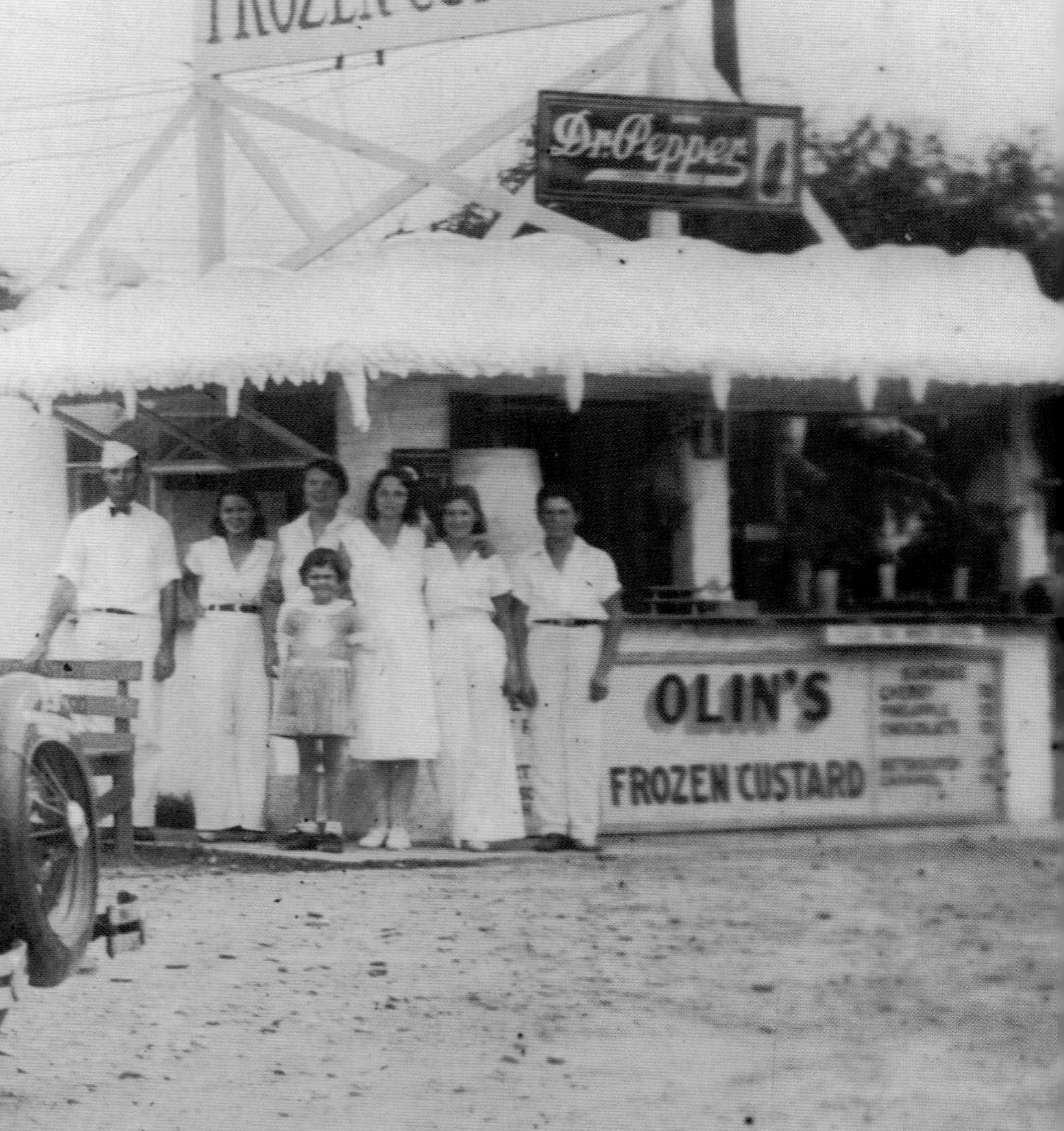
OLIN'S
FROZEN CUSTARD
Dr Pepper
OLIN'S
FROZEN CUSTARD

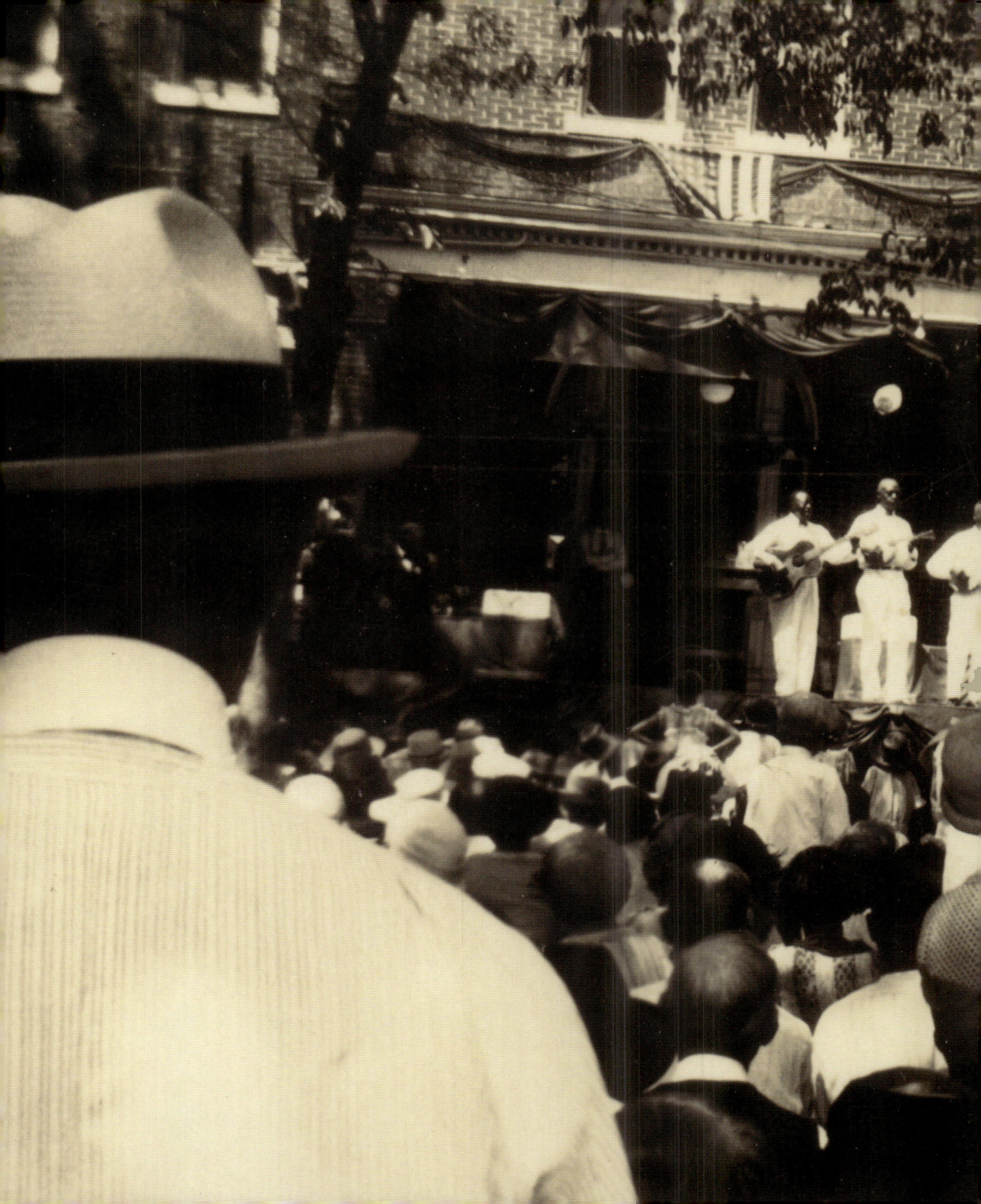

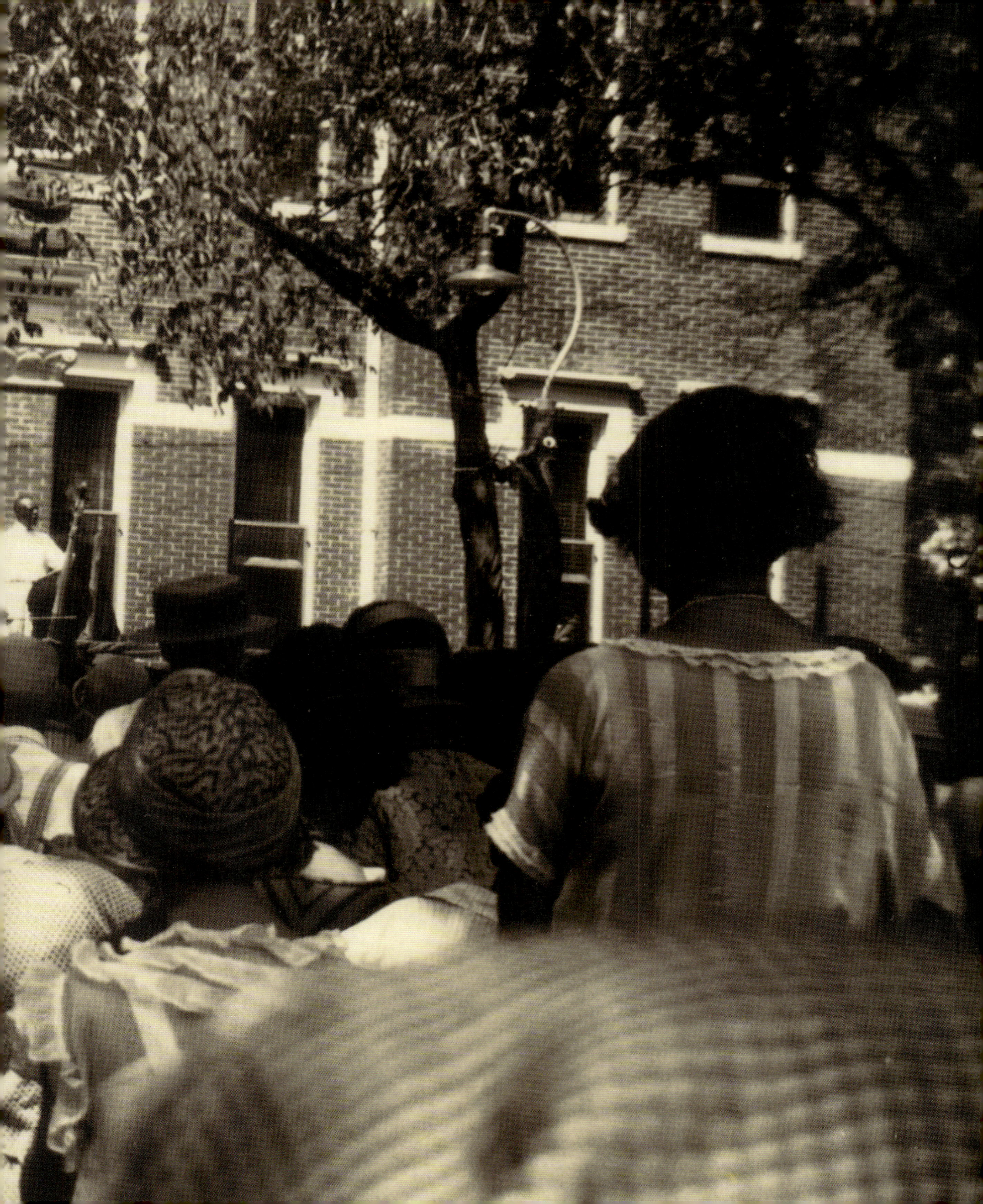

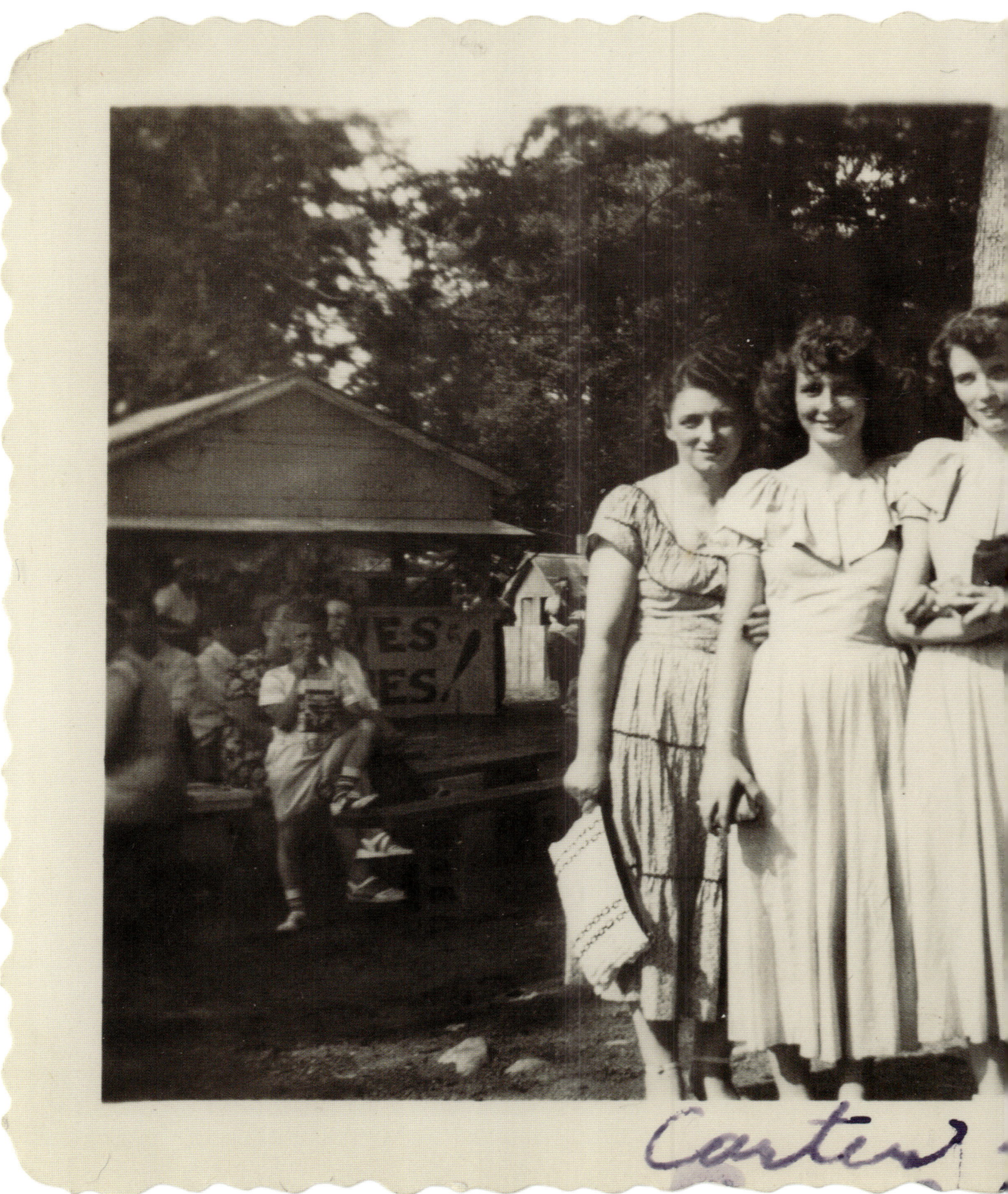

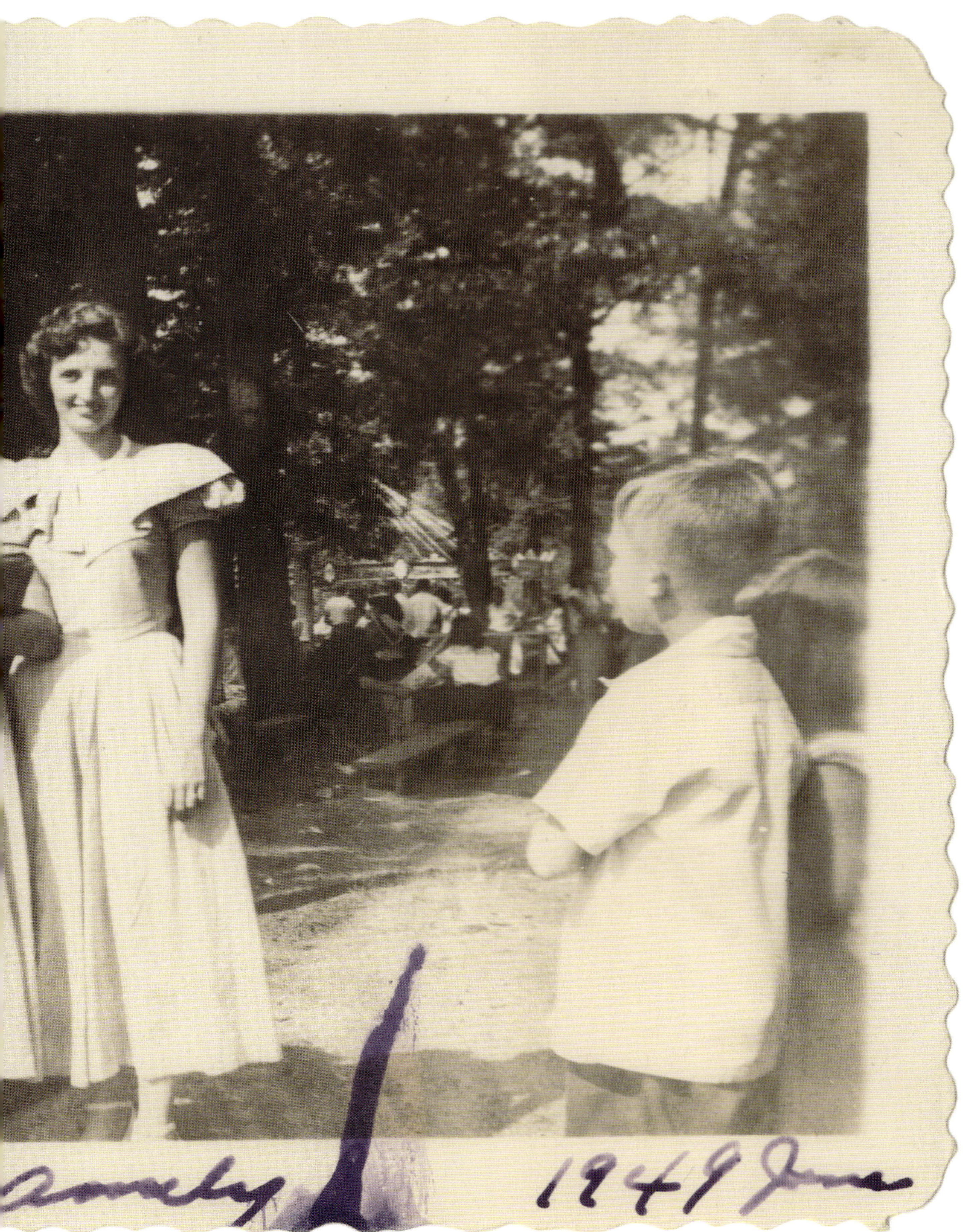
1949 June

Merle + her musician

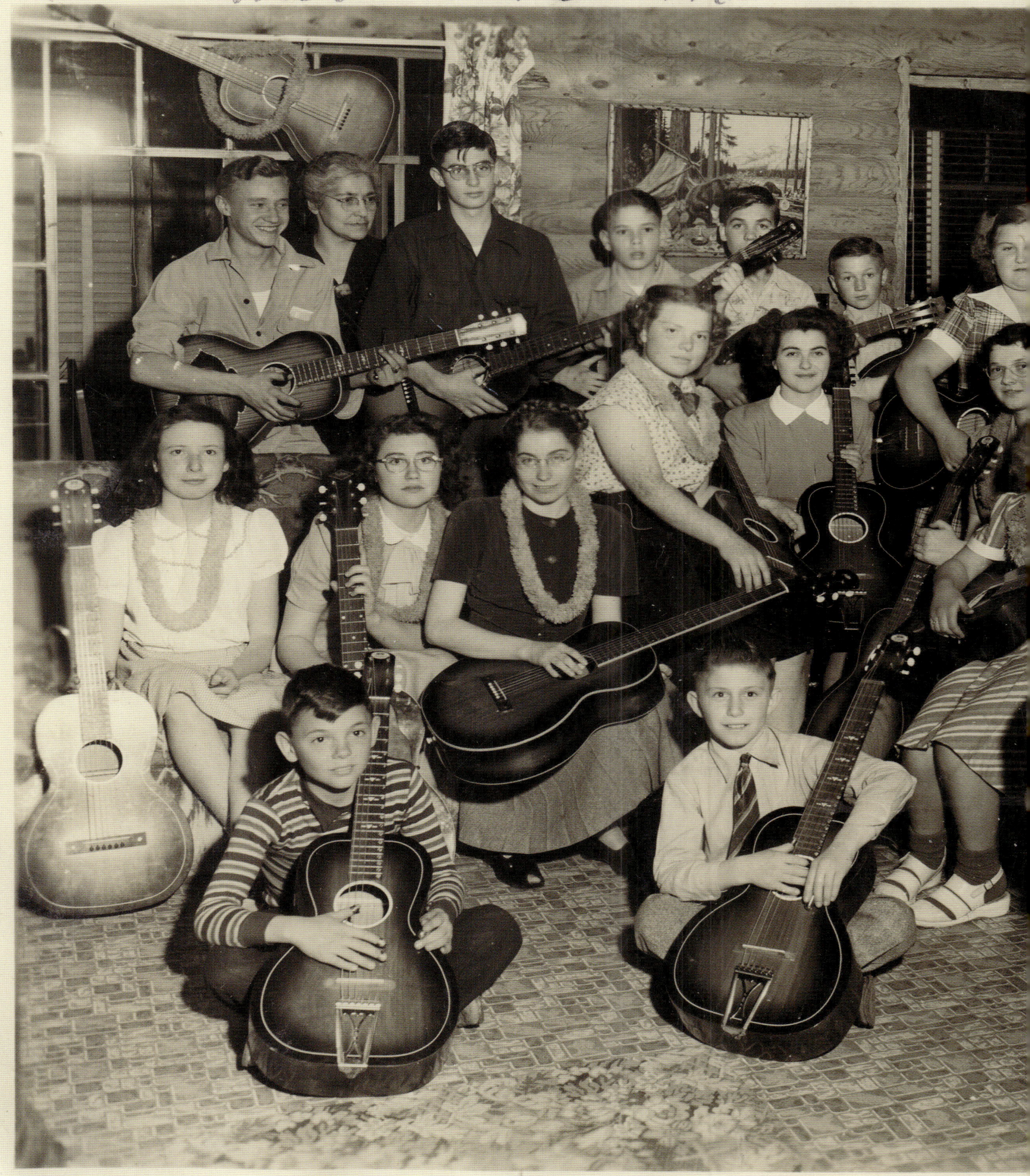

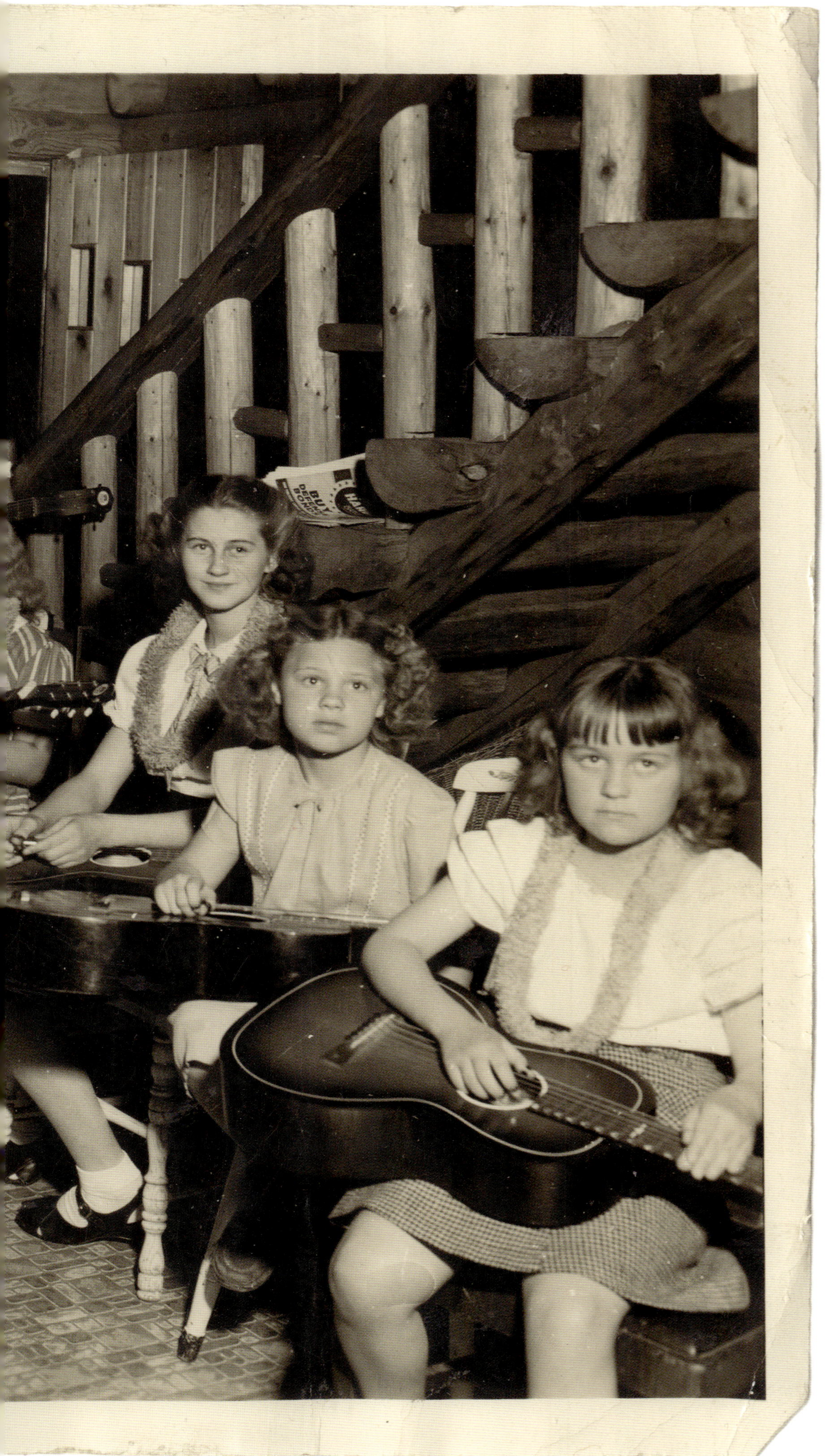
BUY

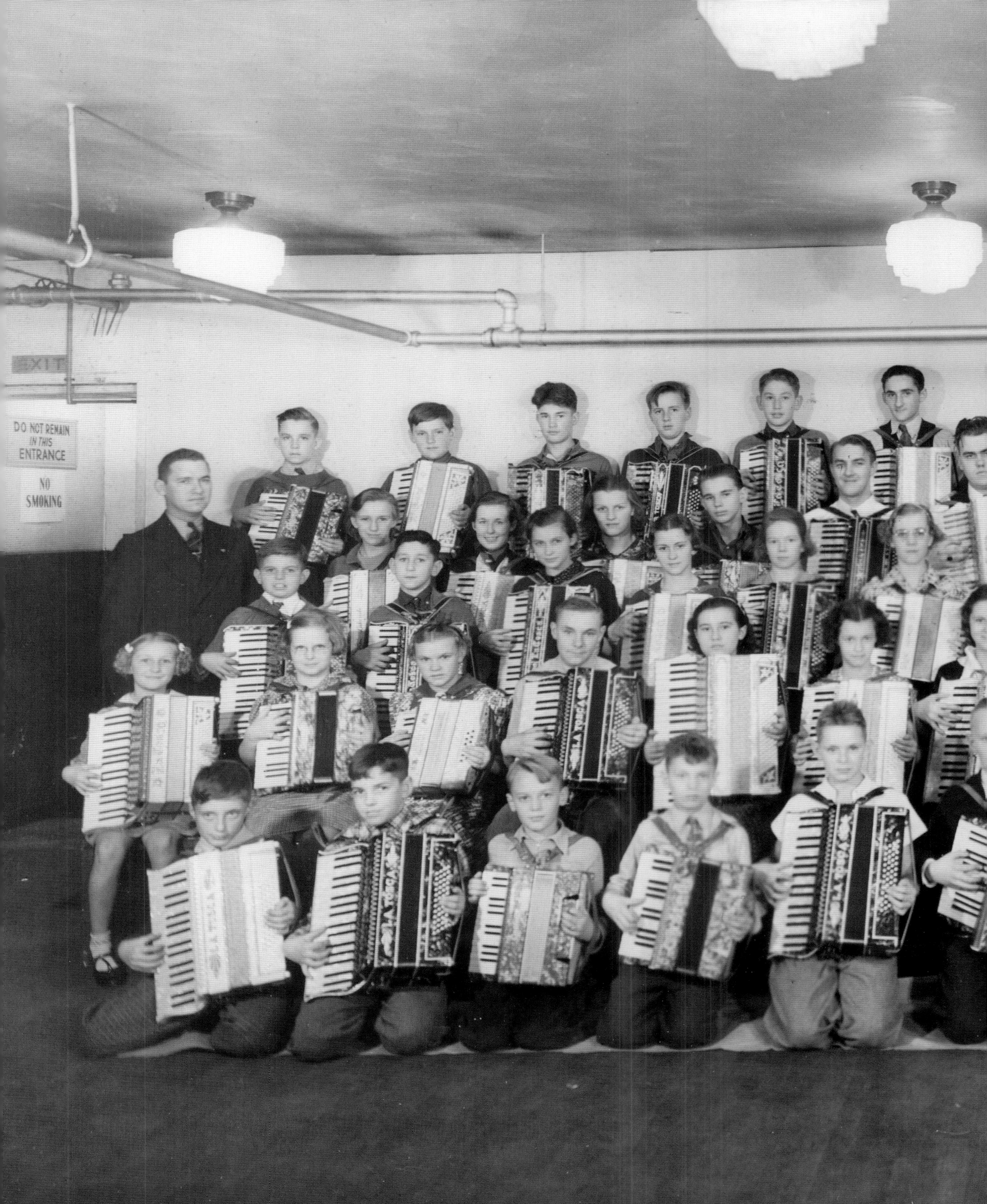
EXIT
DO NOT REMAIN
IN THIS
ENTRANCE
NO
SMOKING

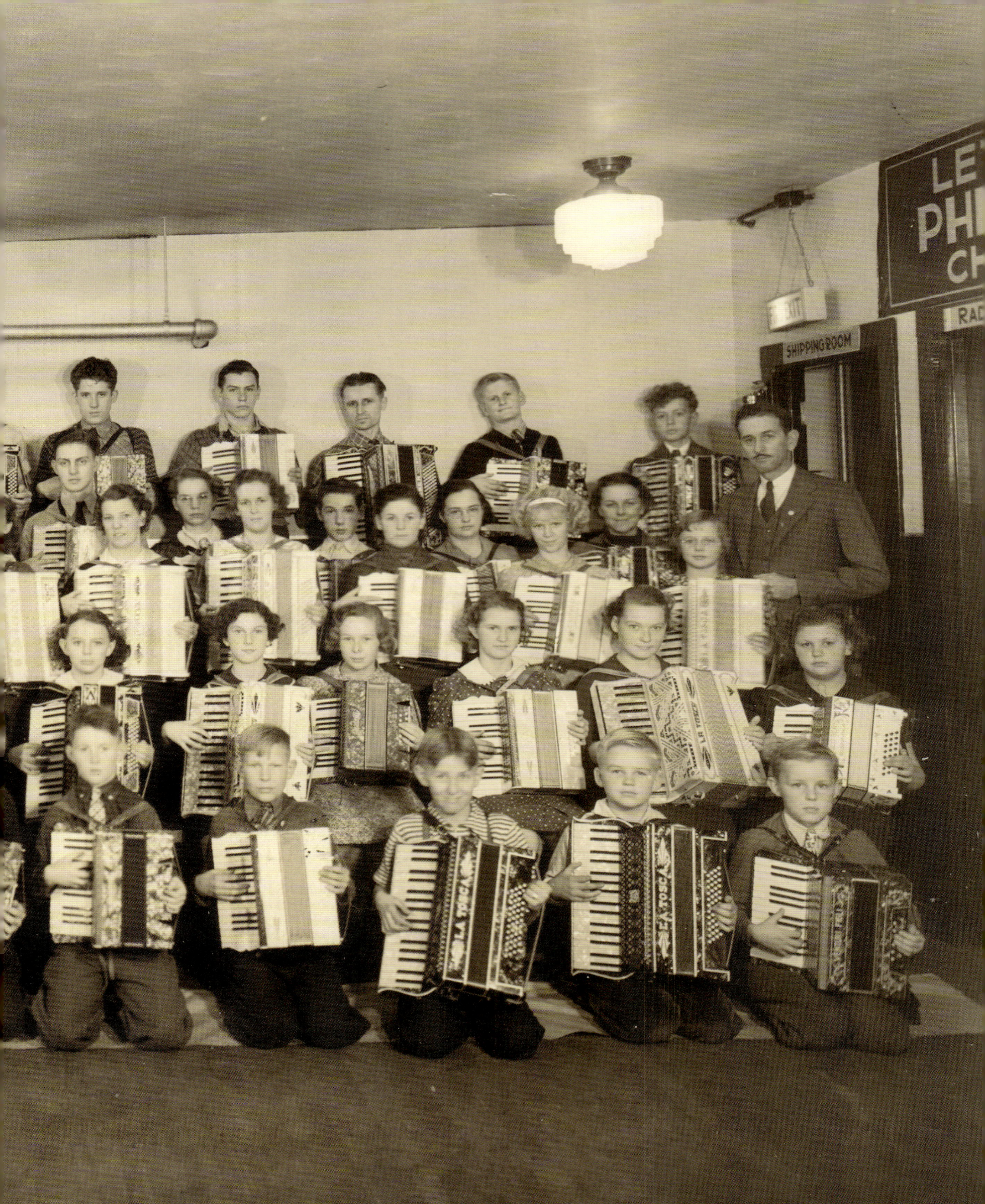
SHIPPING ROOM
LA TOSCA
LA TOSCA

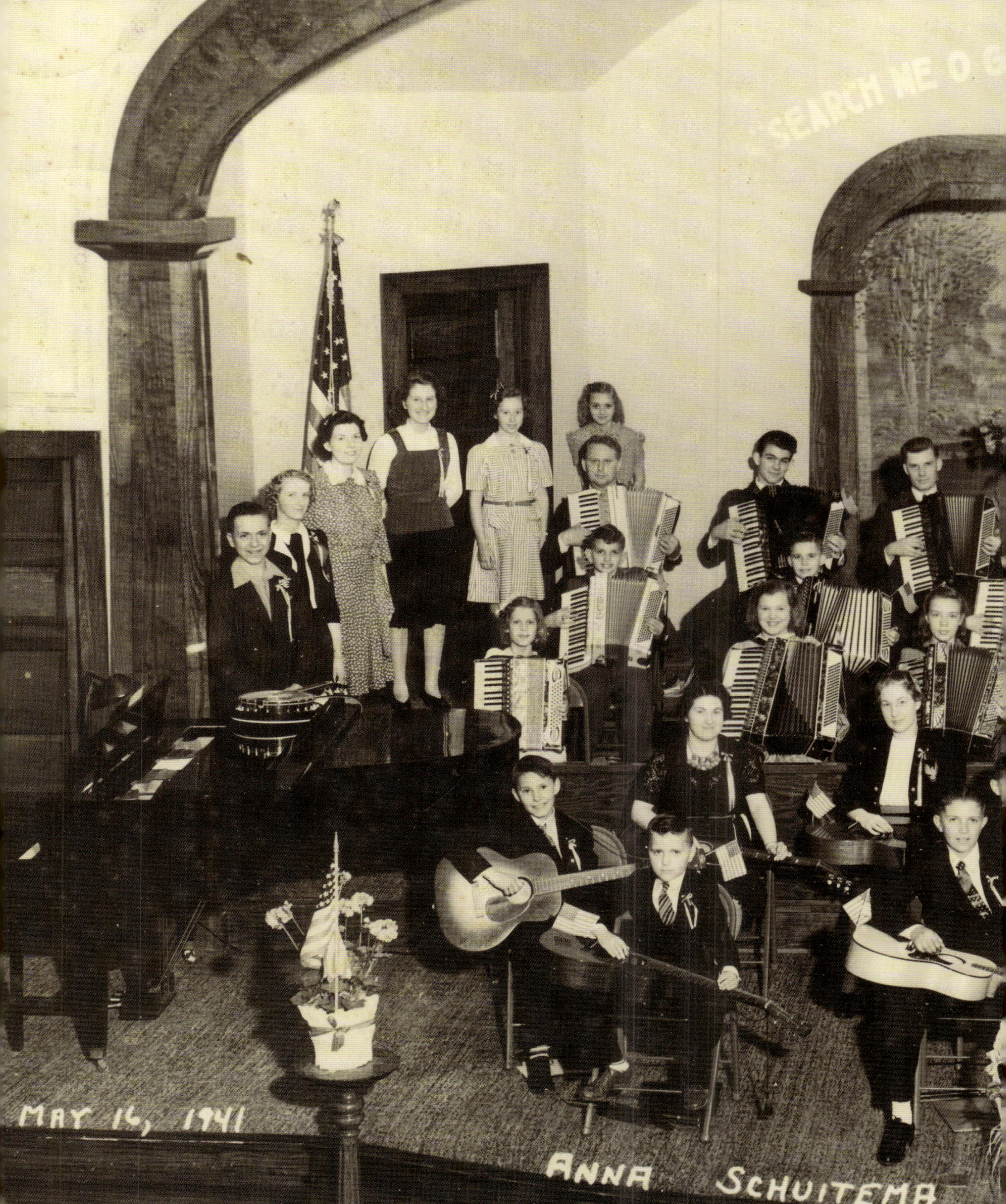
"SEARCH ME O
MAY 16, 1941
ANNA SCHUITEMA

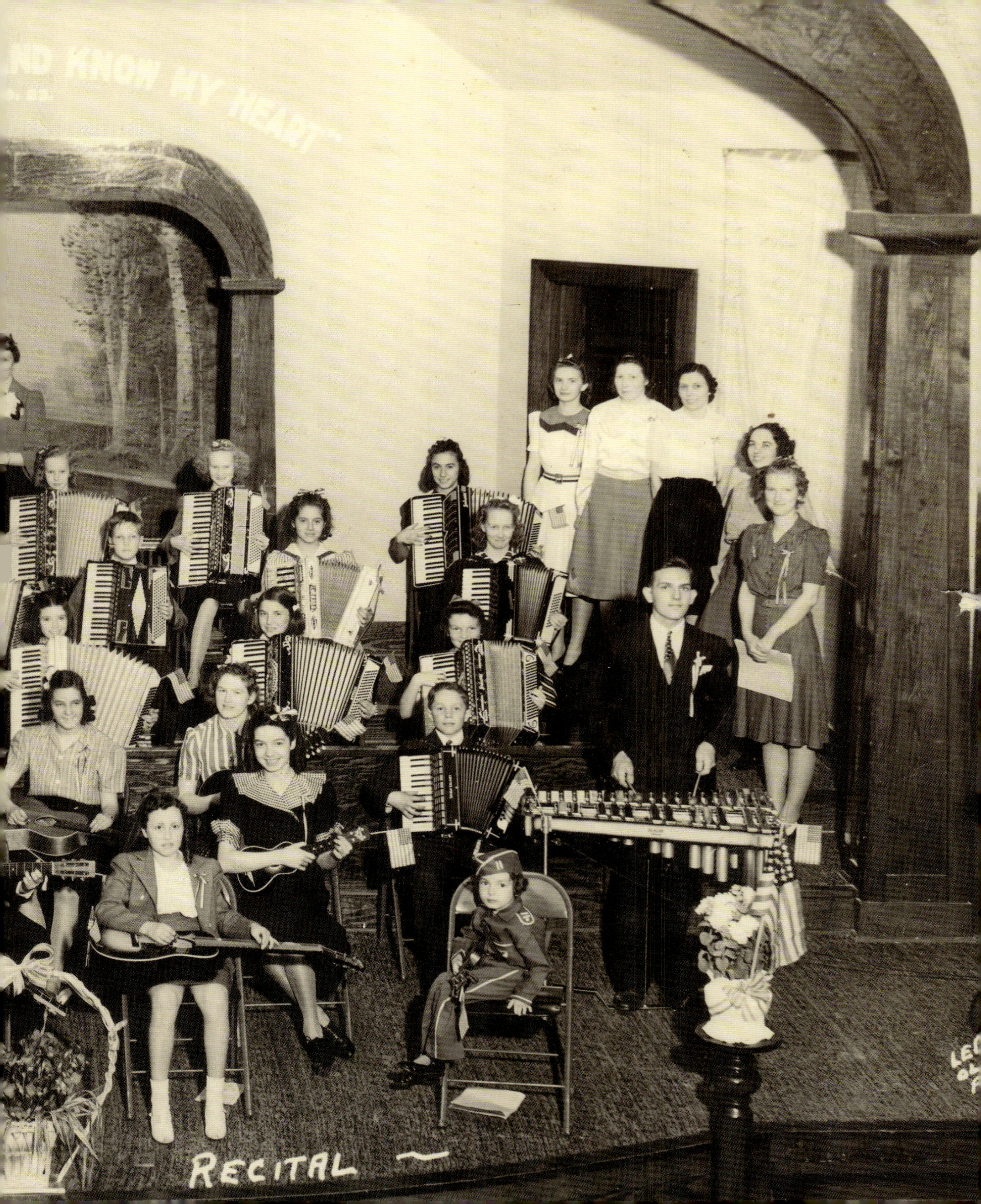
ND KNOW MY HEART"
RECITAL

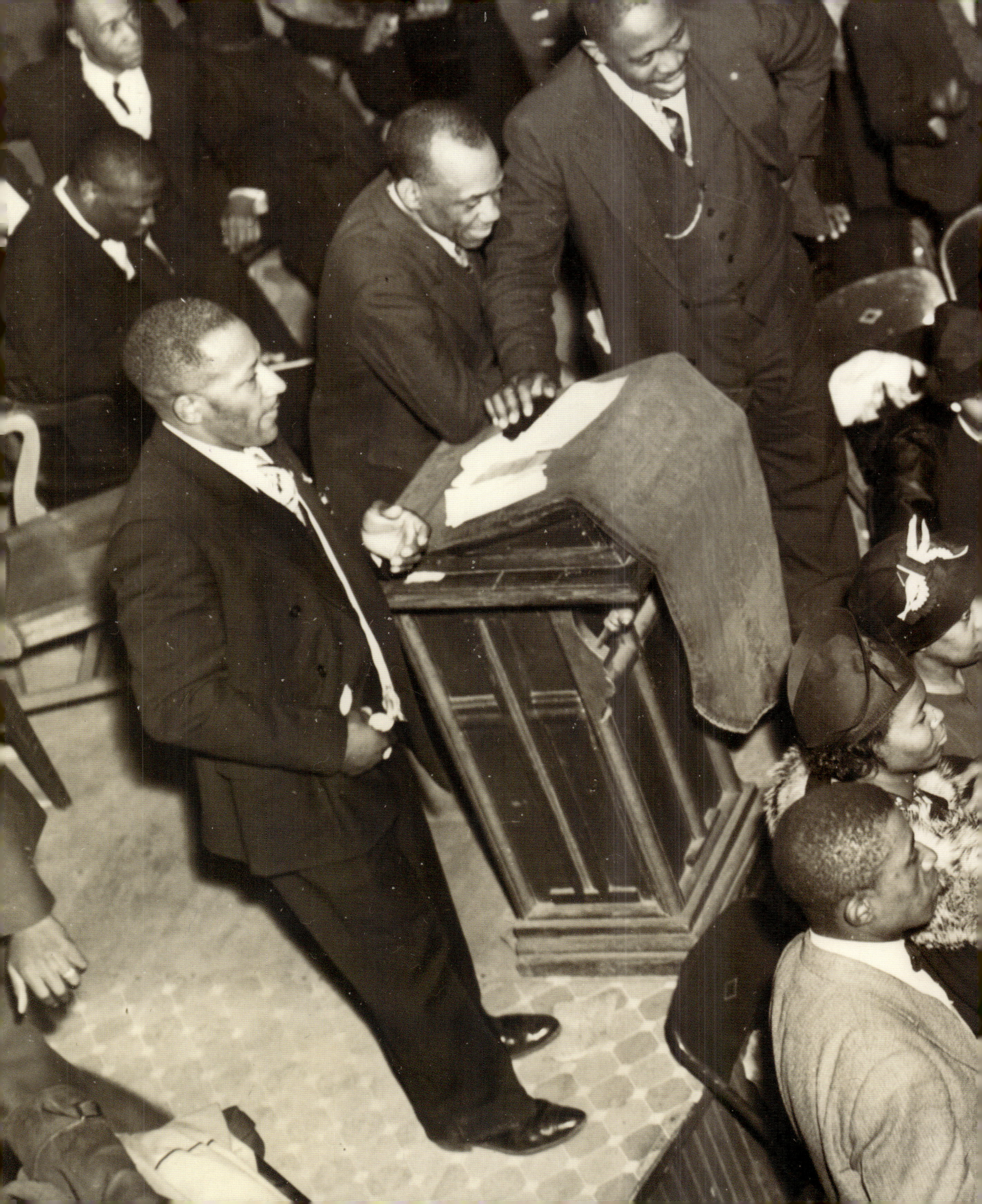

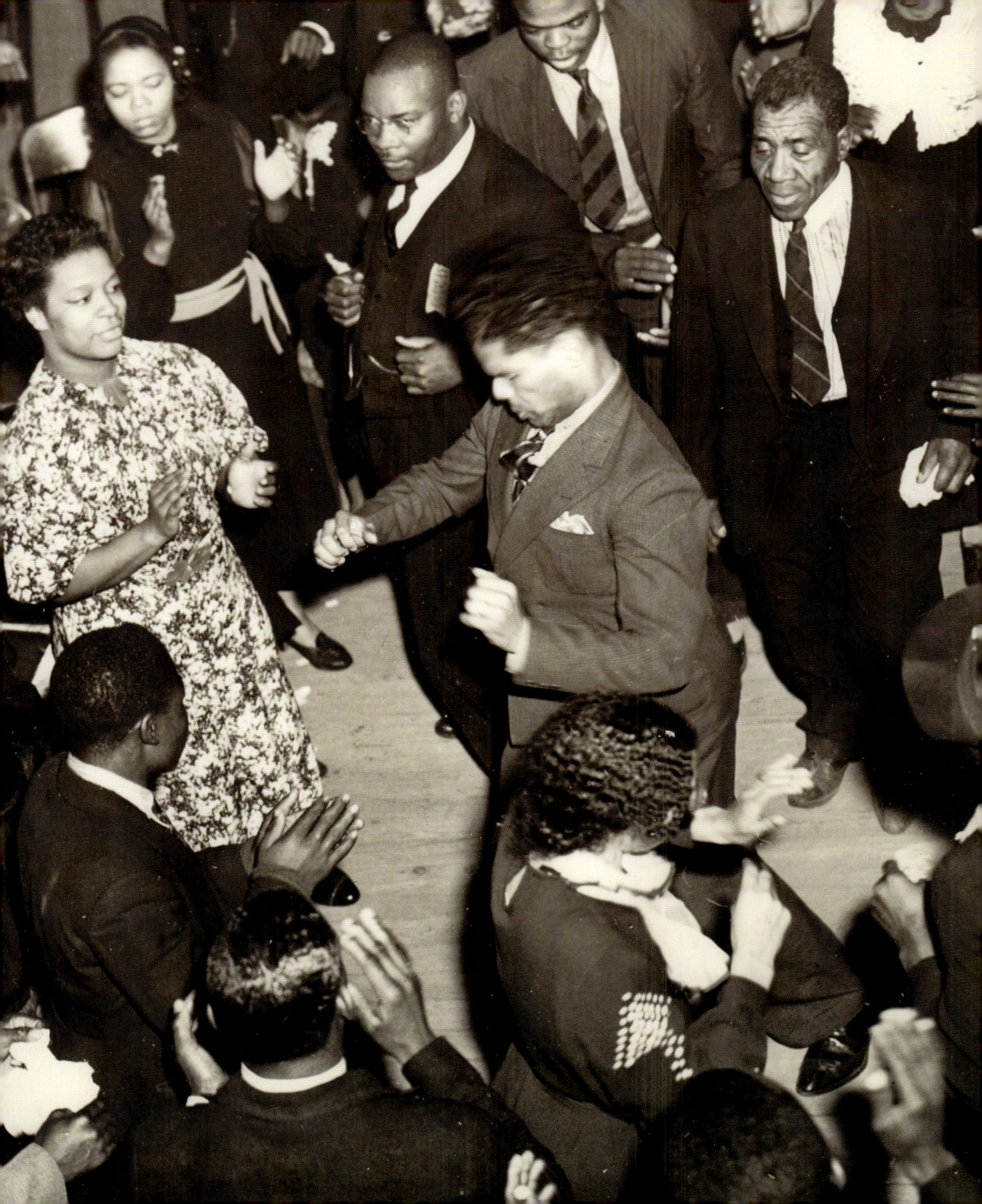

3635

MEM42

THE

MEM423932

THE SPIRIT TOUCHES

NEGRO DELEGATES TO THE CONVENTION COULD HOLD THEIR SEATS JUST SO LONG. WHEN A PIANO PLAYER RAN HIS FINGERS SOFTLY OVER THE KEYS, THIS YOUNG NEGRO IN THE CENTER JUMPED UP IN FRONT OF THE ALTAR AND WENT INTO THE BIG APPLE. HE SOON WAS SURROUNDED BY OTHER MEMBERS OF THE CONGREGATION WHO KEPT TIME BY CLAPPING THEIR HANDS. THIS IS WHAT THEY CALL "BEING TOUCHED BY THE SPIRIT" AND IT SEEMS TO HAVE PLEASED THE SPEAKING PREACHER, EXTREME LEFT.

CREDIT LINE (ACME)

ACME ROTO SERVICE FOR IMMEDIATE RELEASE

A225 - Religion

Negro Religion & Church

5-

When the preacher wishes to stop the dancing he has a big bell which he rings. But sometimes it fails;; the spirit has too much of a hold upon them and all the ringing in the world wouldn't stop----so it just winds up in the bell being rung in a rhytmatic manner and the ~~spirit~~ emotions overcome the preachers who too begin dancing.

The Church of God in Christ

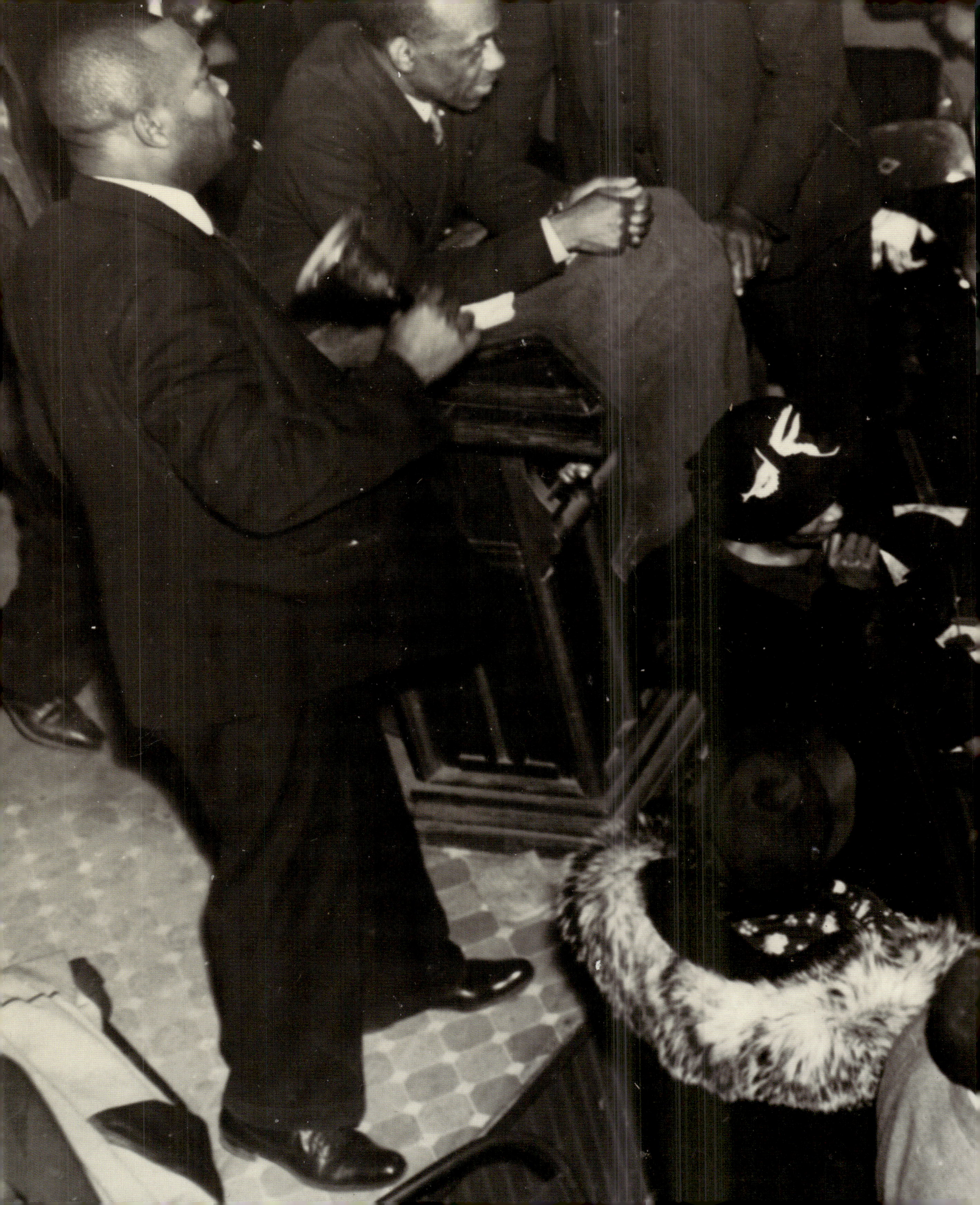

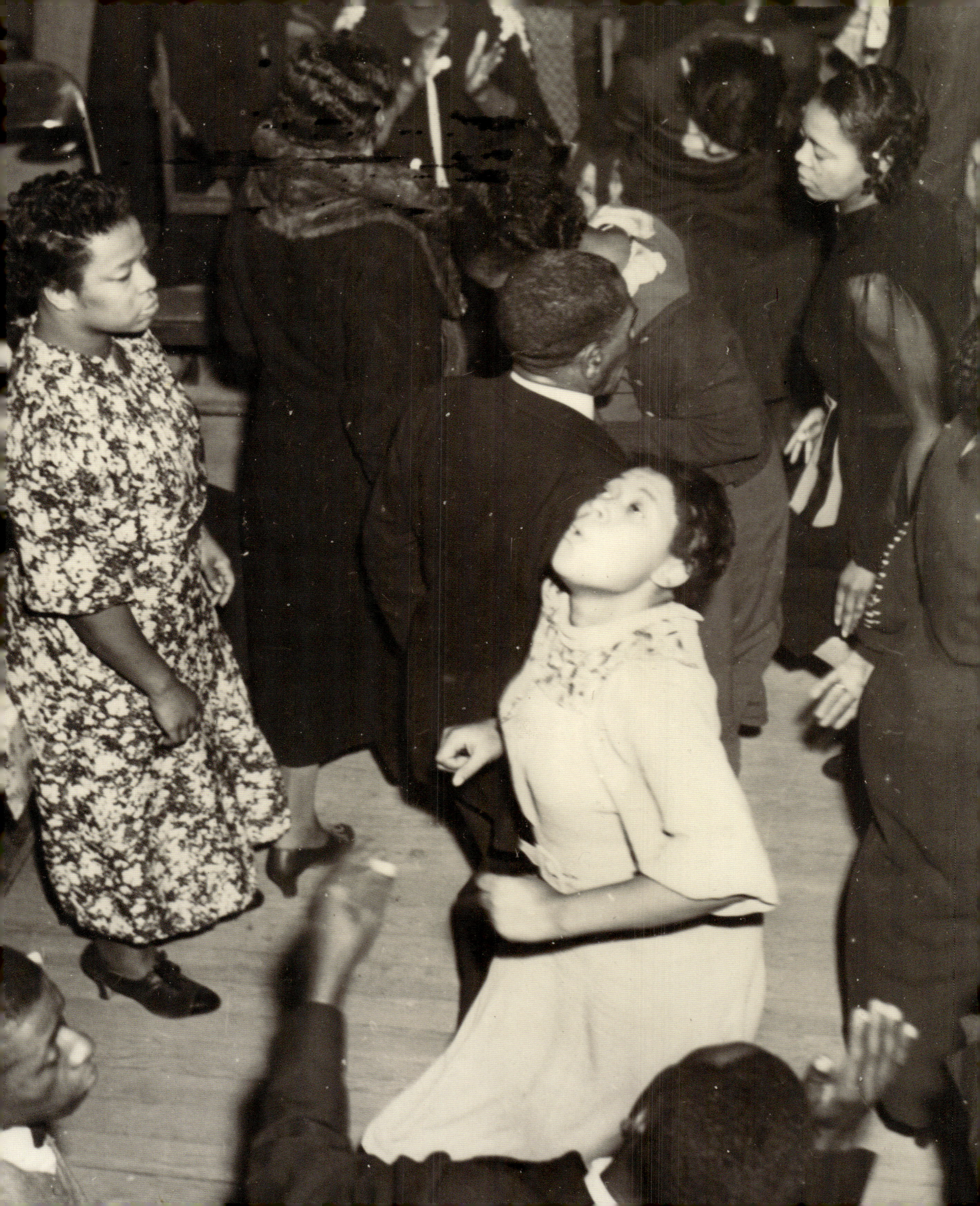

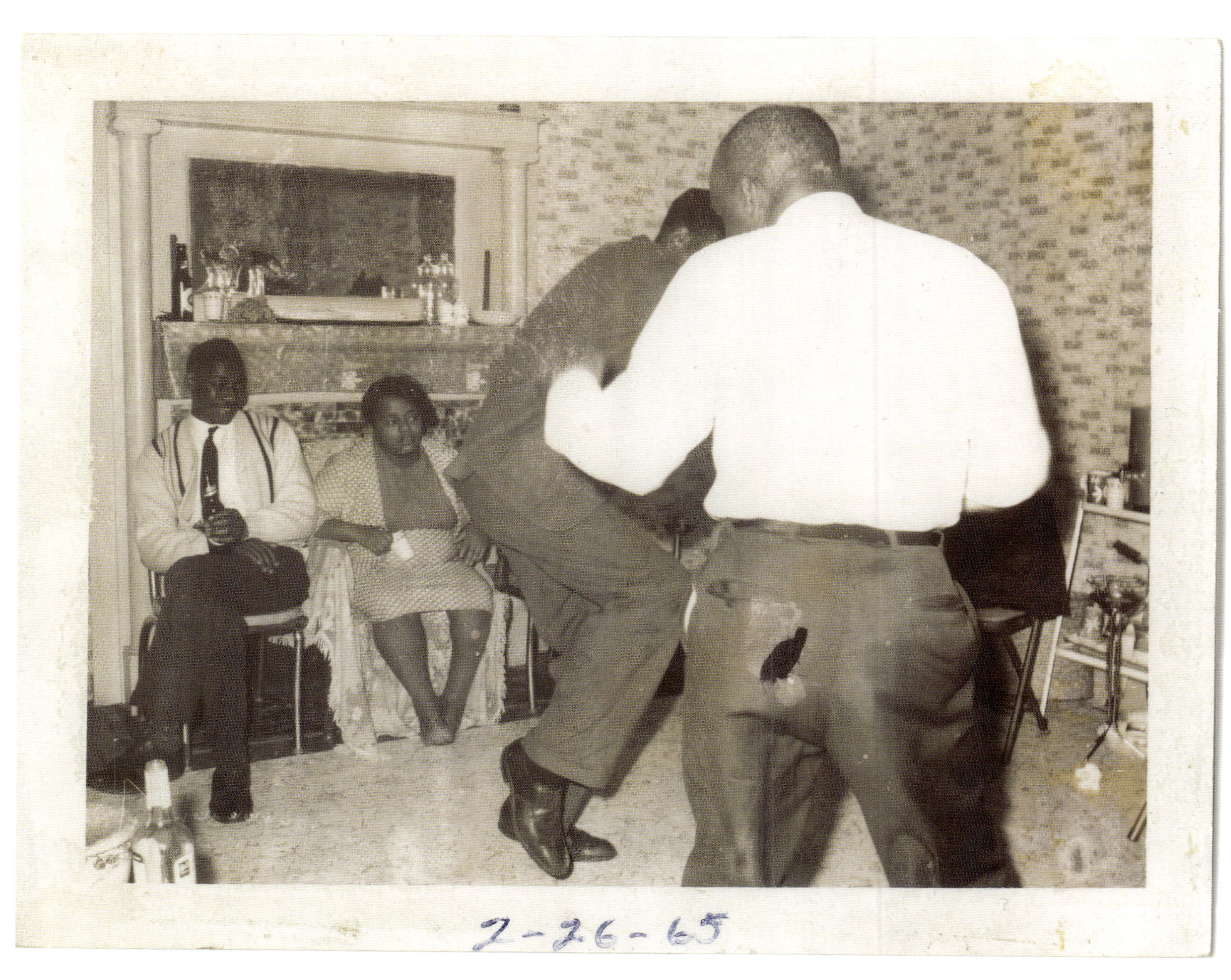
2-26-65

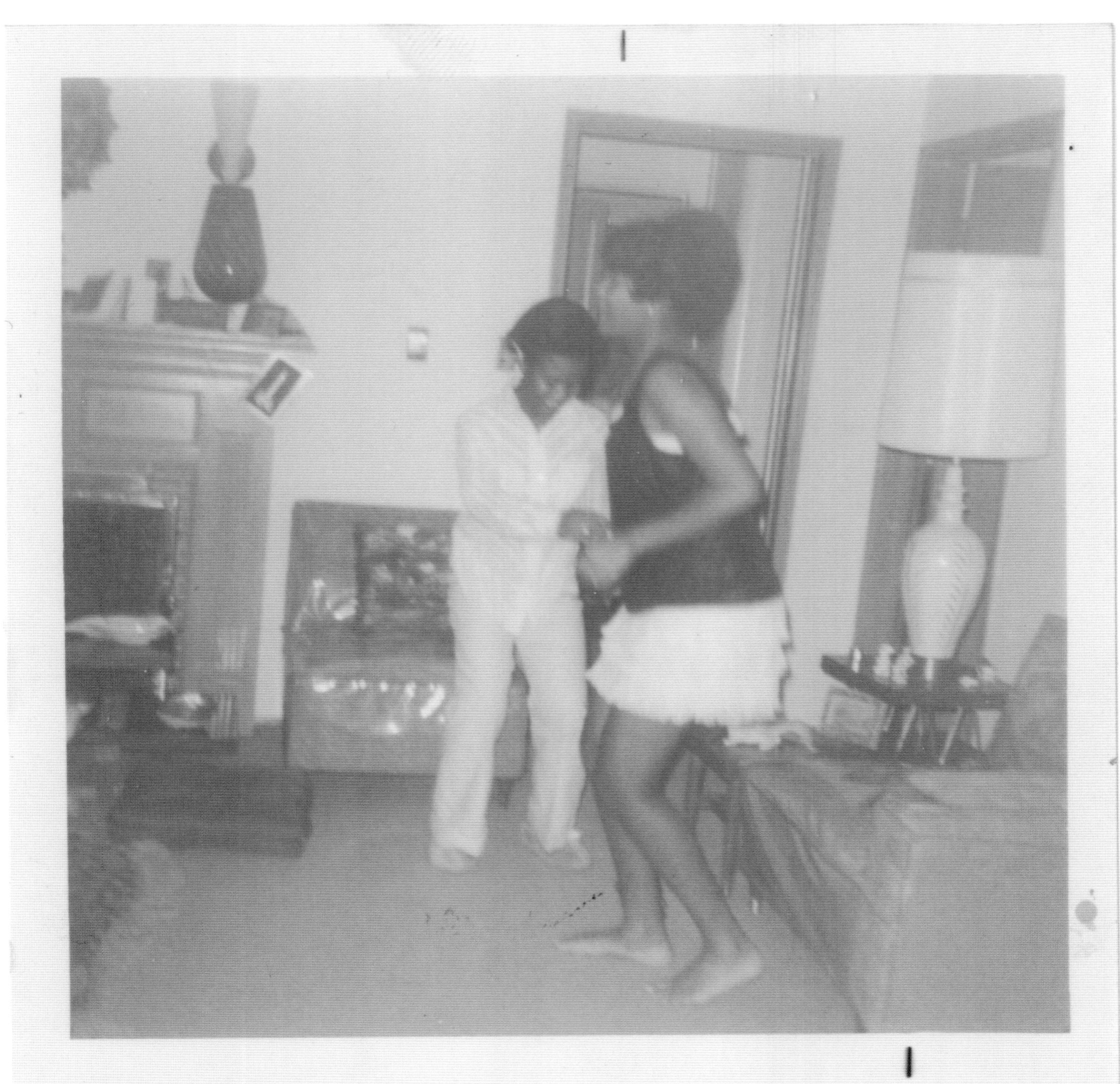

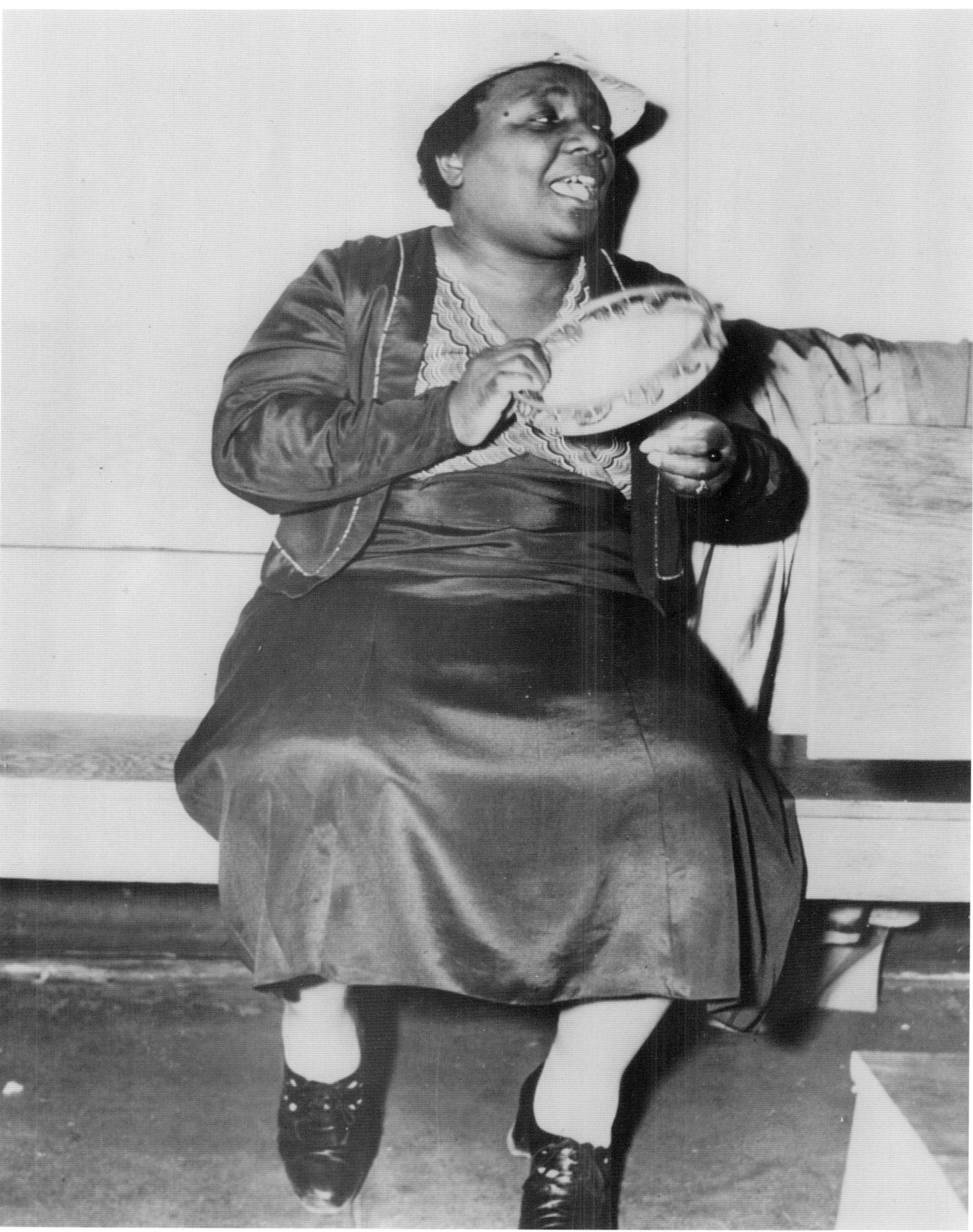

A225

A CAMERA CLICKS IN 'HEAVEN'

AN ACME CAMERAMAN WENT TO "HEAVEN" -- FATHER DIVINE'S LOCAL HEADQUARTERS IN LOS ANGELES, CALIF. THIS EXCLUSIVE LAYOUT OF PICTURES SHOWS A FEW OF THE ACTIVITIES IN THE LOS ANGELES "KINGDOM." BOTH NEGROES AND WHITES WORK TOGETHER IN THE ESTABLISHMENT, PREPARING AND EATING THEIR MEALS, CHANTING THEIR SONGS, GOING TO SCHOOL AND GIVING TRIBUTE TO "FATHER," THE NEGRO WHOM THEY LOOK UPON AS "GOD."

CREDIT LINE (ACME) 4/21/37

LA 390687

PHOTO SHOWS: A BUXOM NEGRO "MAMMY" POUNDING ON A TAMBOURINE AND CHANTING TO THE STRAINS OF A DIVINE HYMN.

CREDIT LINE (ACME) 4/21/37

2-

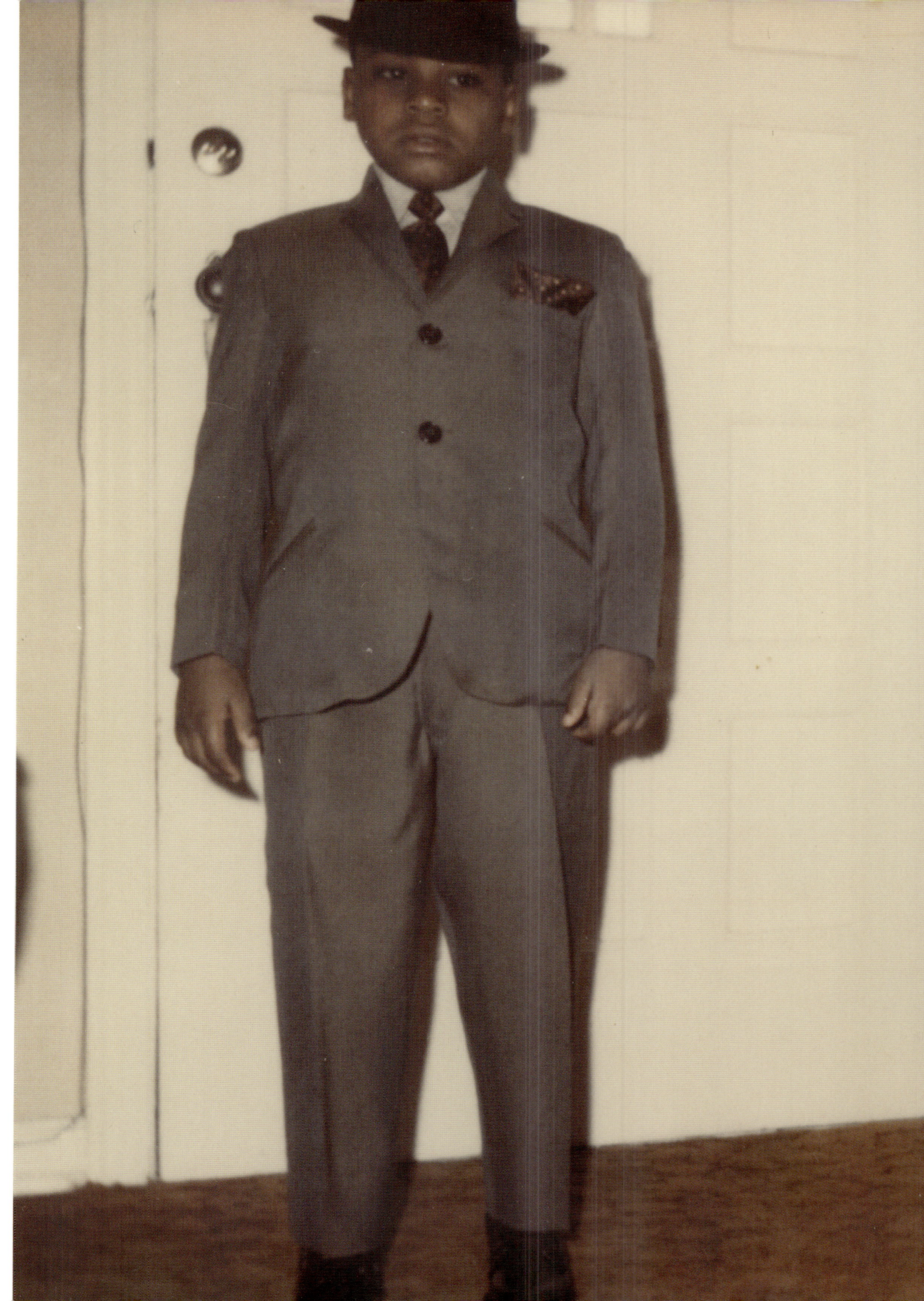

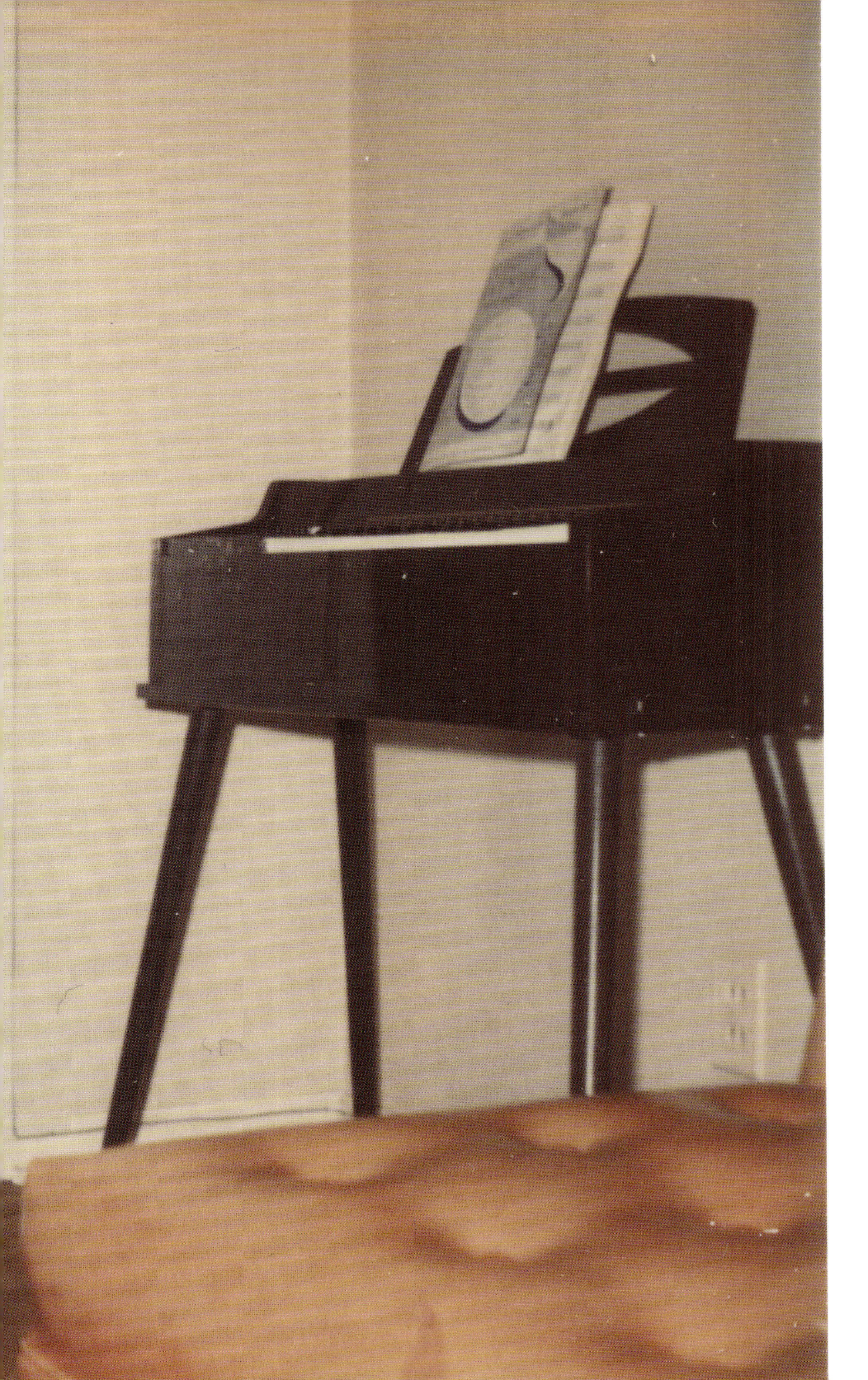

Gooley Family Playing.

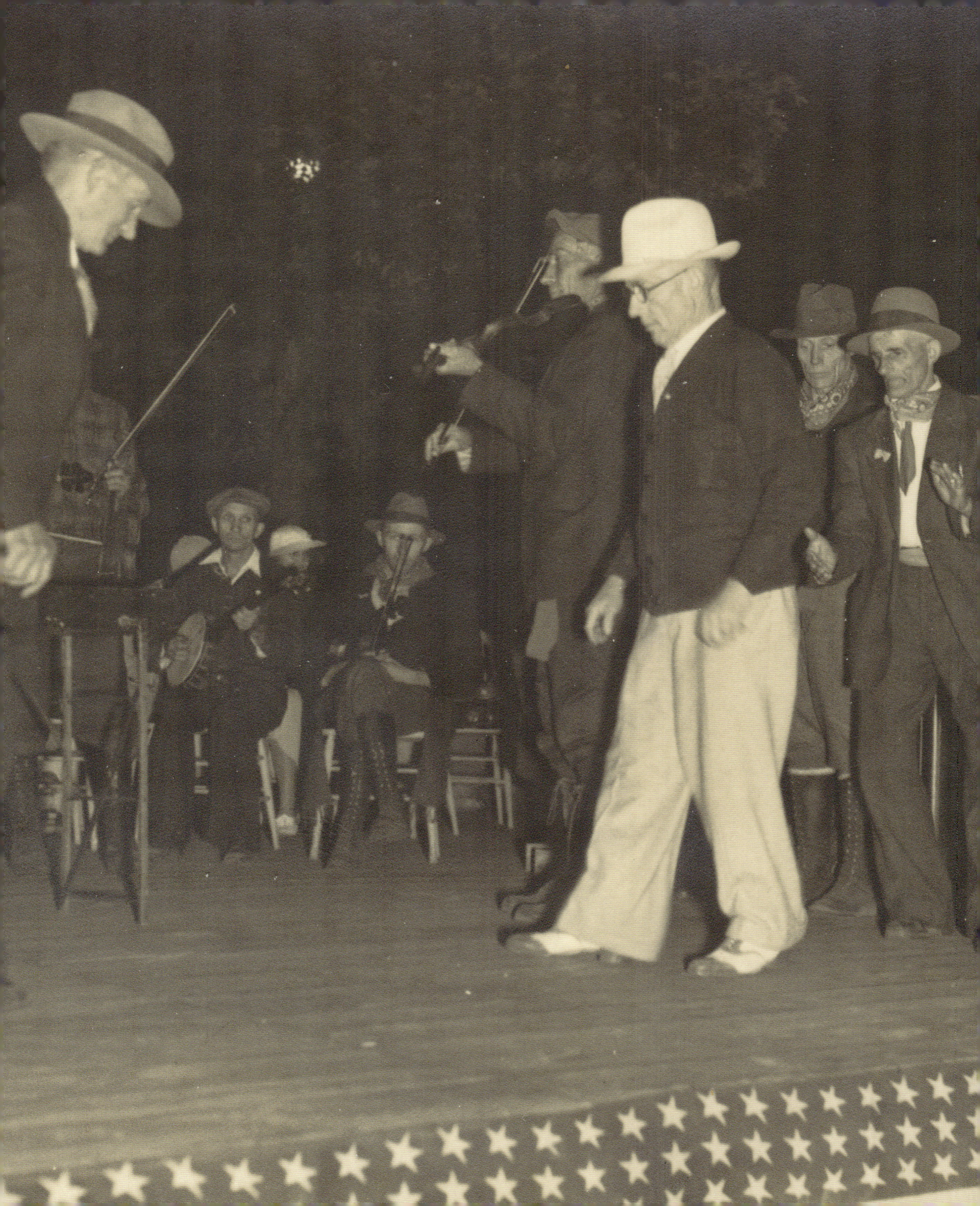

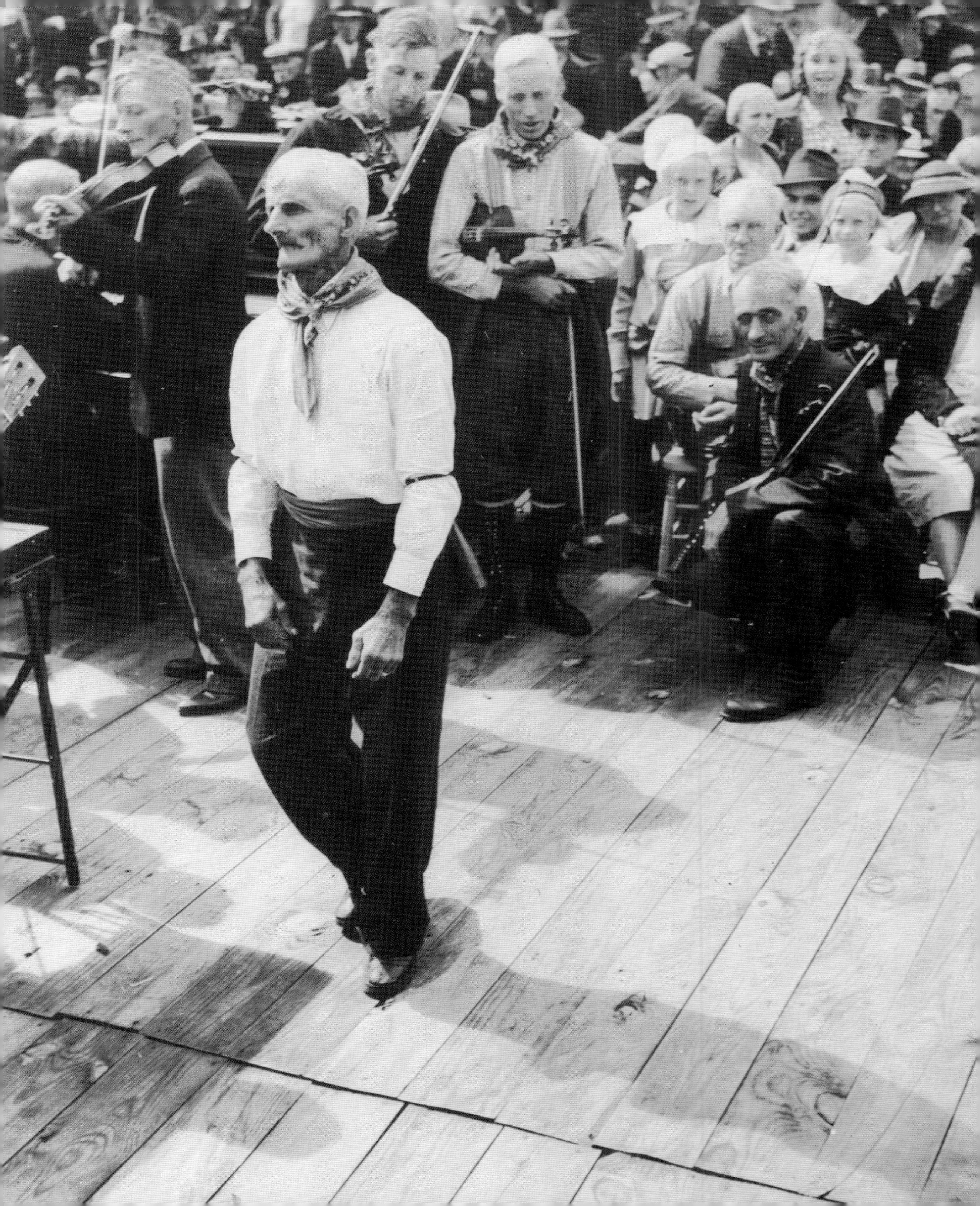

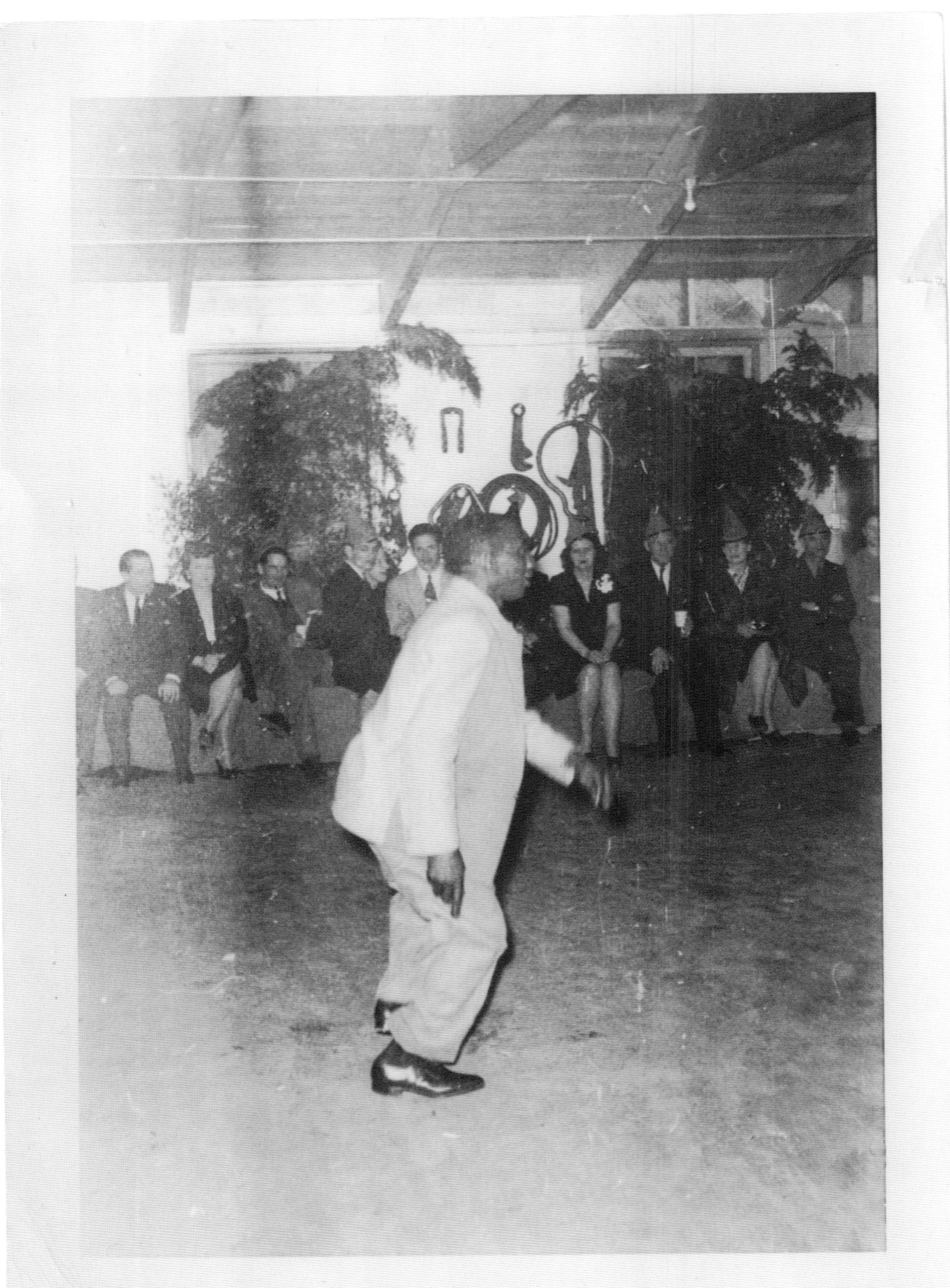

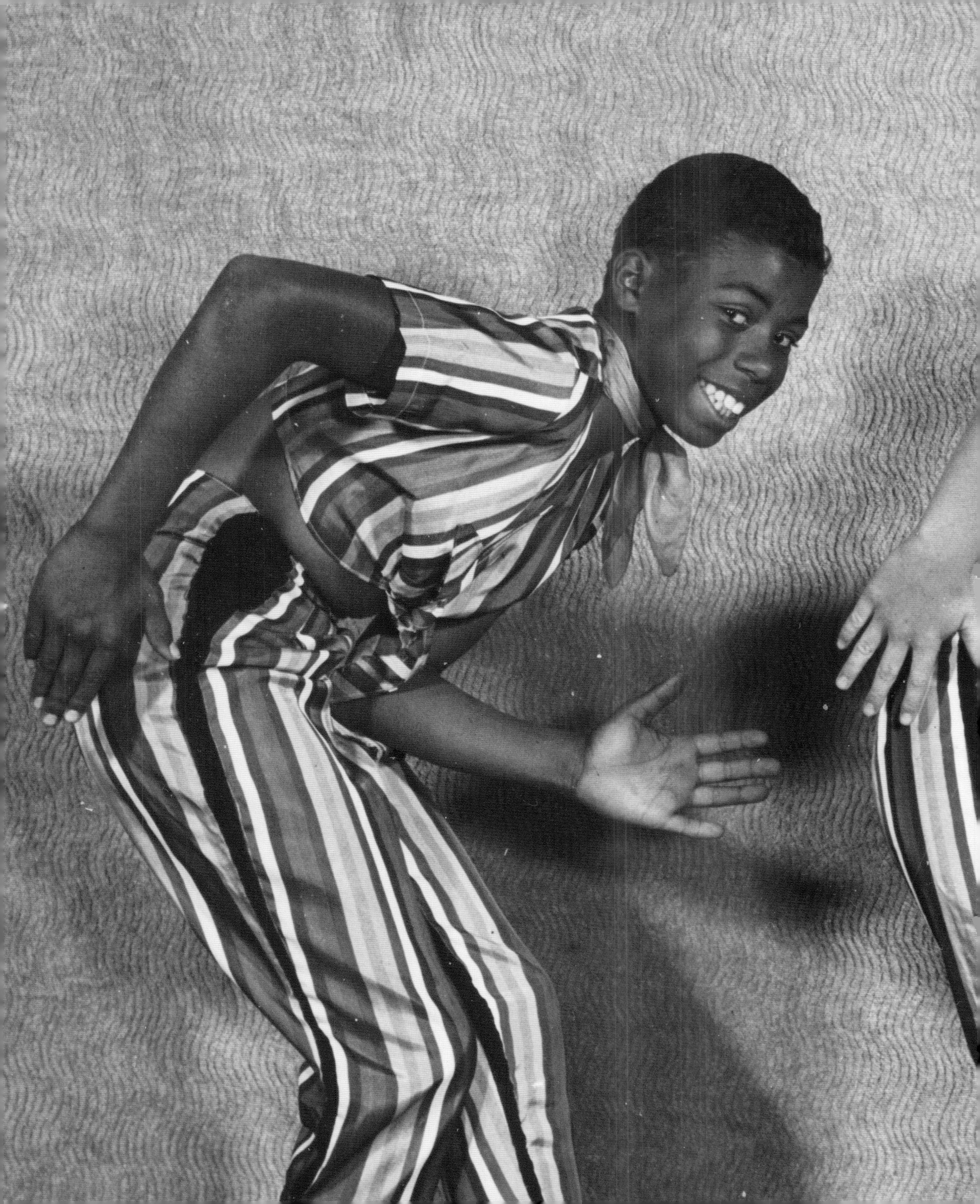

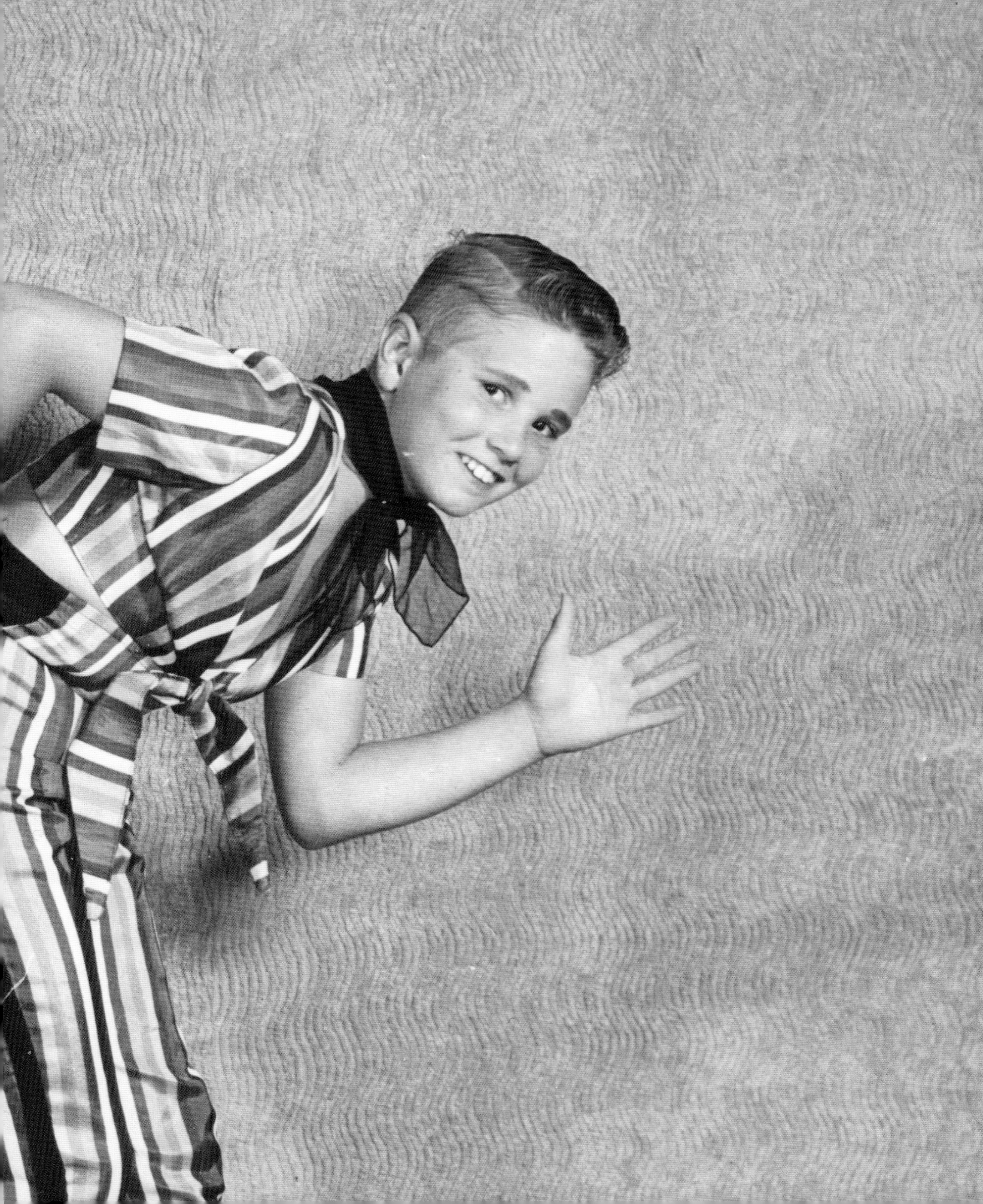

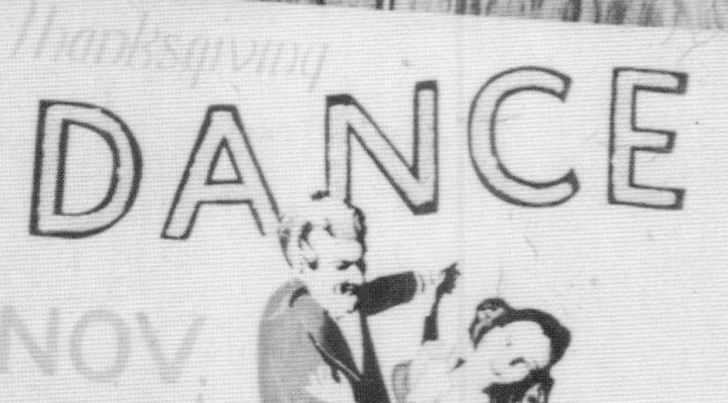
Thanksgiving
DANCE
NOV 27th
25¢
7.30 to 1100
SPONSORED BY EDISON STUDENT COUNCIL
NOV27

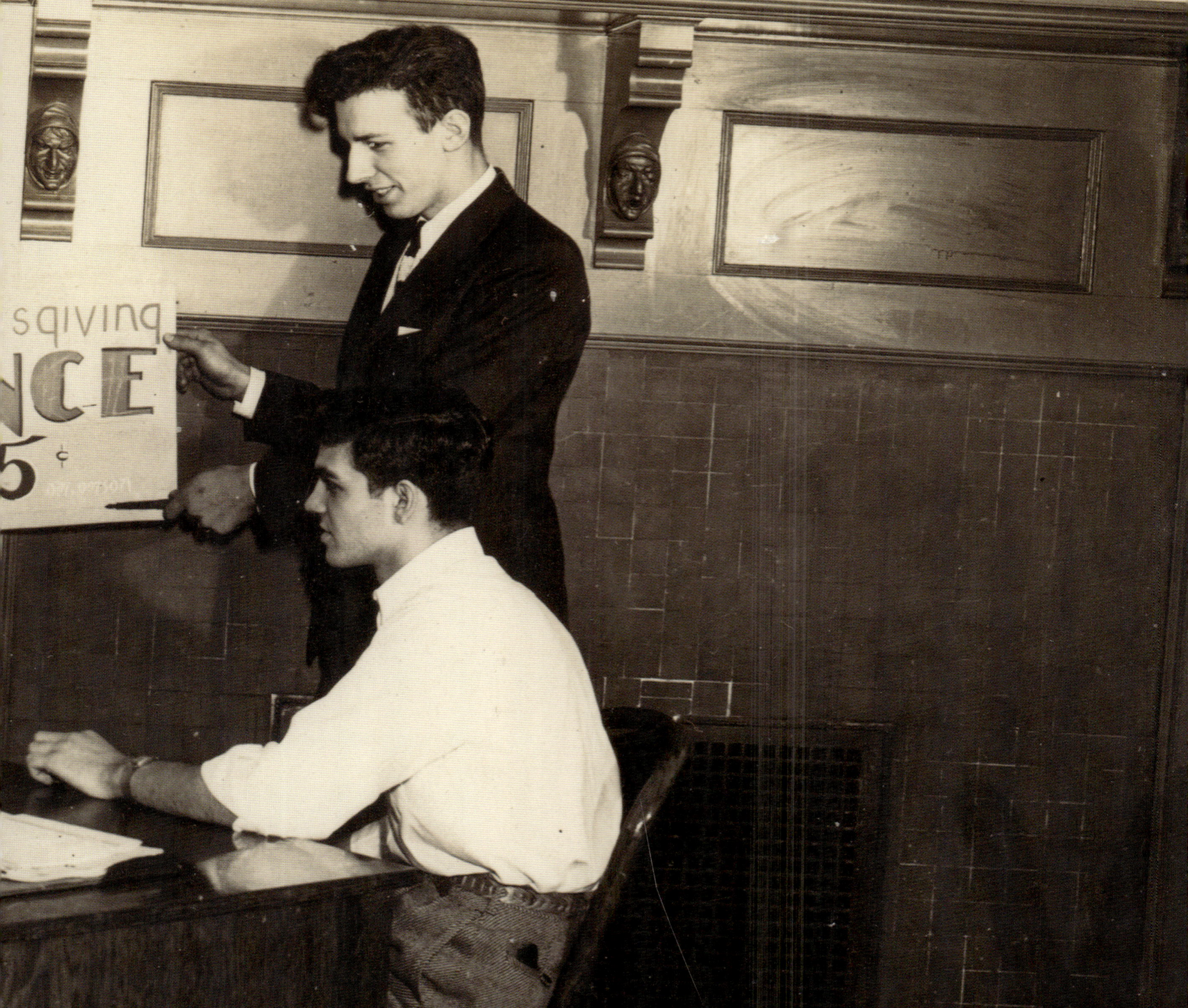
STUDENT COUNCIL
FOOTBALL DANCE
8:00 to 11:30 P.M.
OCT. 23 rd.
DANCE
NOV. 27th
7:30 to 11:00
25¢

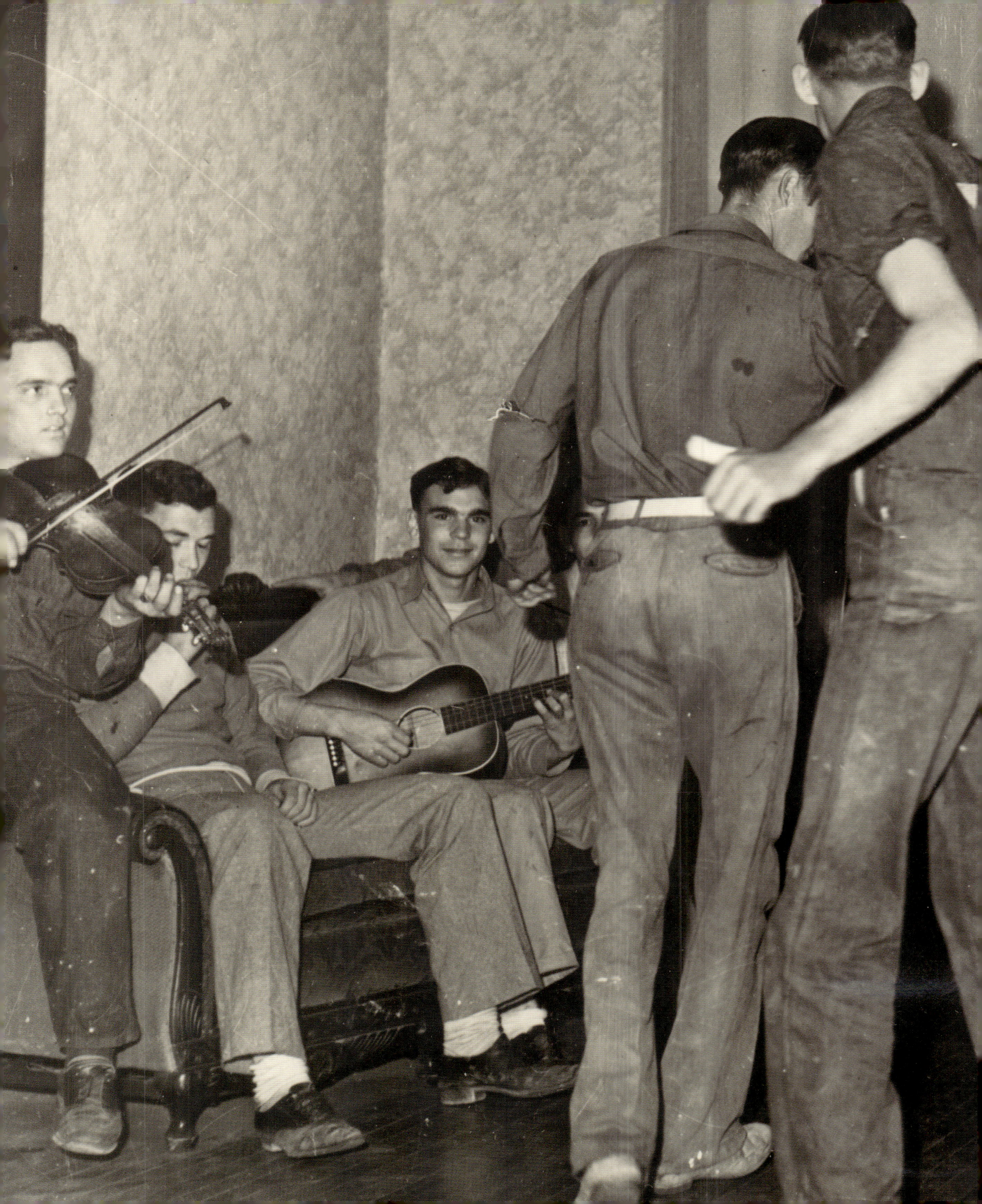

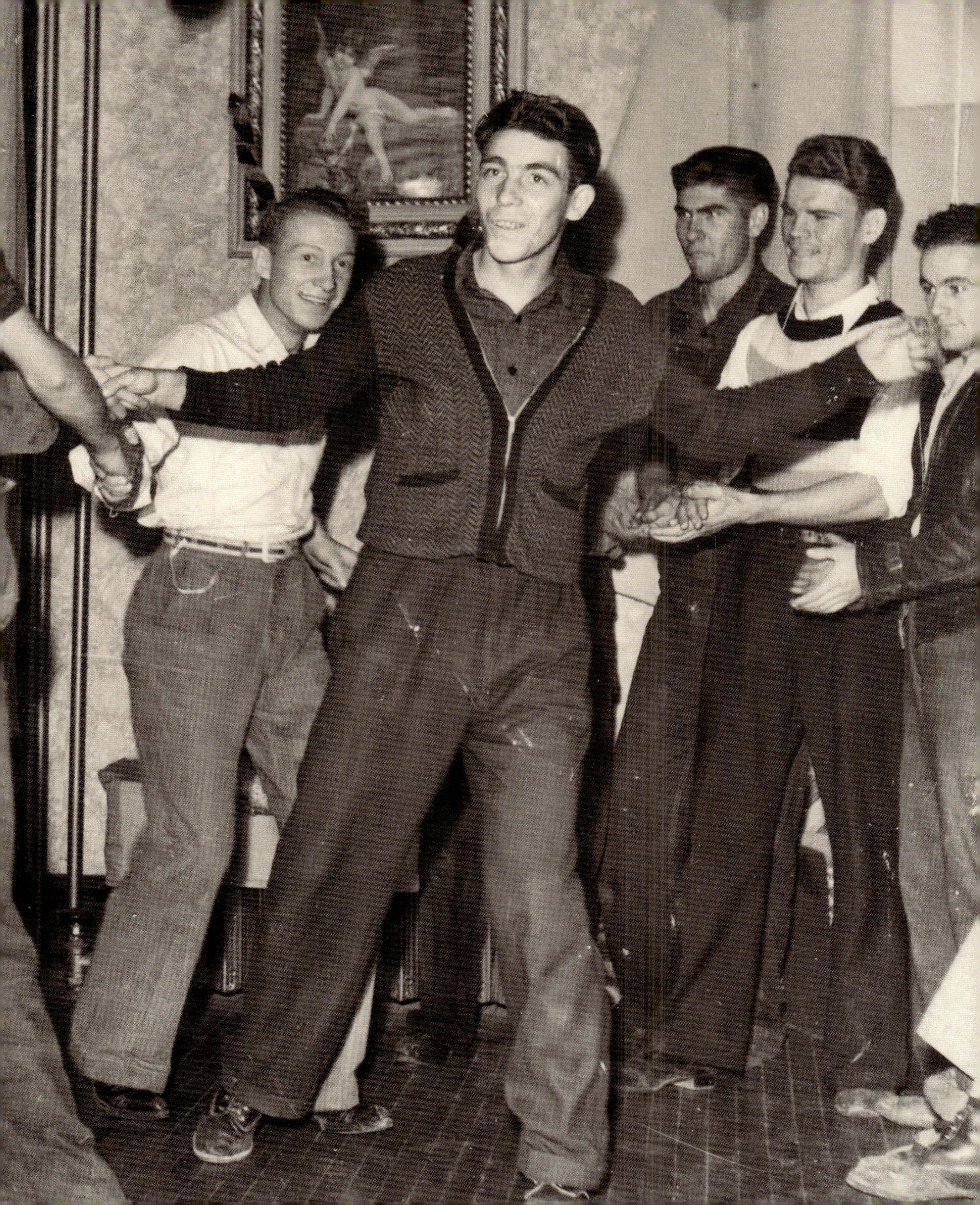

WATCH RELEASE DATE
WIDE WORLD PHOTO : PLEASE WATCH CREDIT

SPECIAL FEATURE SERIES, 905521 to 905527, FOR RELEASE MARCH 5.

2

905523 NATION'S YOUTH CARVE OWN CAREERS

CARBONDALE, Ill.-- There's nothing jitterbuggish about these big country lads and when recreation time comes around, the good old-fashioned square dance is the thing. There are no house rules posted--the boys have a gentleman's agreement when they enter the house, and if any of them get out of line, the boys themselves usually take care of the offender in their own inimitable way.

t-2/17/39 (fea) pgd

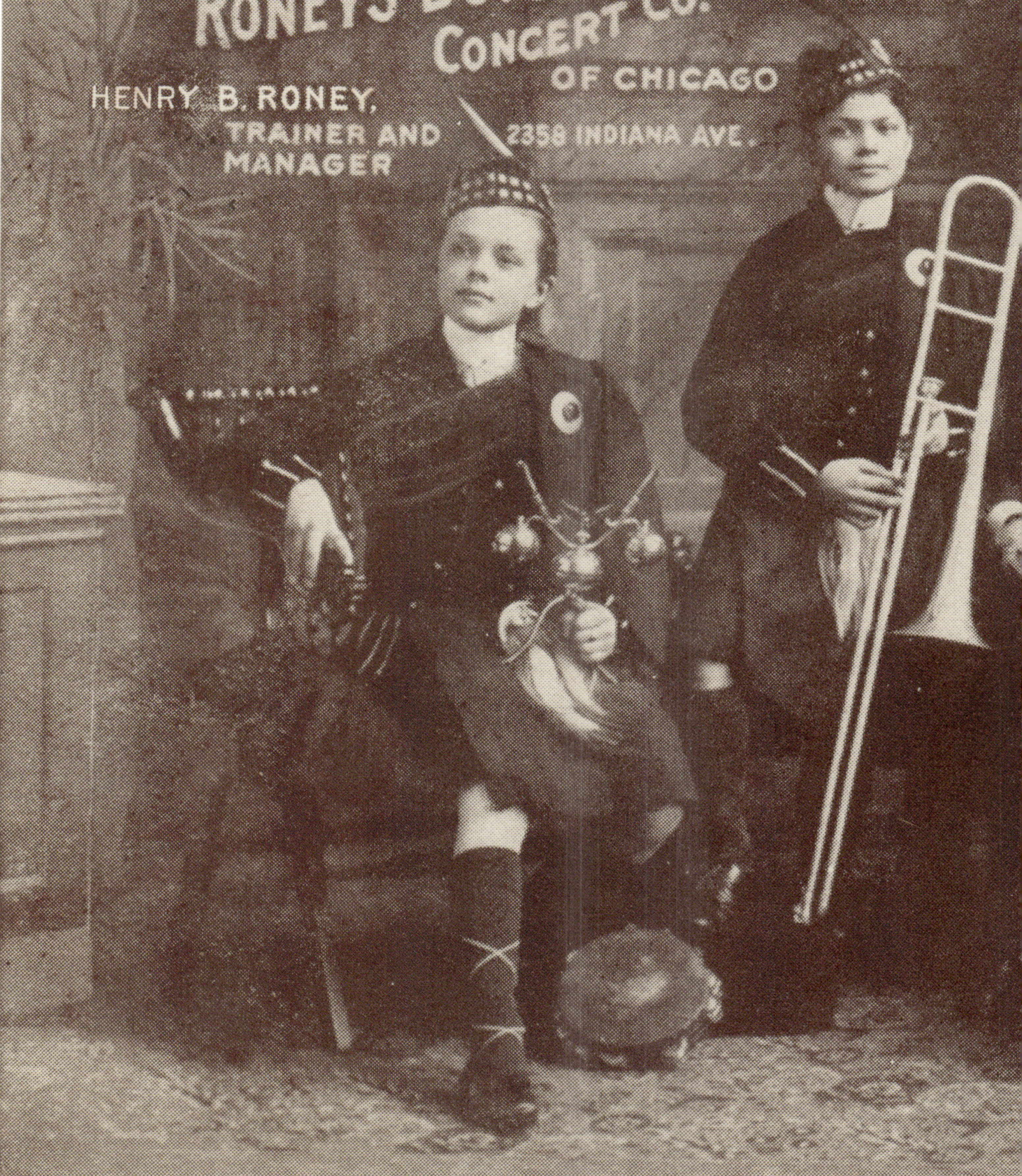

"RONEY'S BOYS"
CONCERT CO.
OF CHICAGO
HENRY B. RONEY,
TRAINER AND
MANAGER
2358 INDIANA AVE.

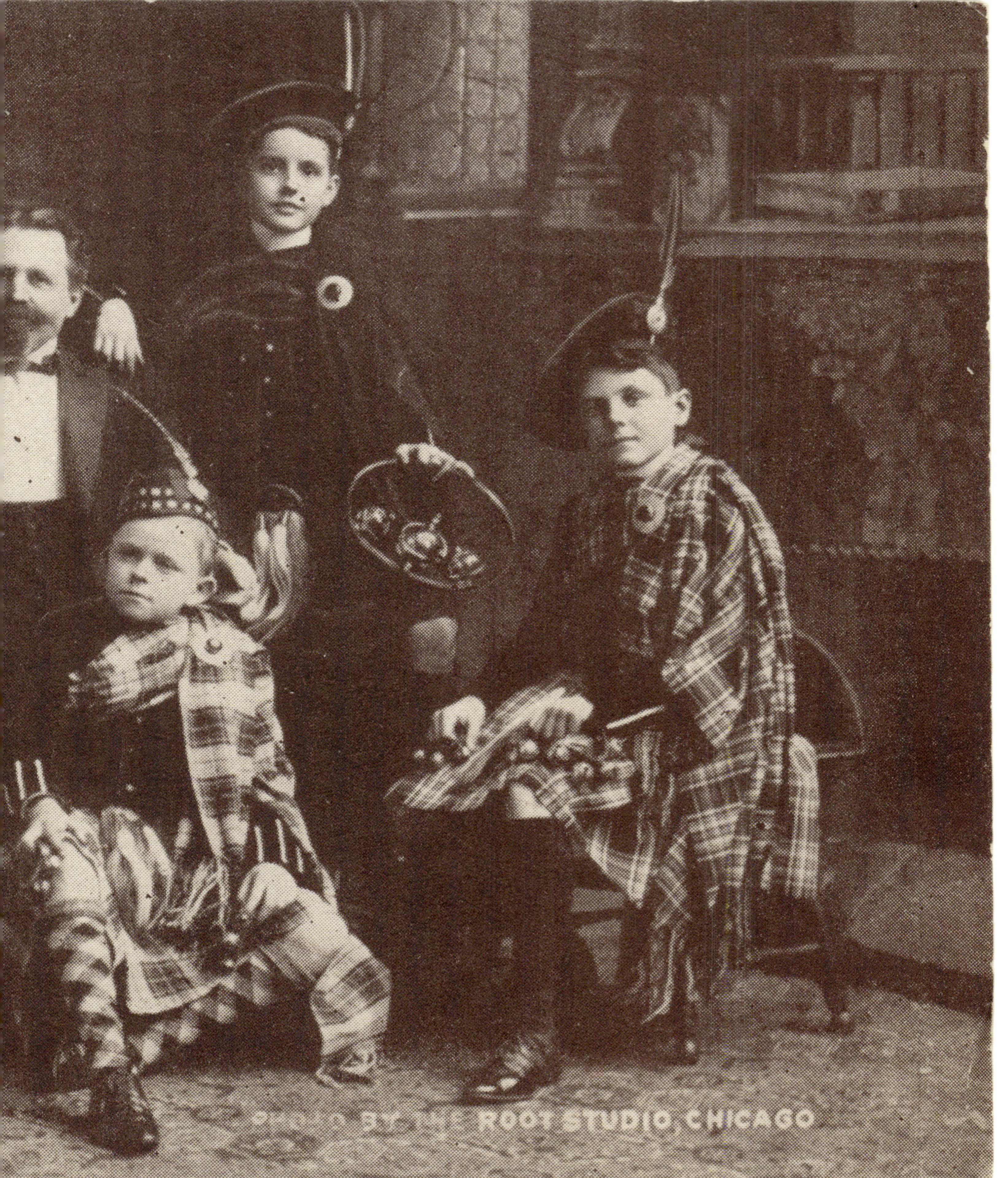
PHOTO BY THE ROOT STUDIO, CHICAGO

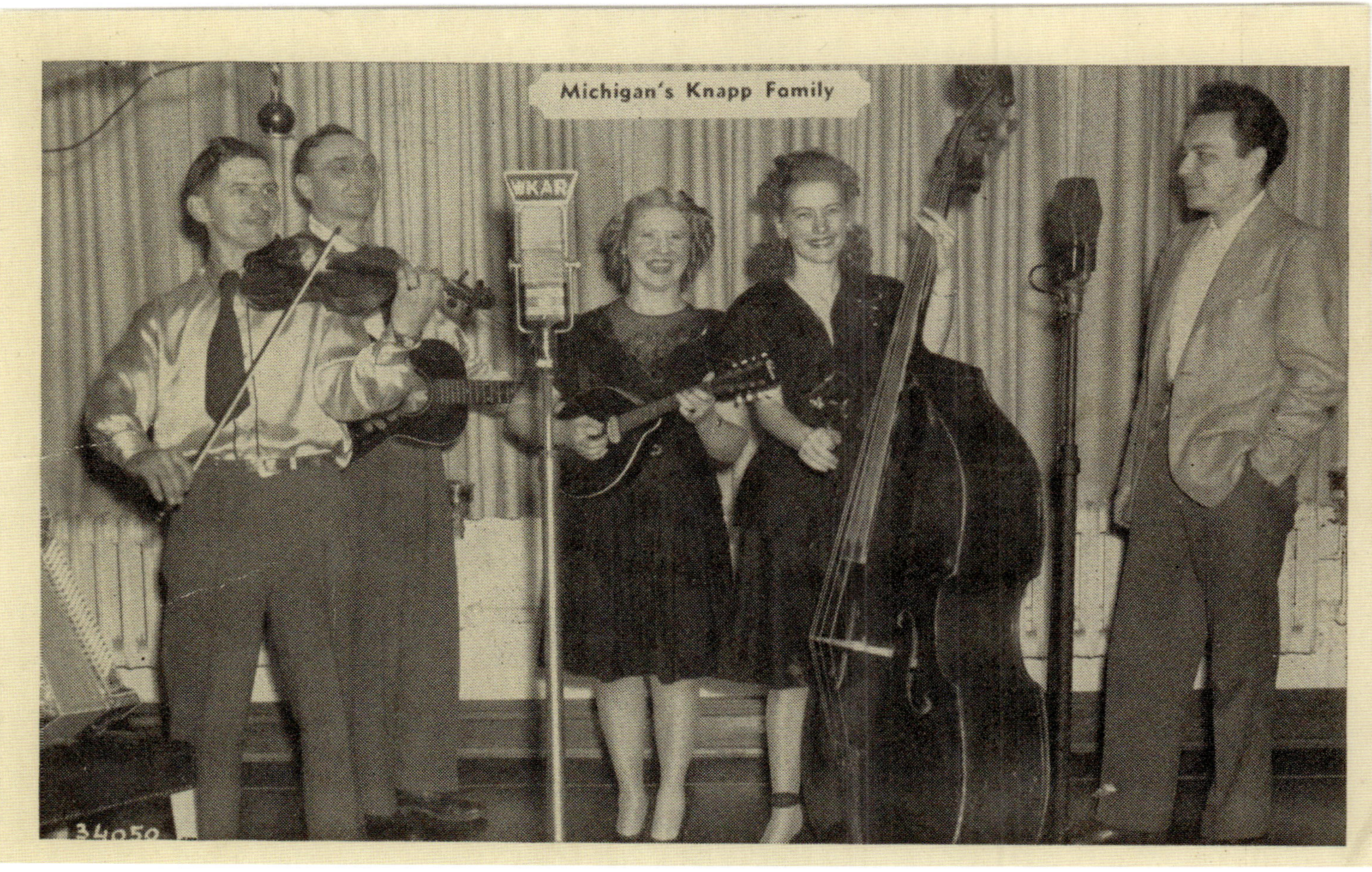
Michigan's Knapp Family
WKAR
34050

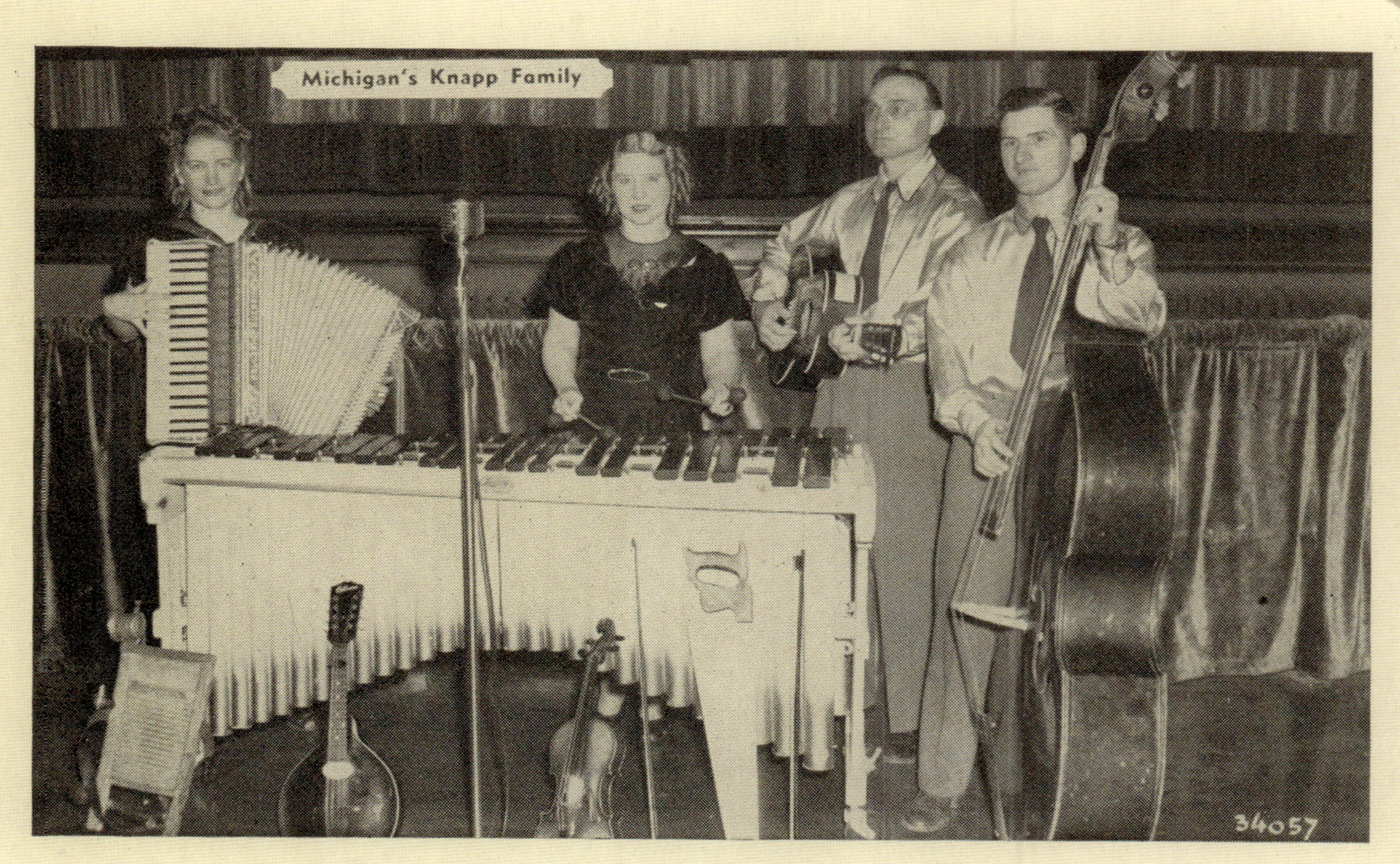
Michigan's Knapp Family
34057

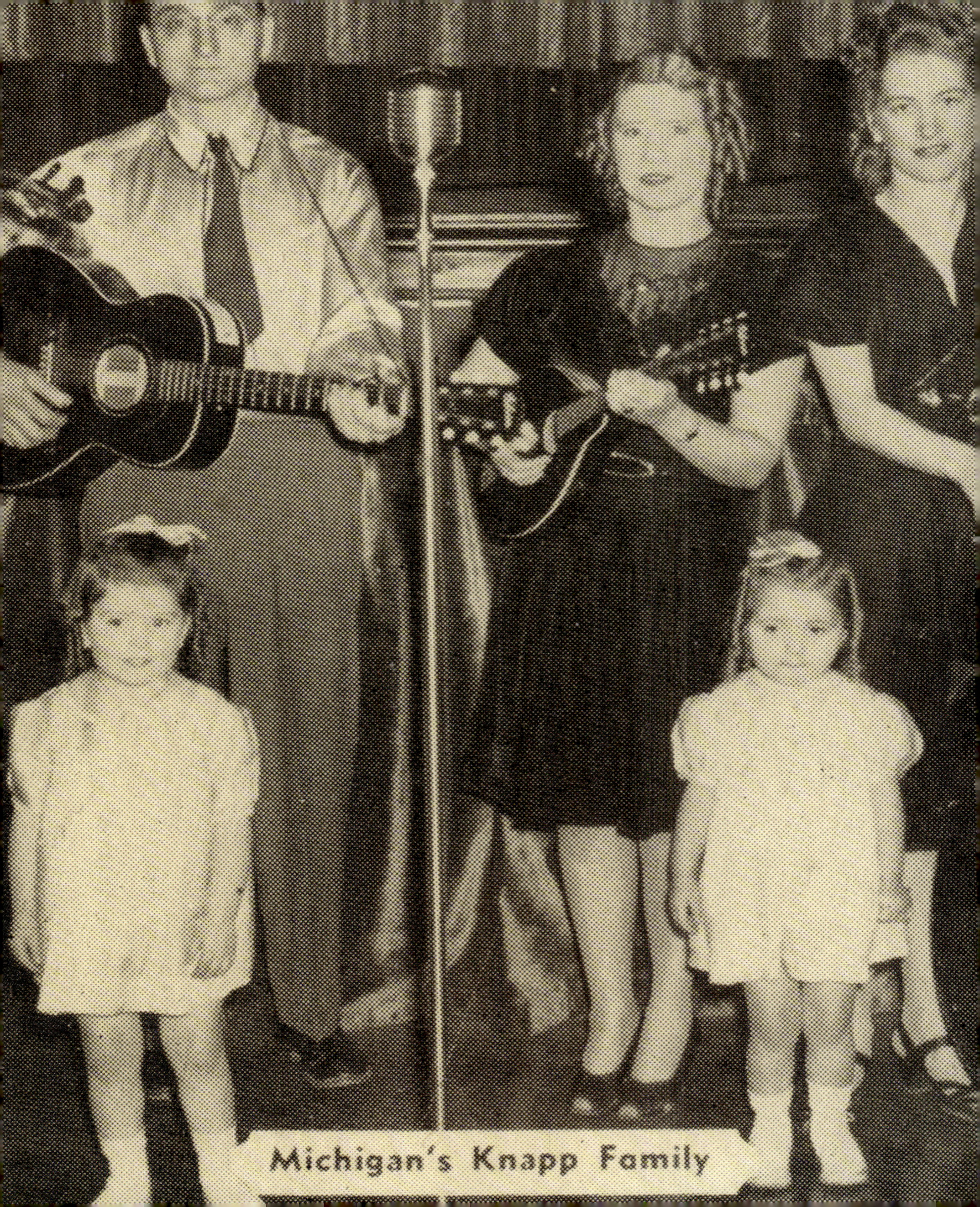

Michigan's Knapp Family

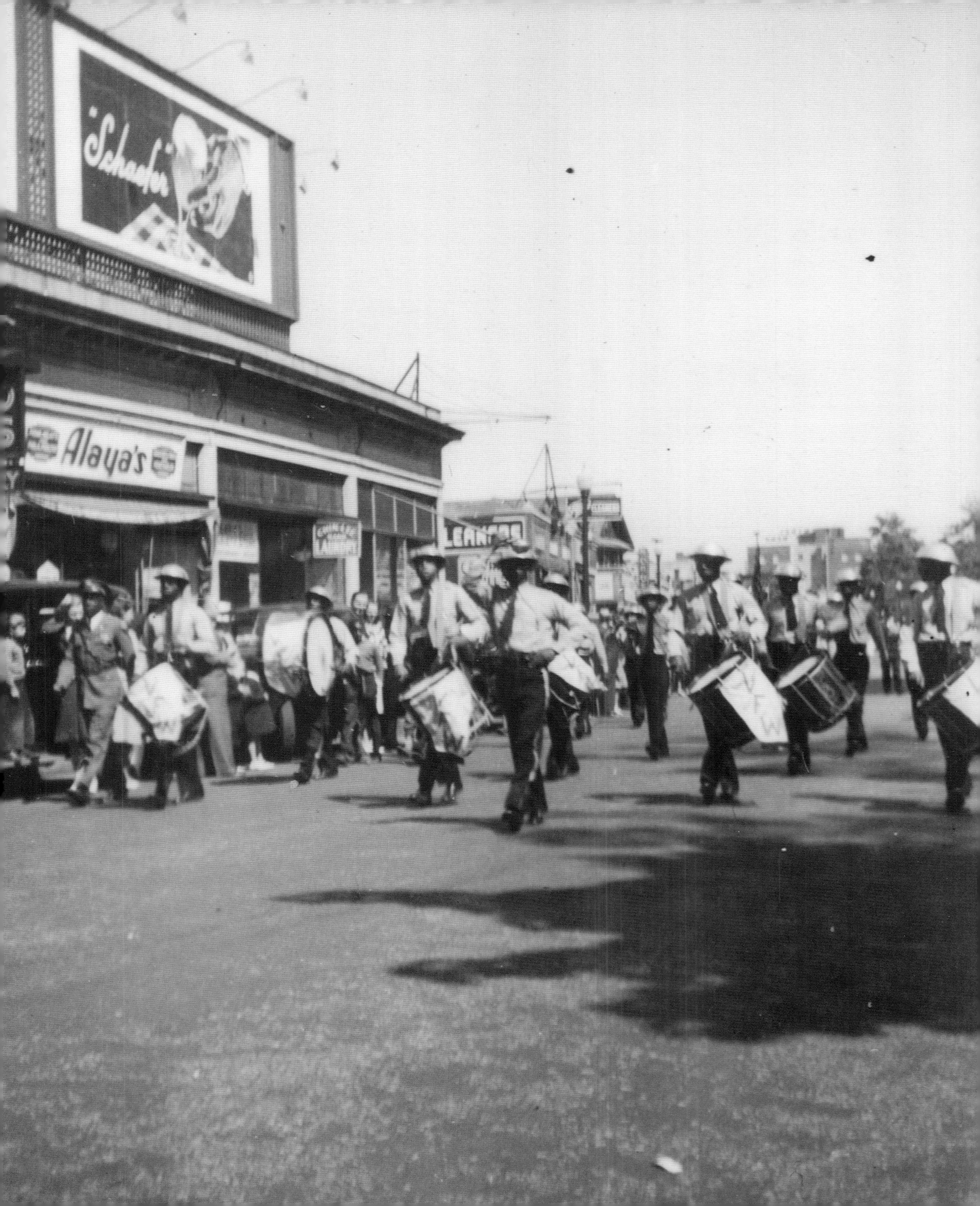
"Schaefer"
Alaya's

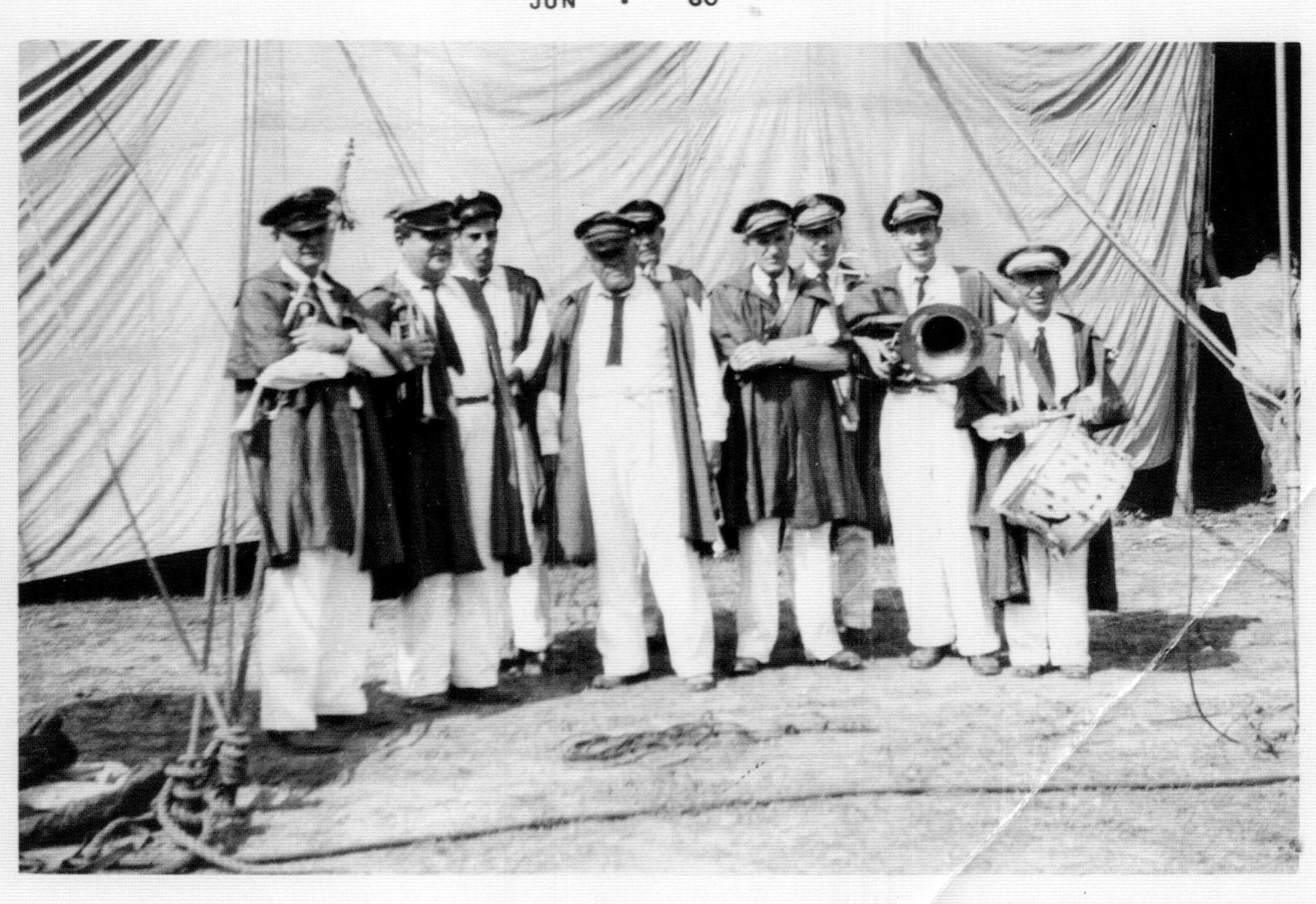
JUN • 60

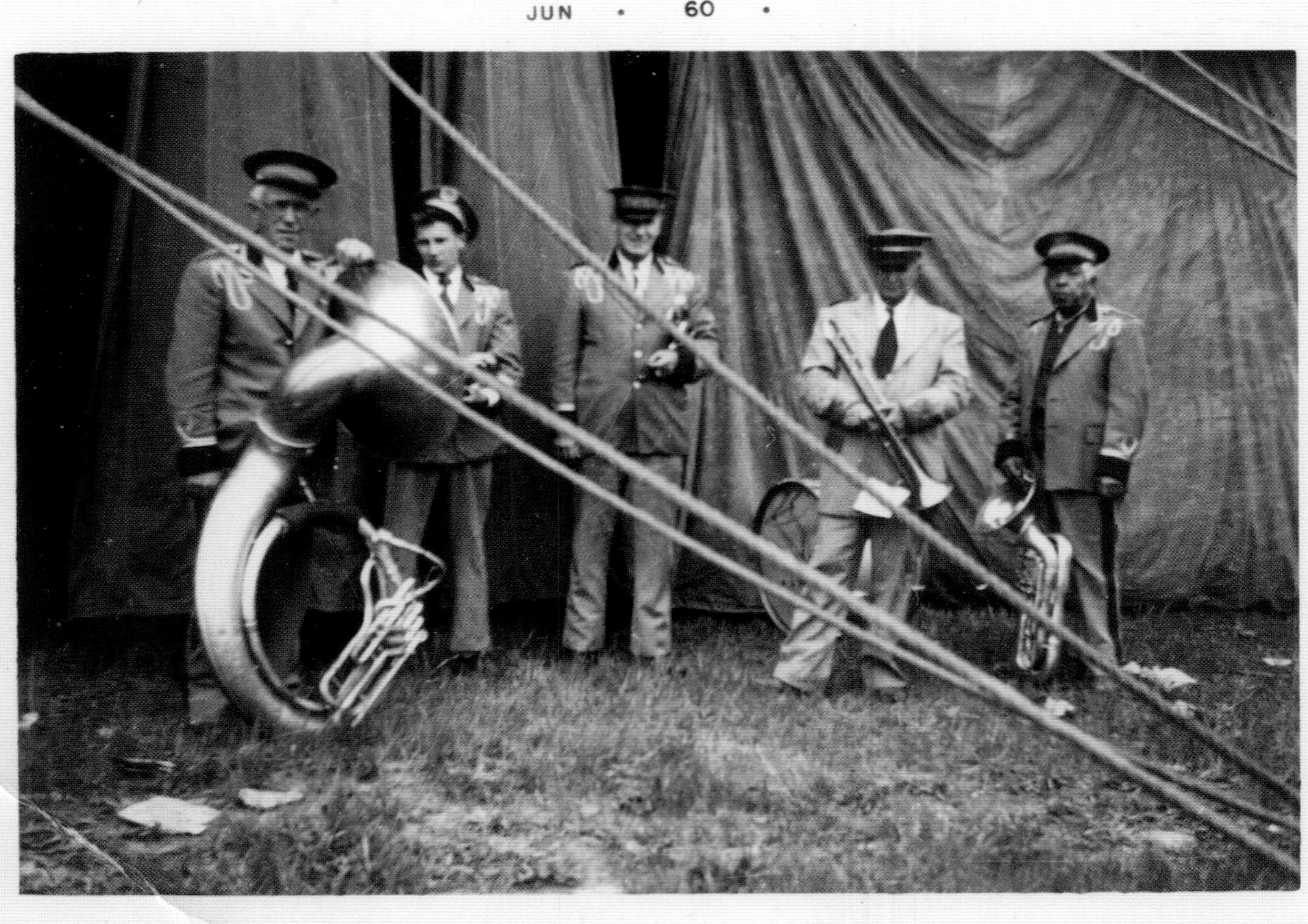
JUN • 60 •

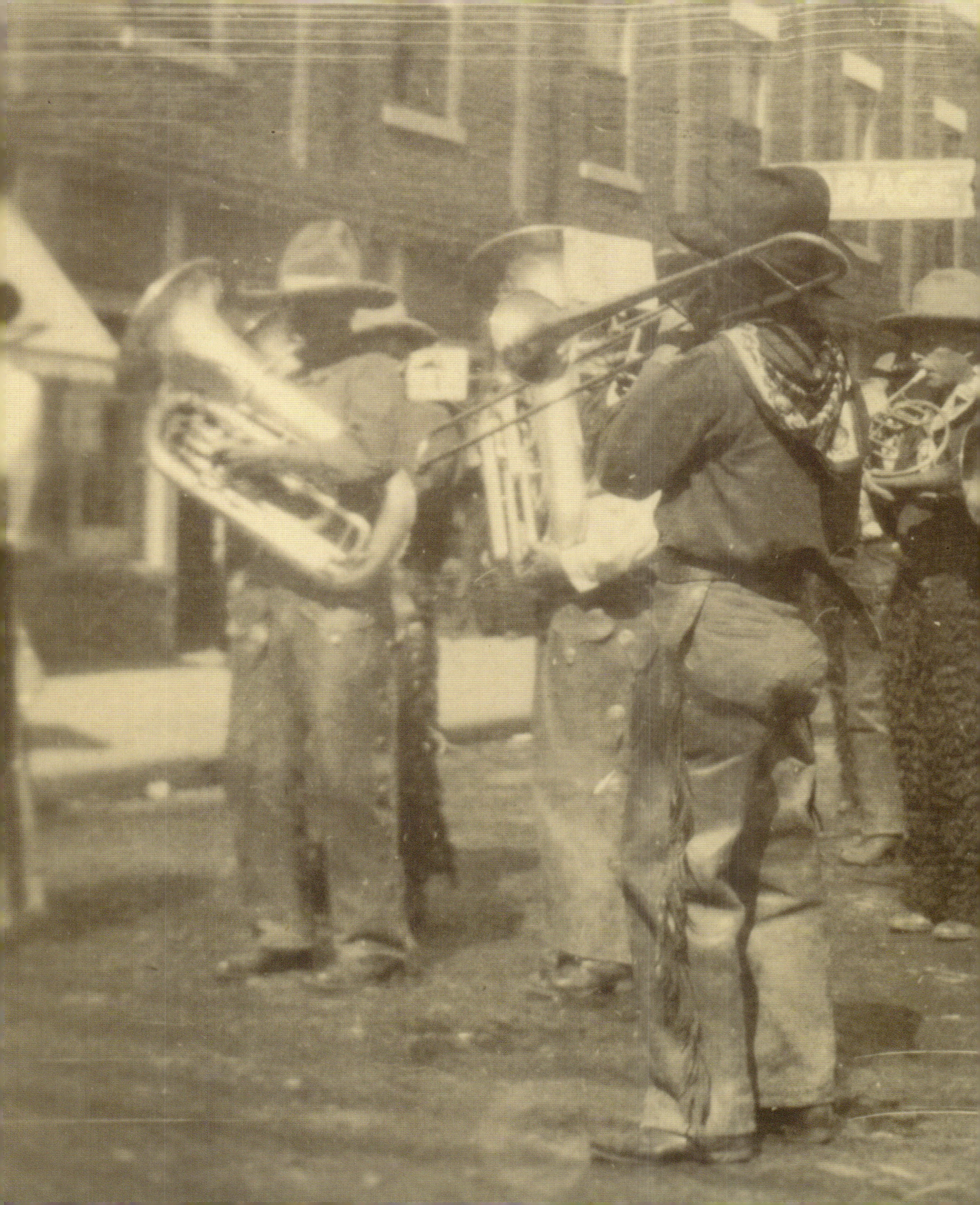

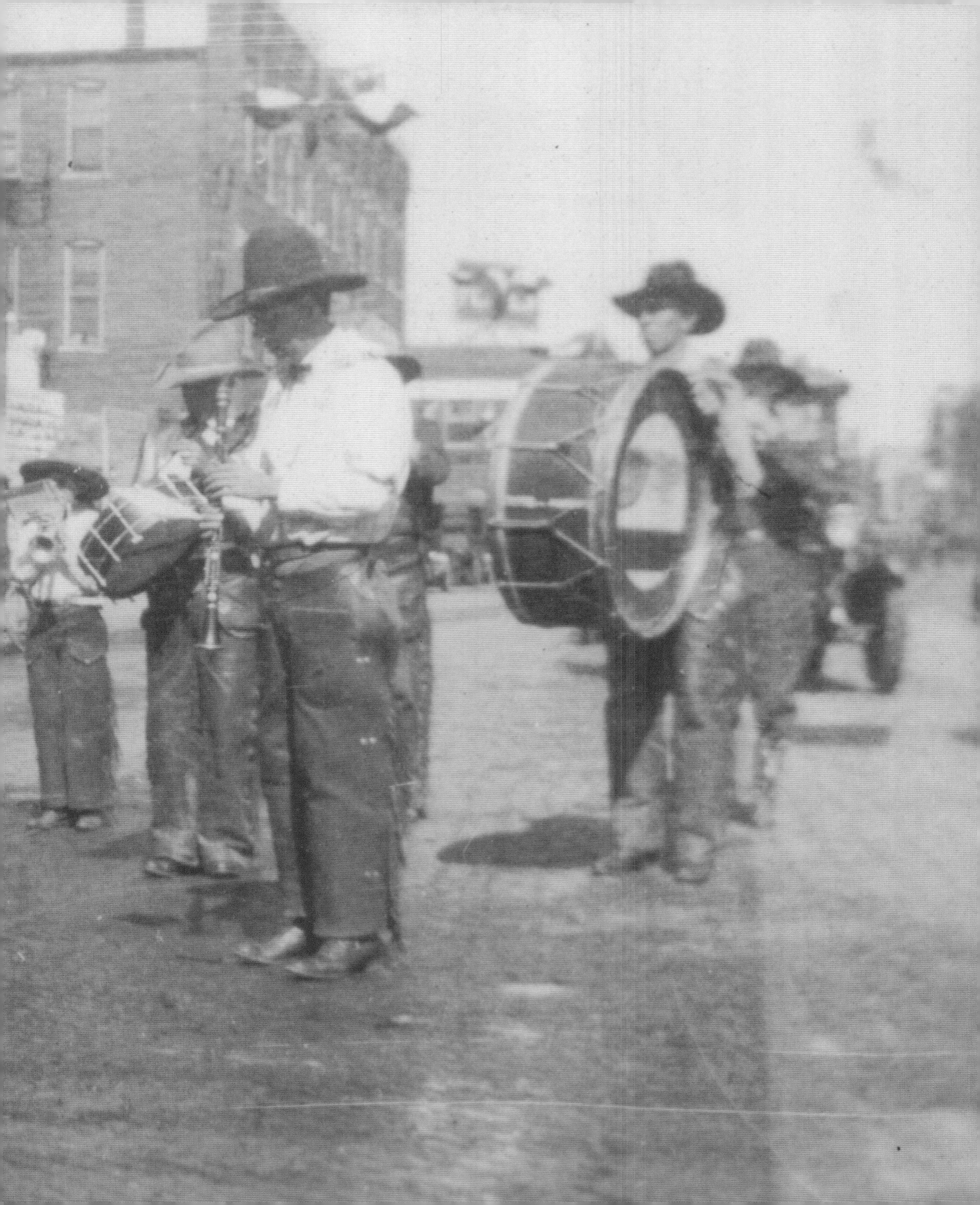

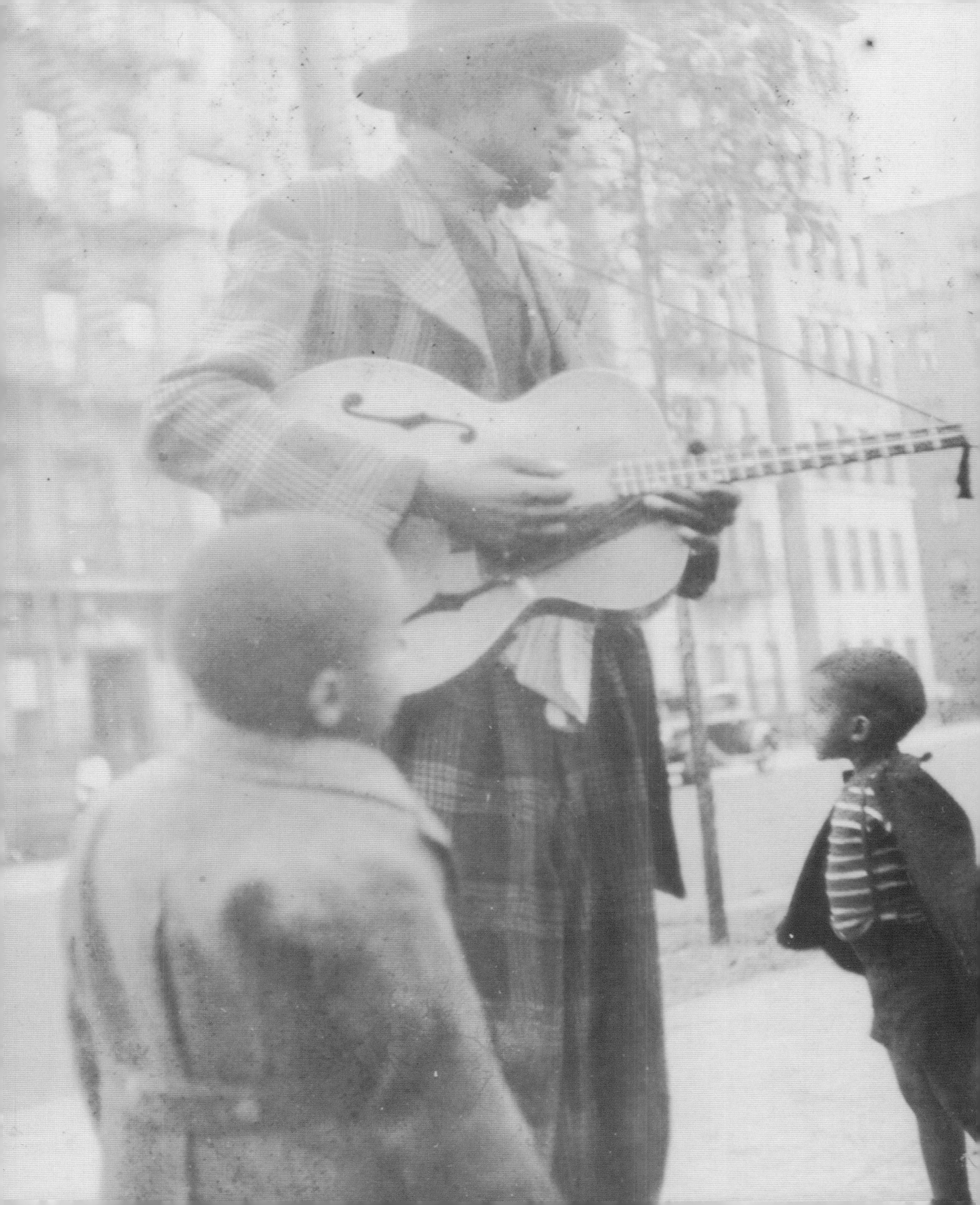

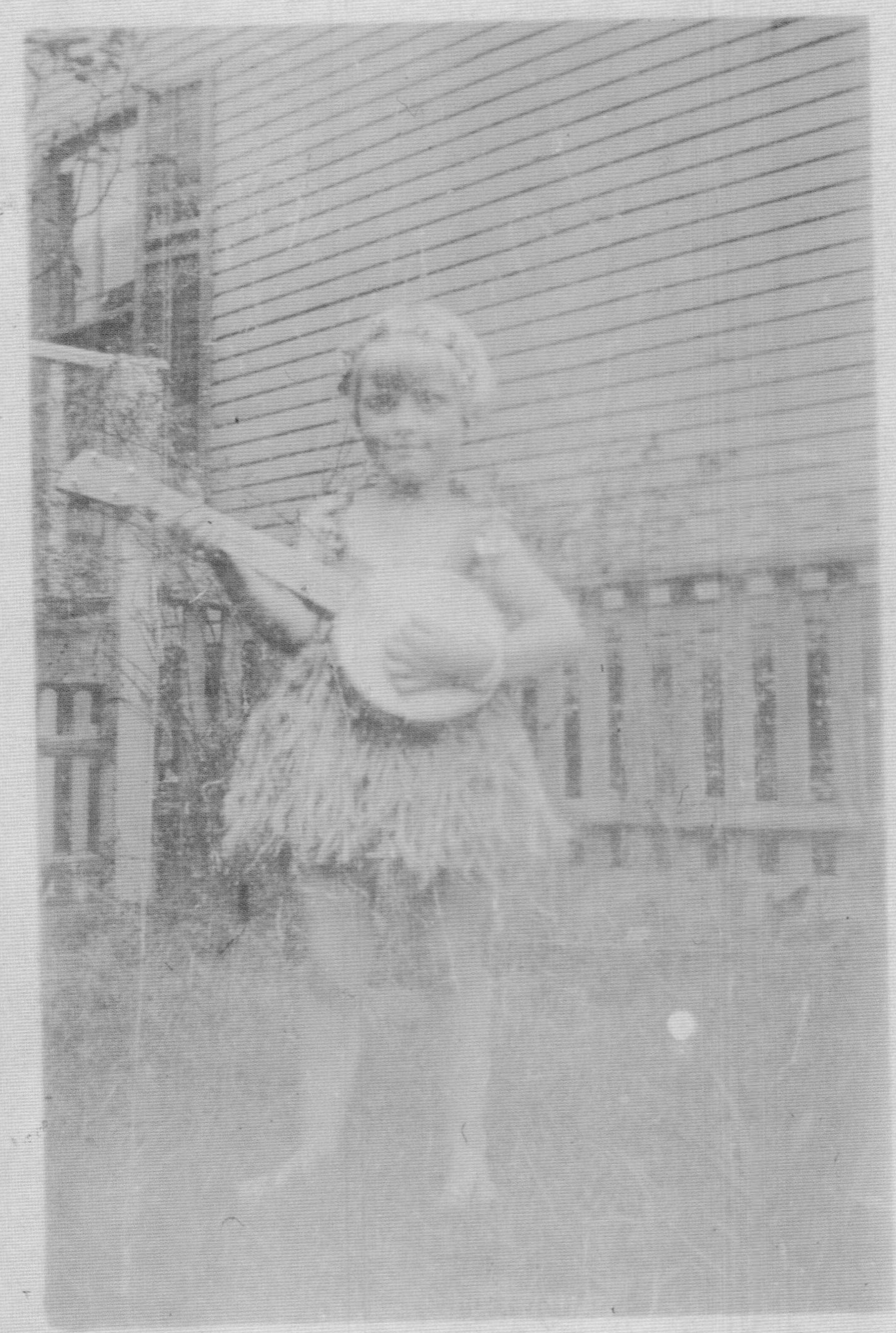

Broad - Channel
Aug. 17. - 1925 -

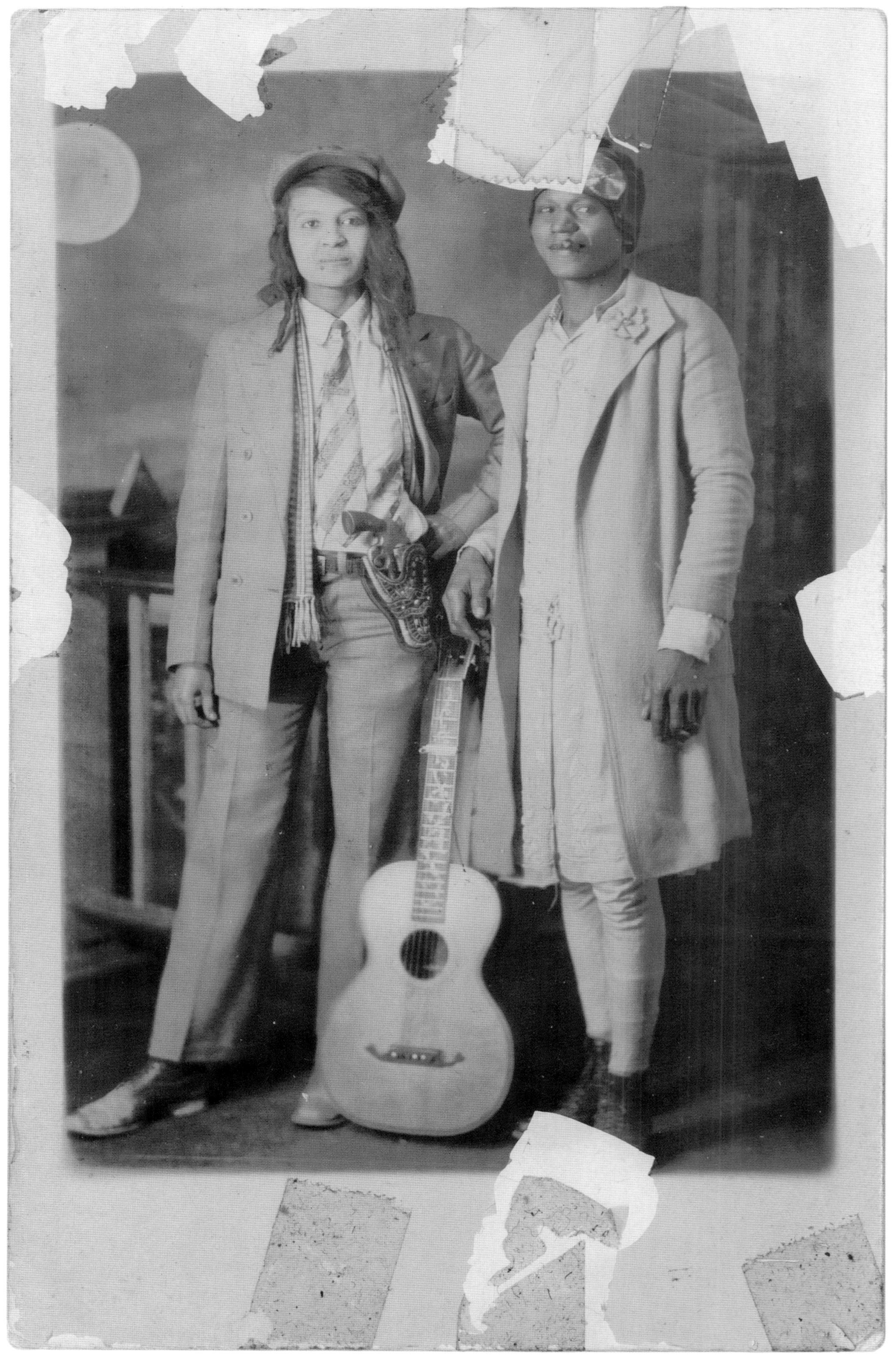

2.

this is what I am
Talk about on
the phone

POST CARD

CORRESPONDENCE ADDRESS

PLACE STAMP HERE

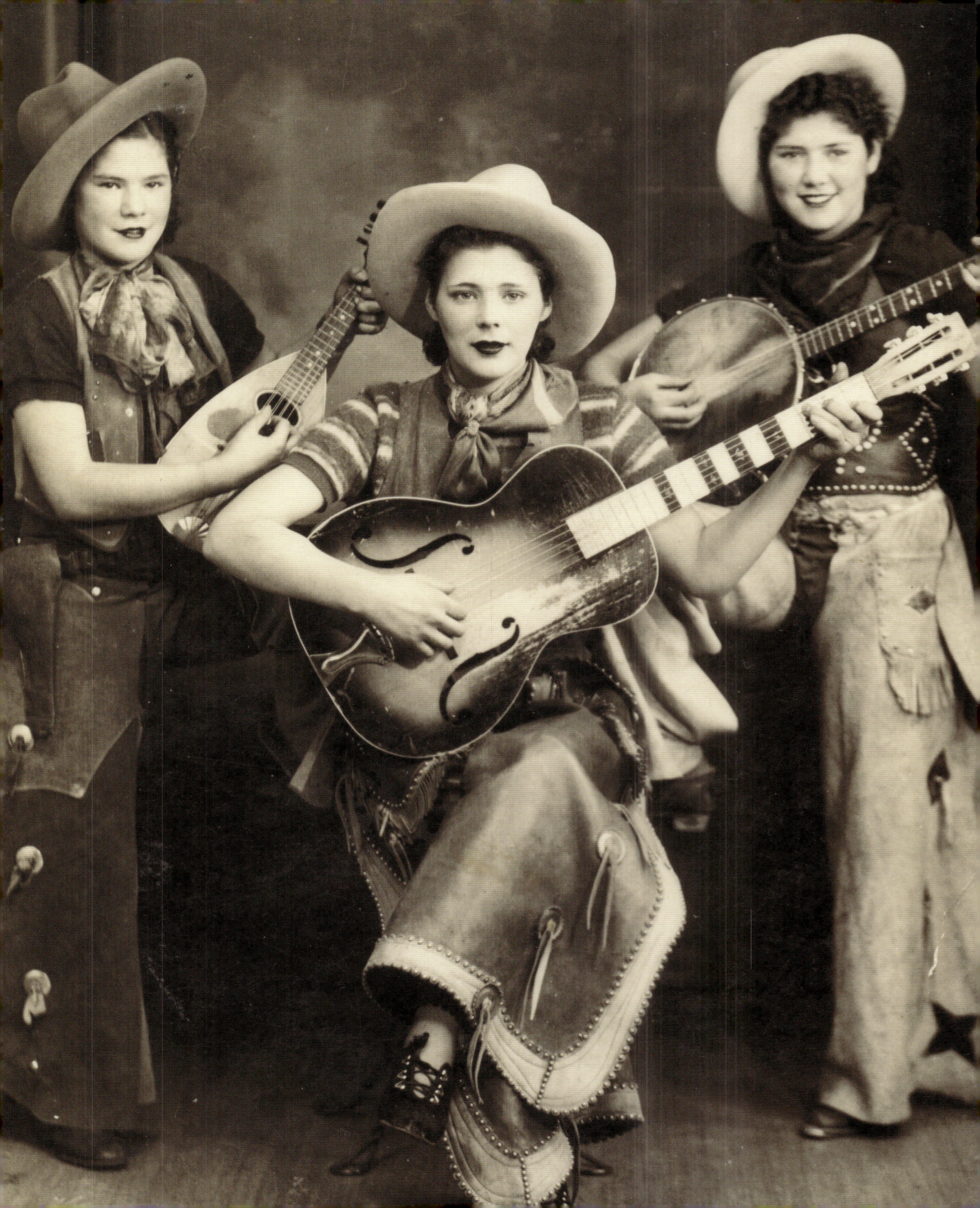

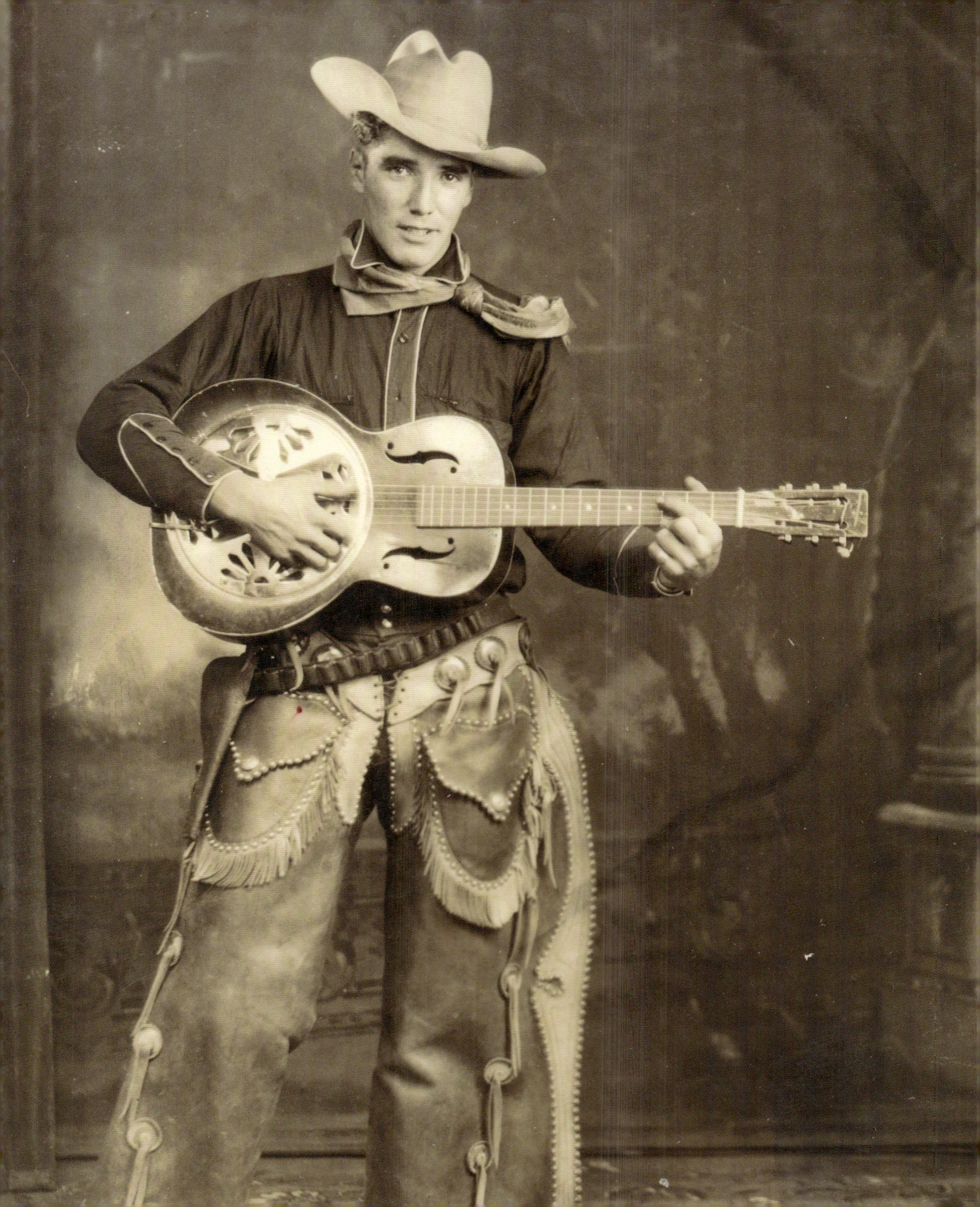

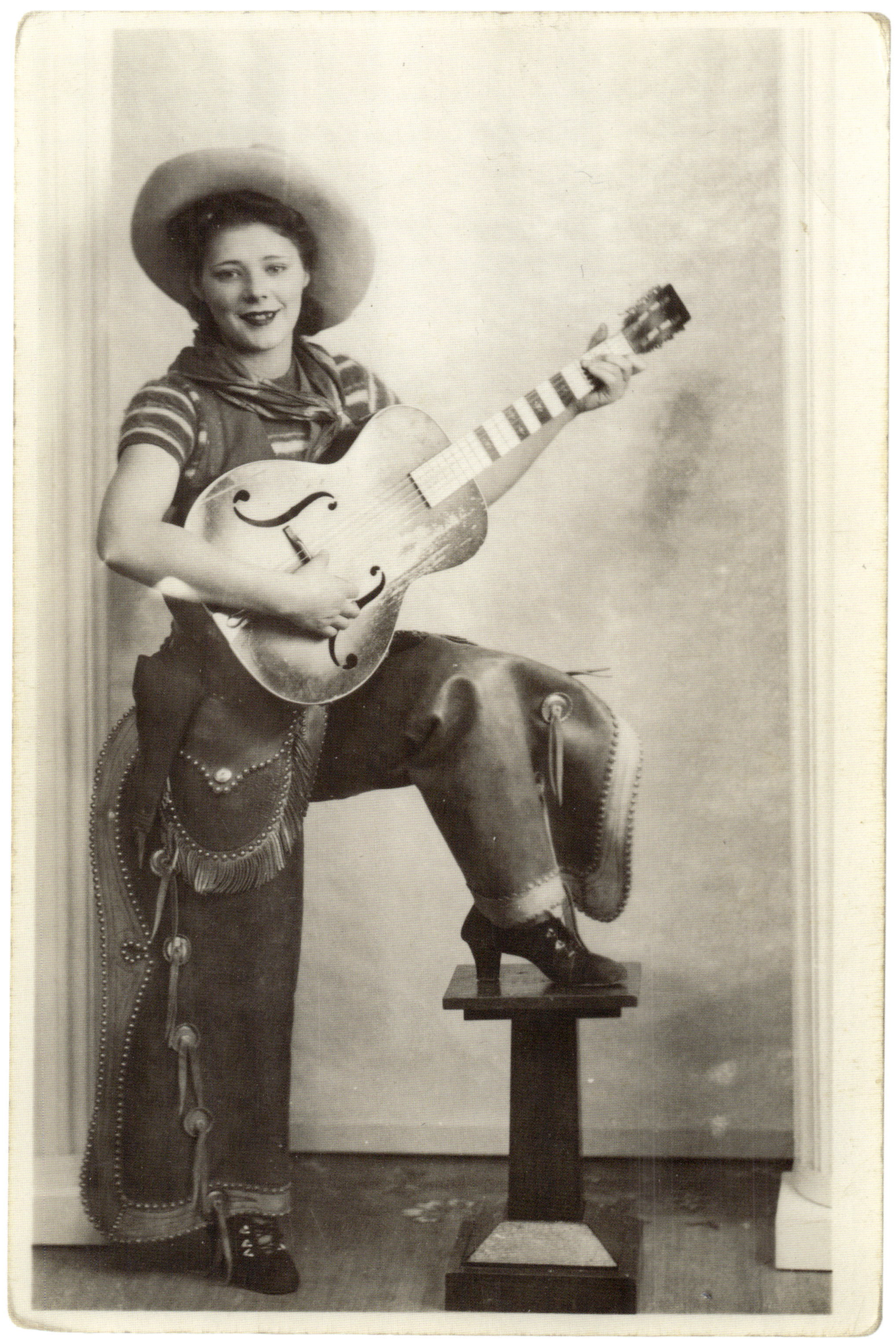

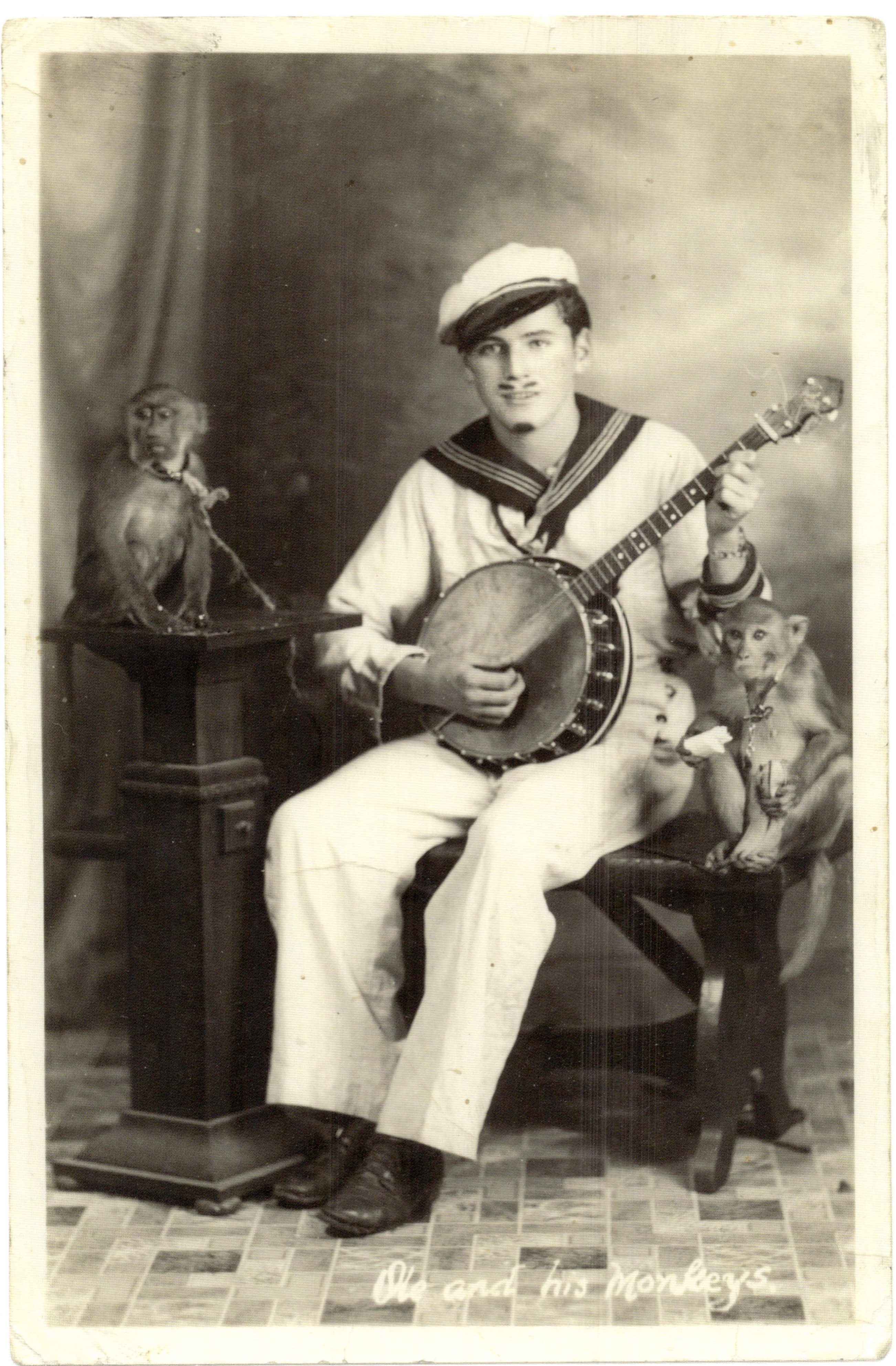
Ole and his Monkeys.

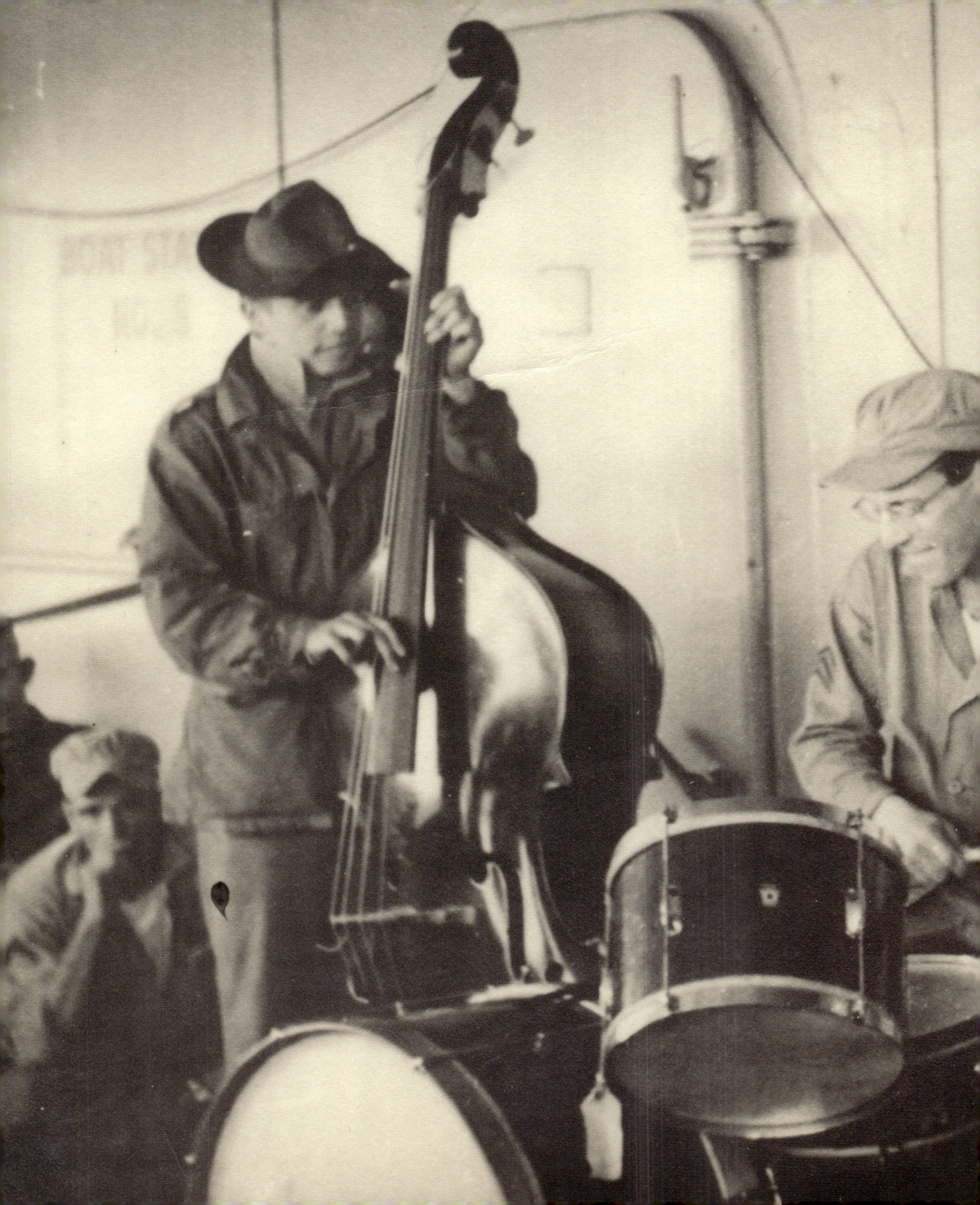
5

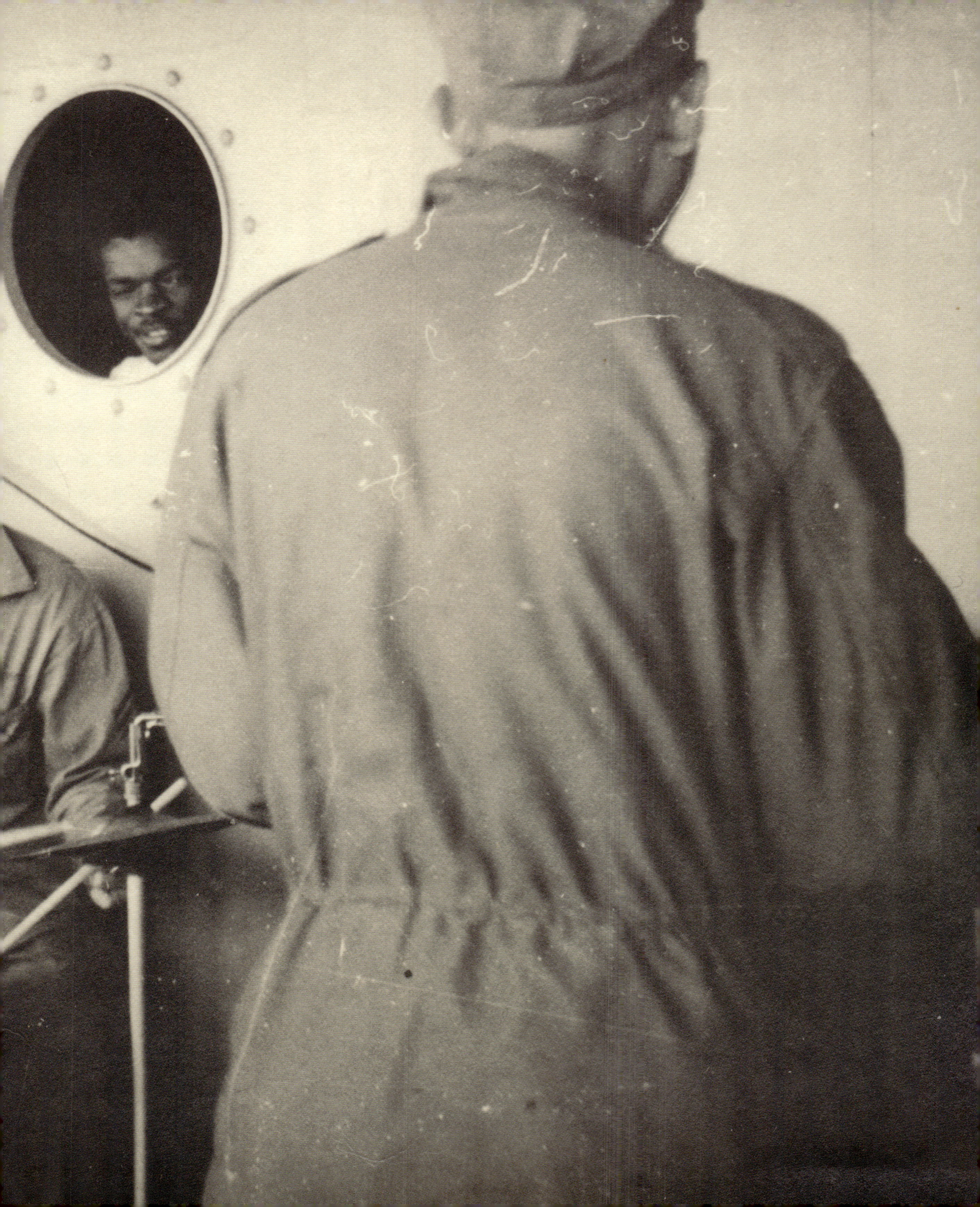

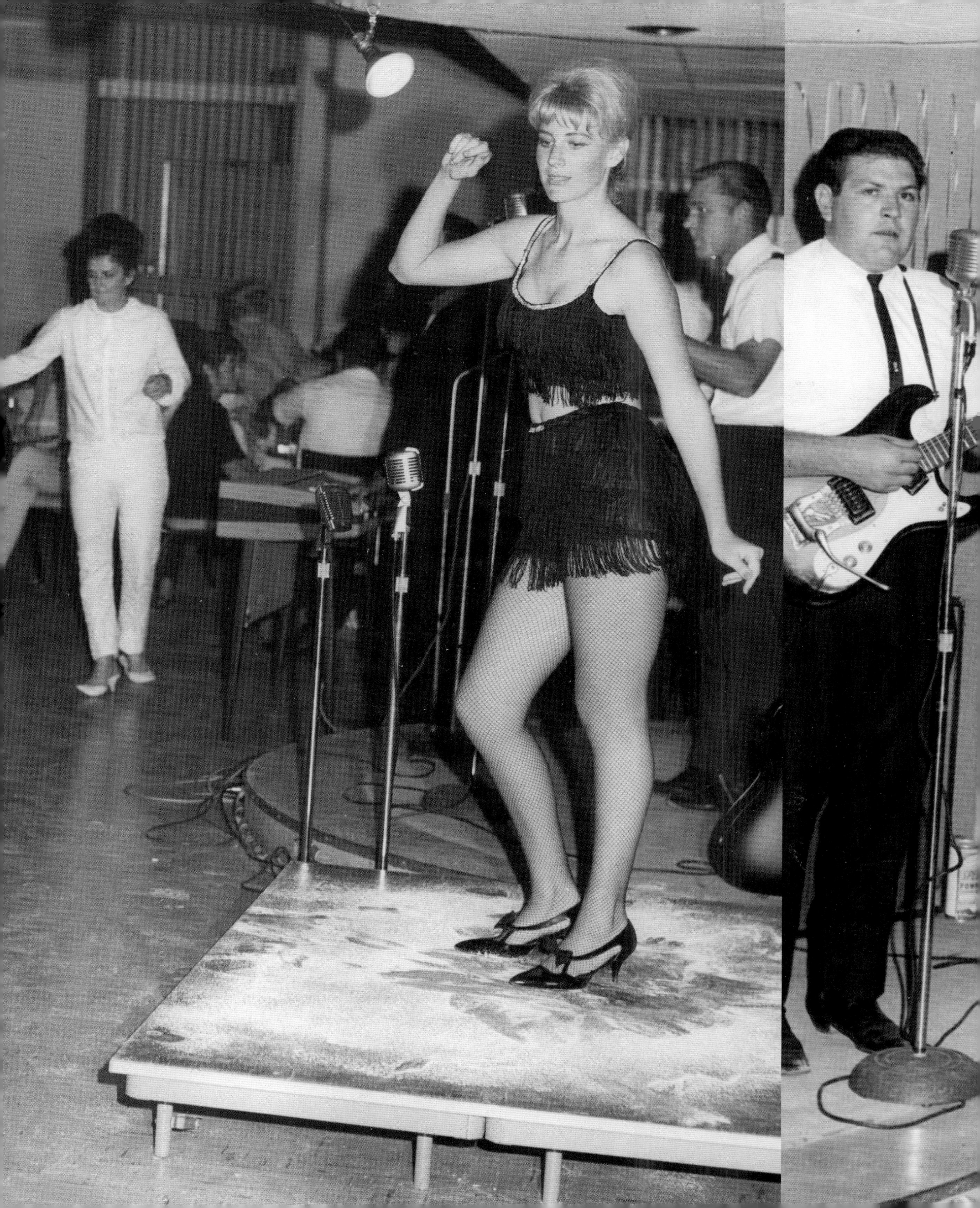

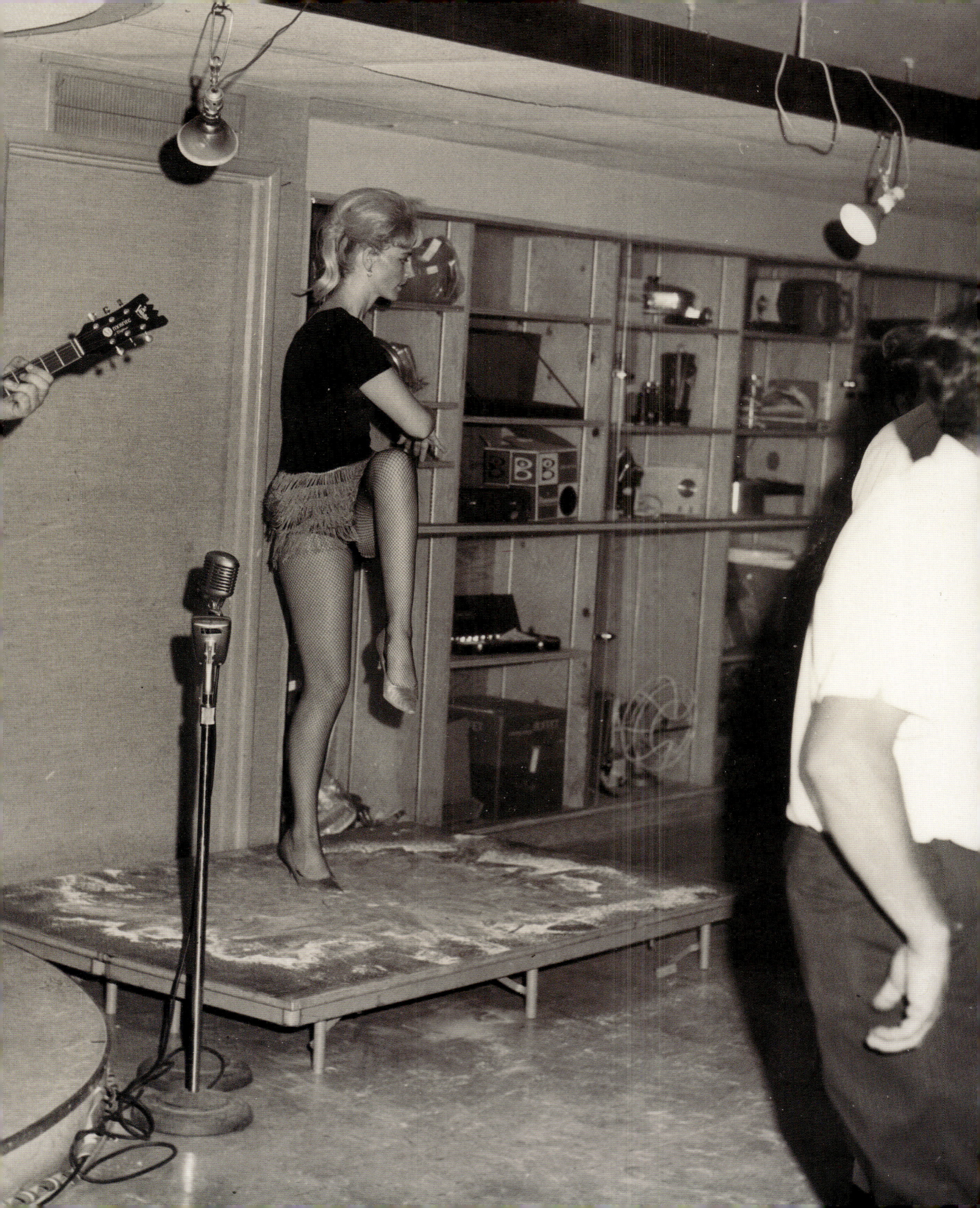

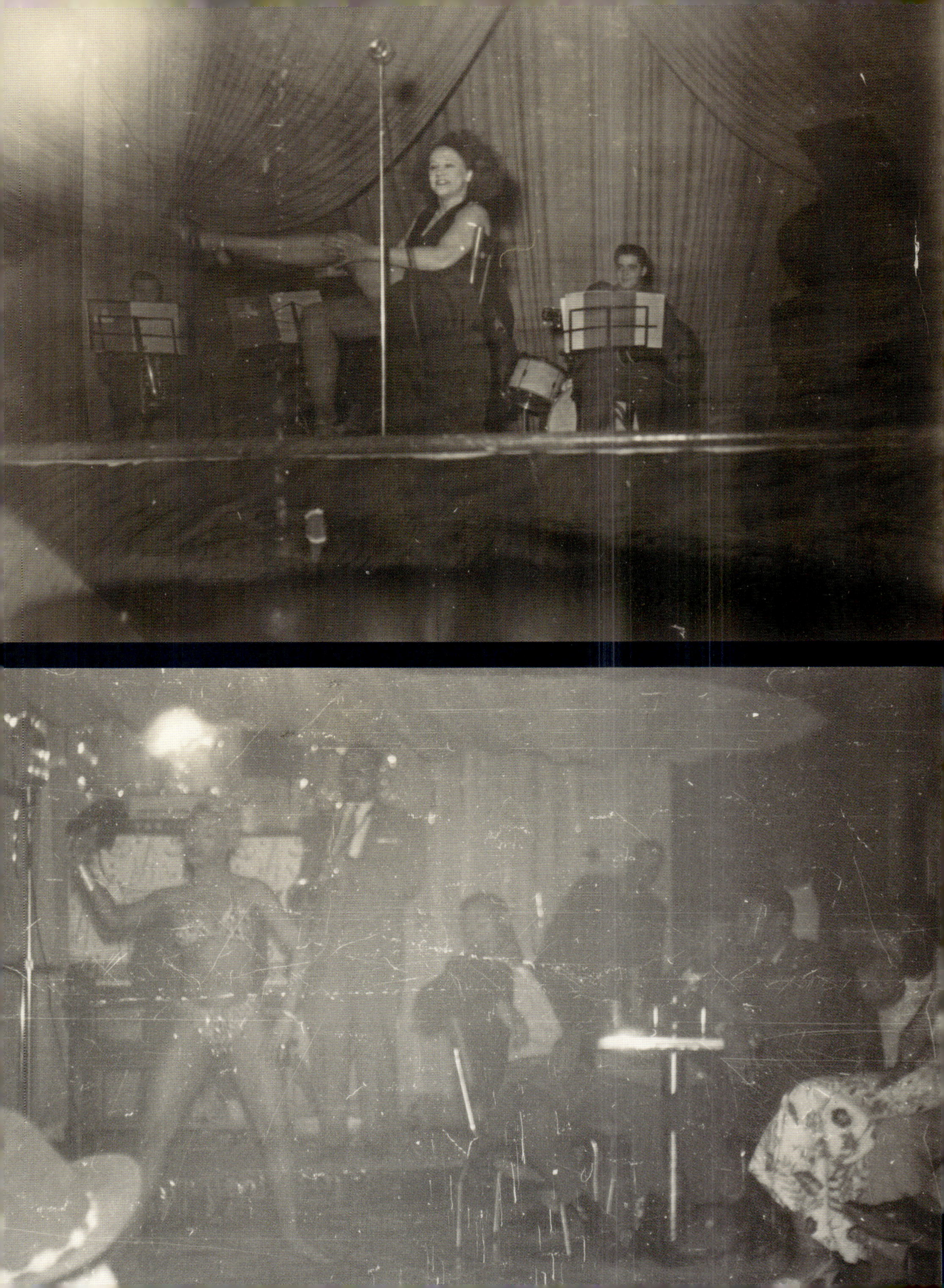

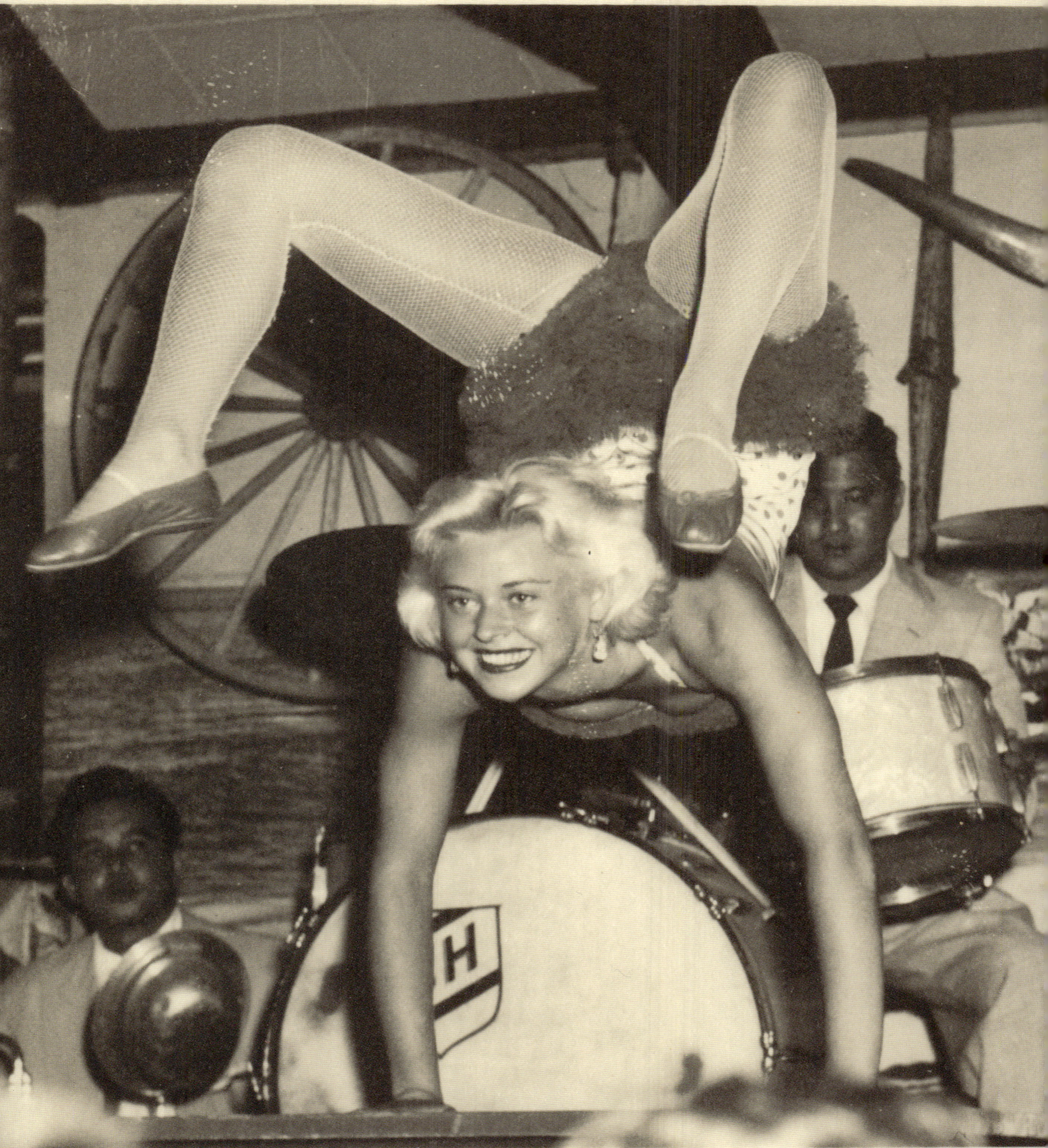

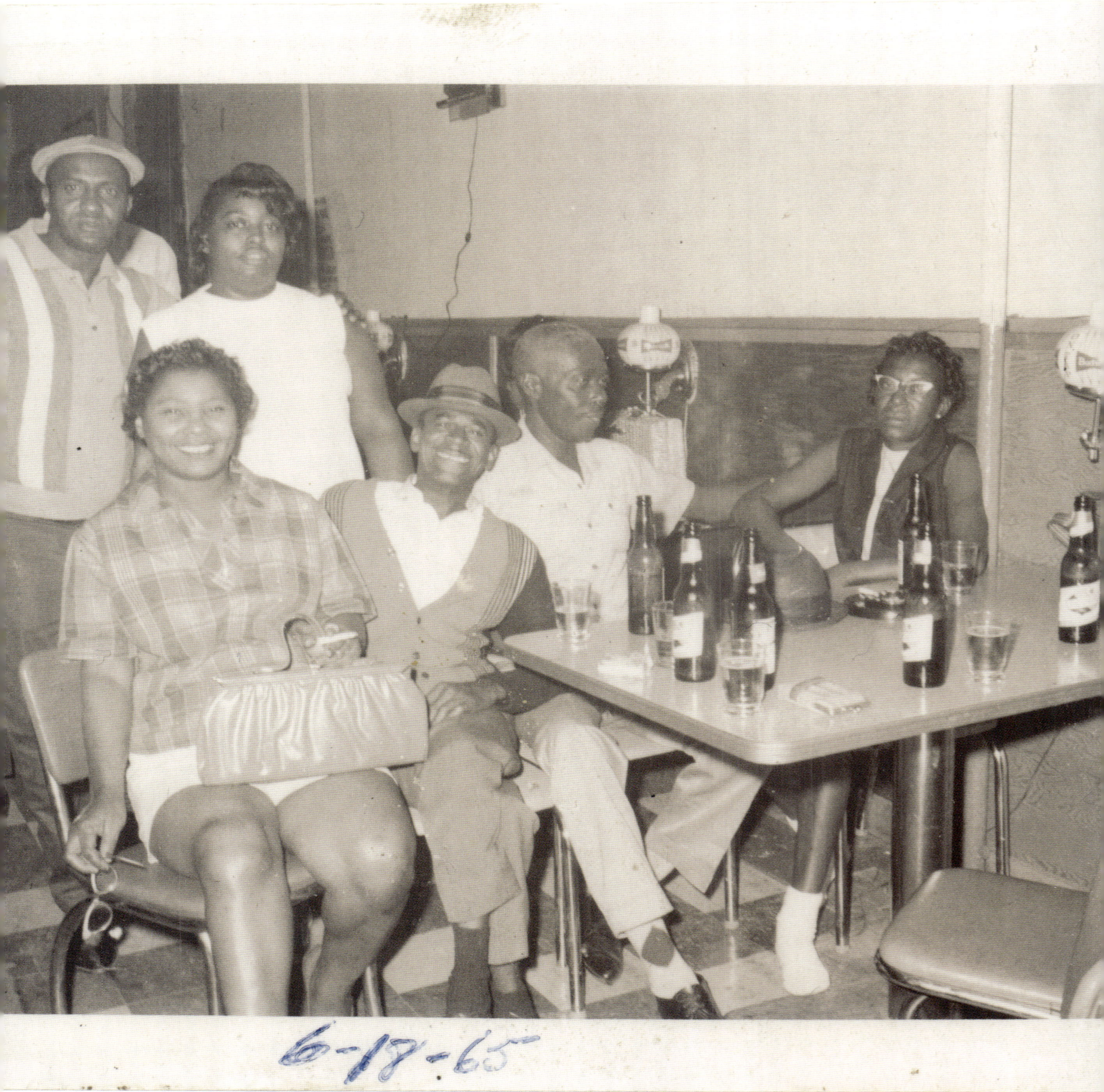
6-18-65

NOV 1959

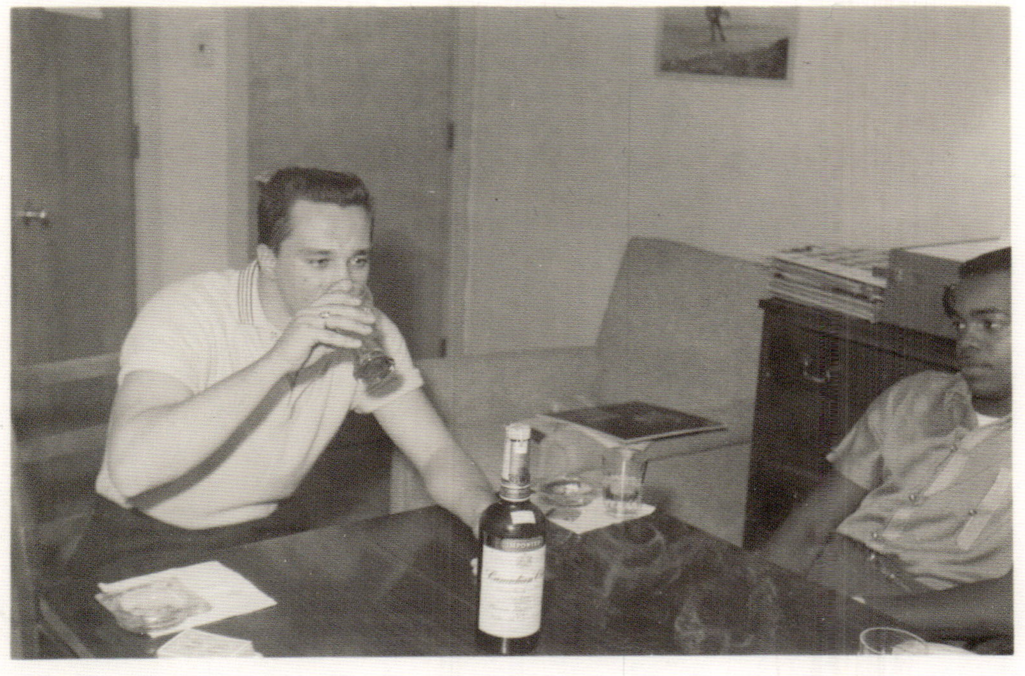

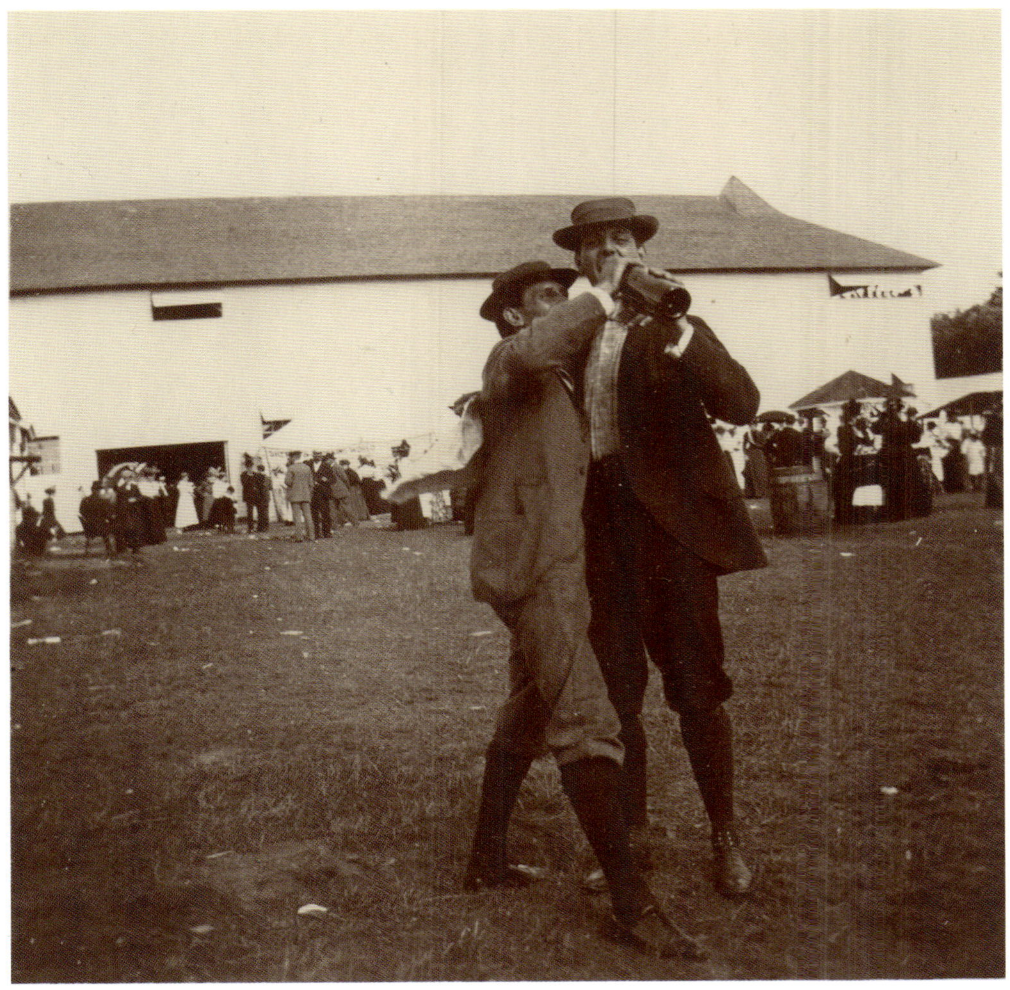

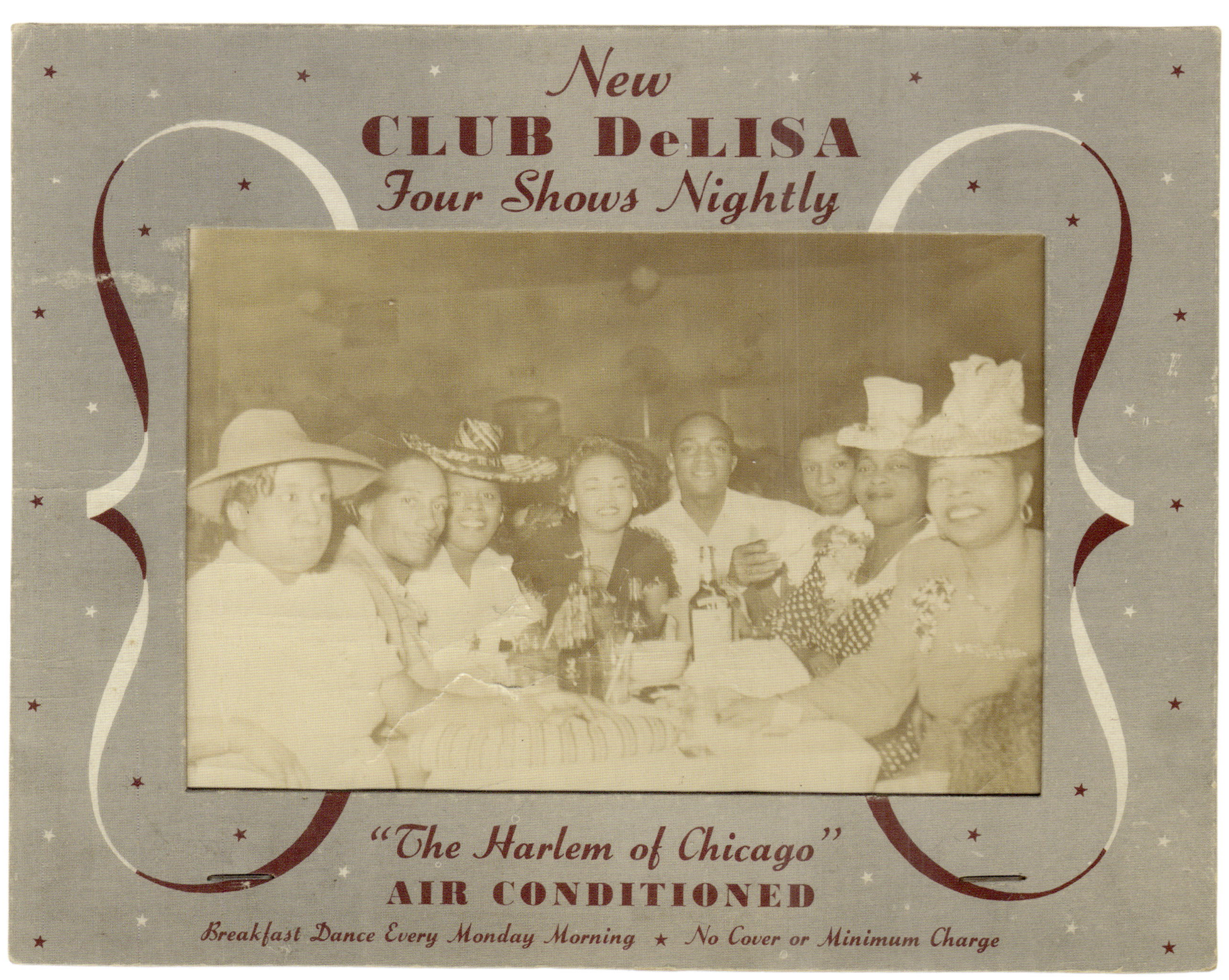
New
CLUB DeLISA
Four Shows Nightly
"The Harlem of Chicago"
AIR CONDITIONED
Breakfast Dance Every Monday Morning ★ No Cover or Minimum Charge

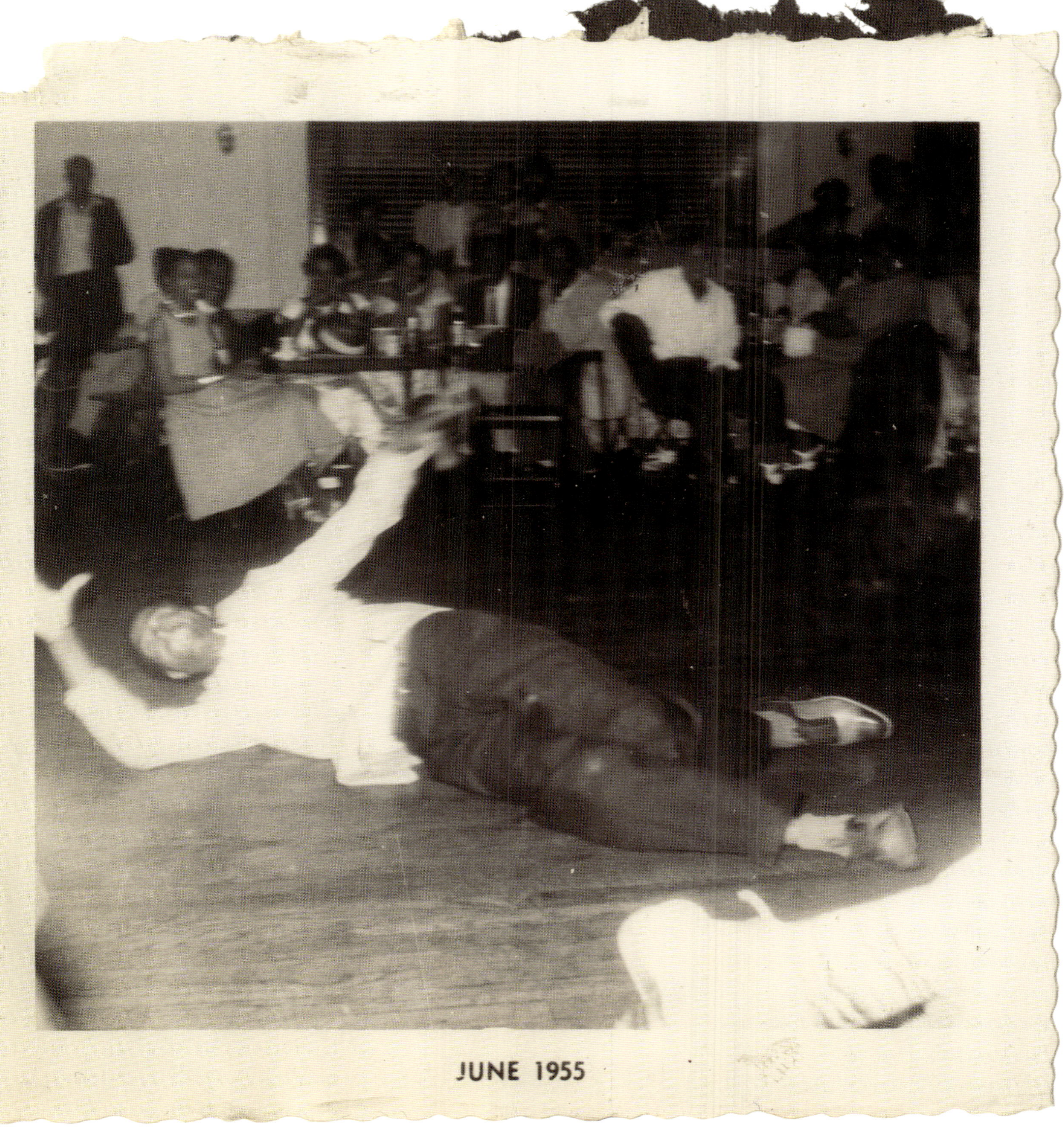

JUNE 1955

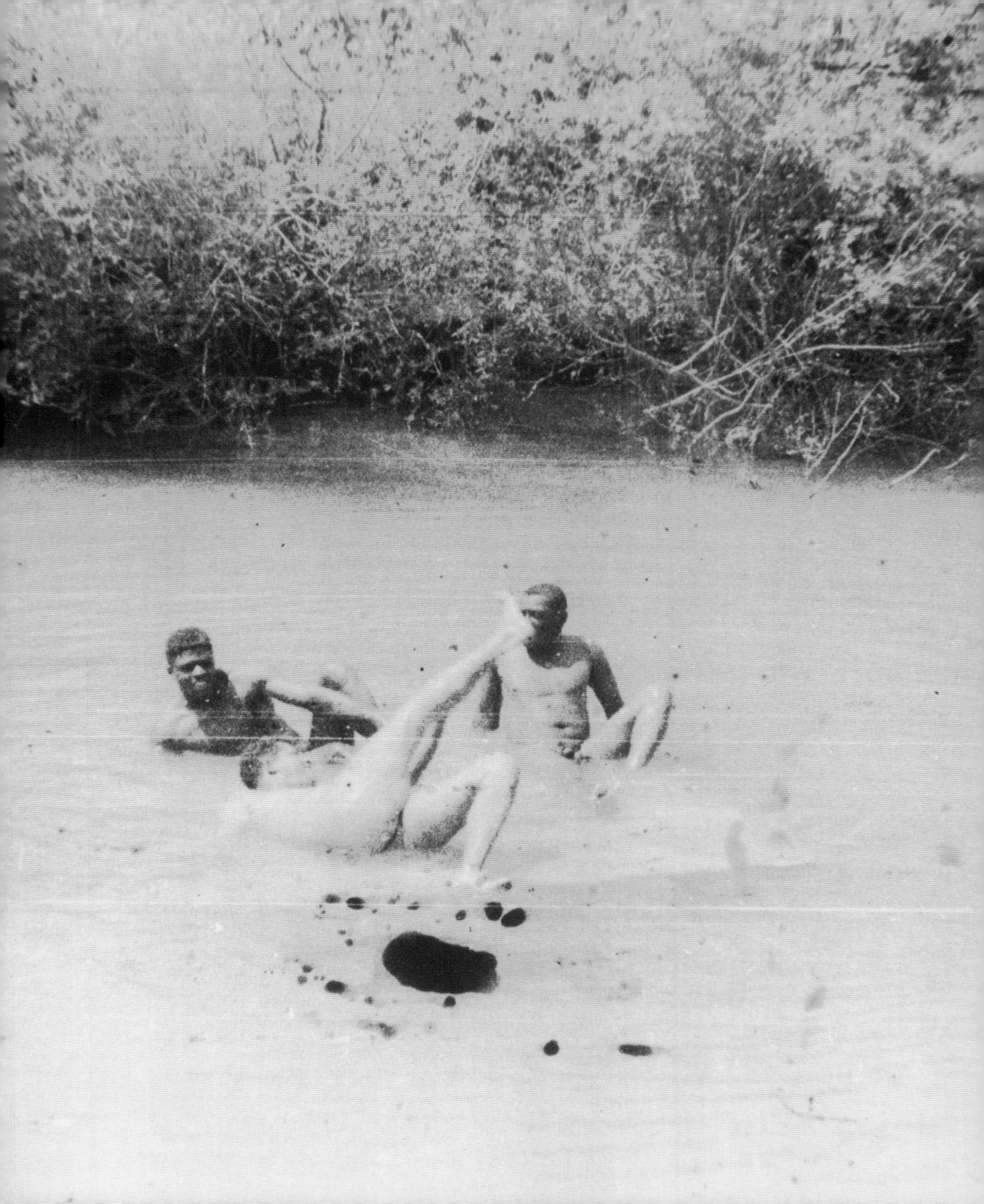

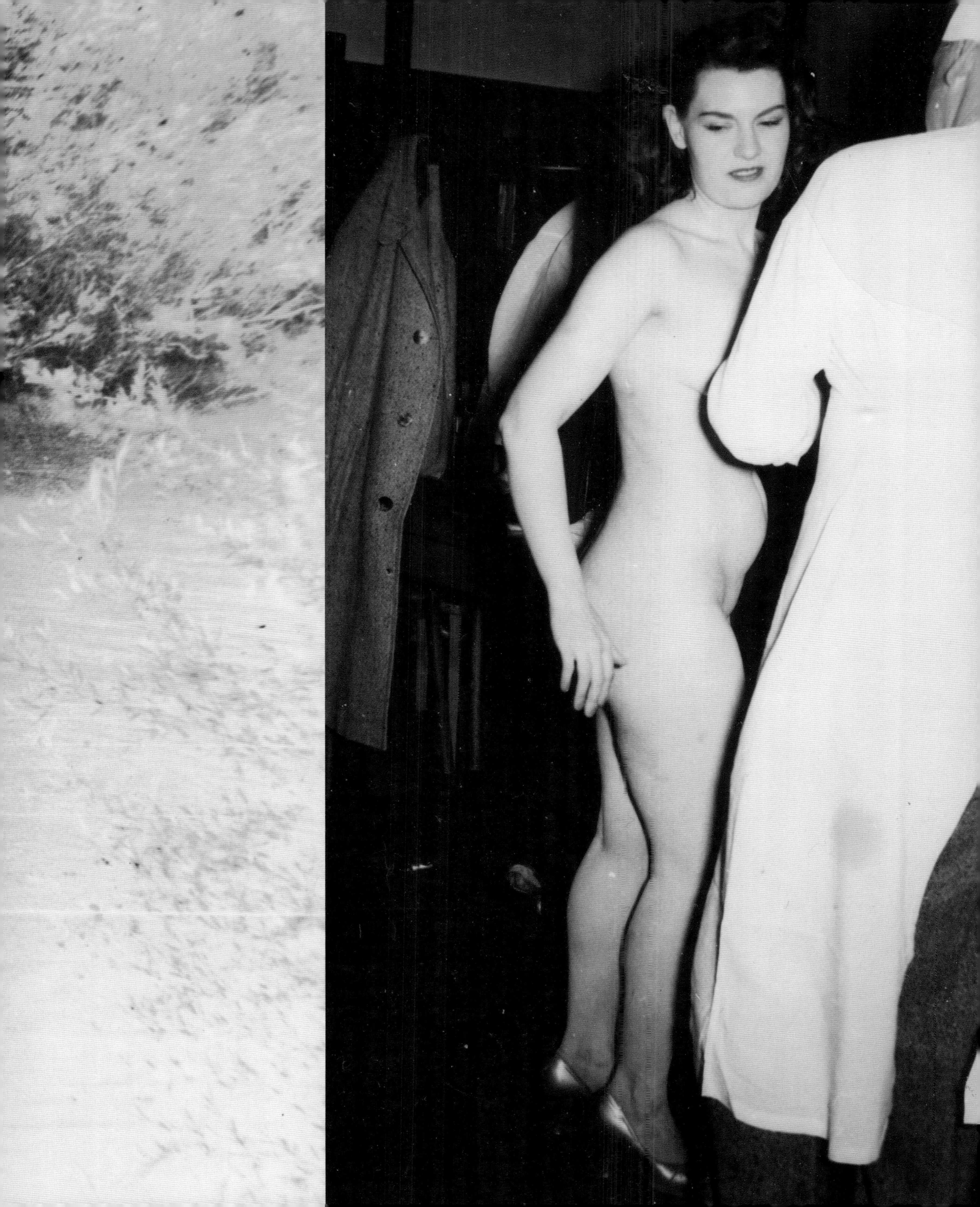

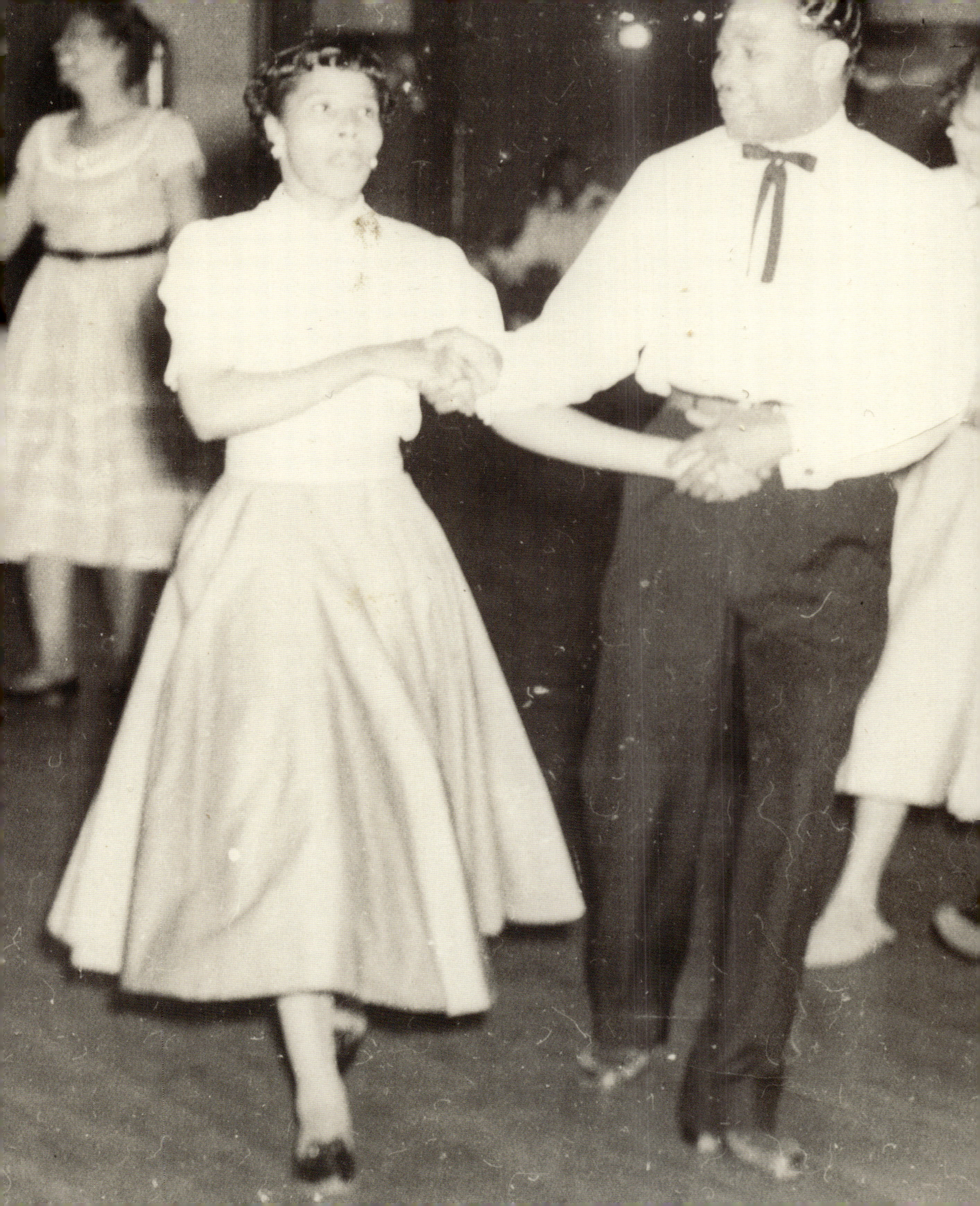

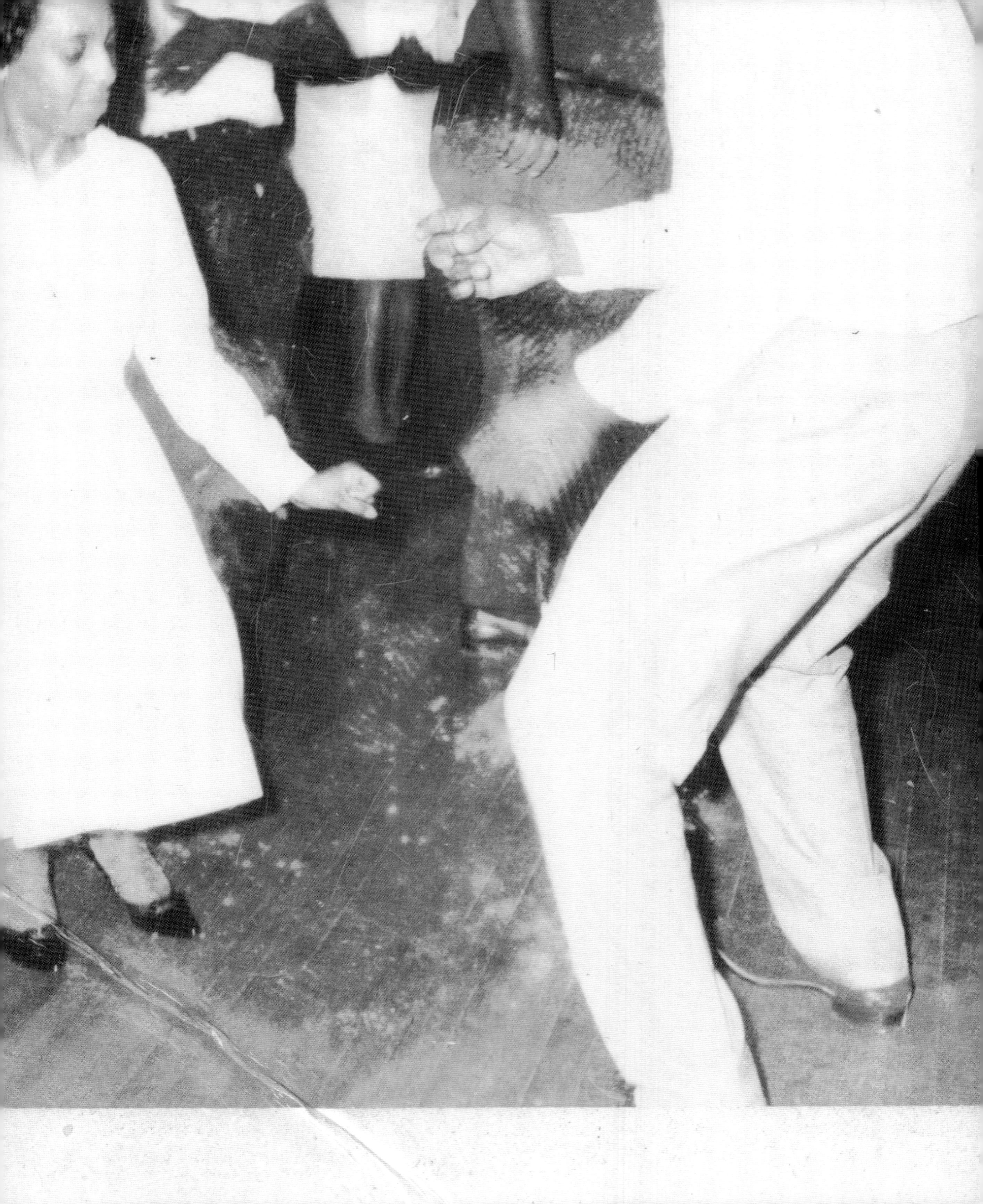

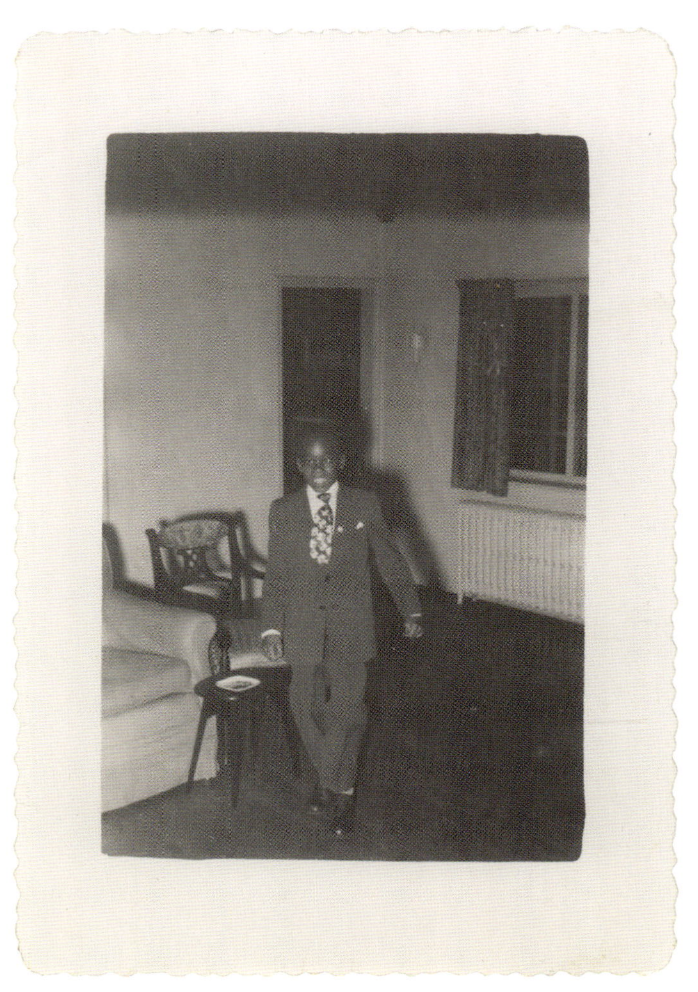

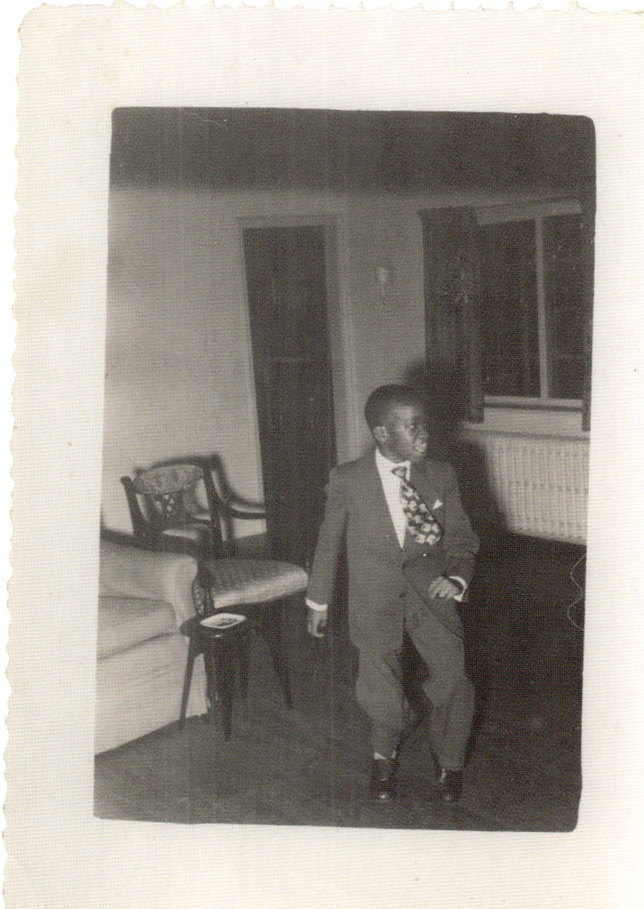

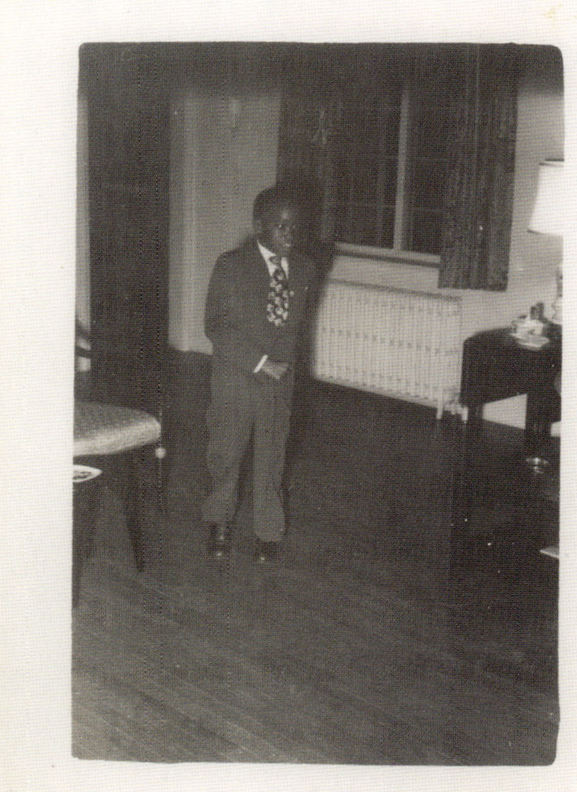

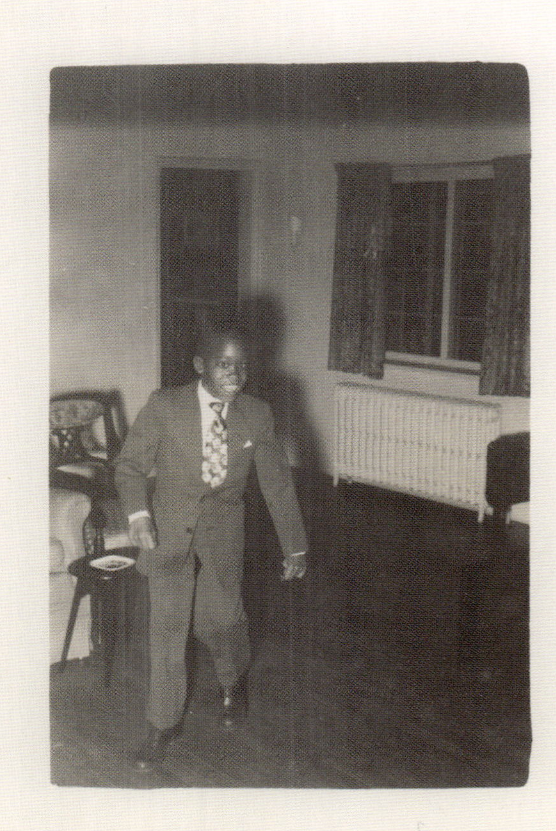

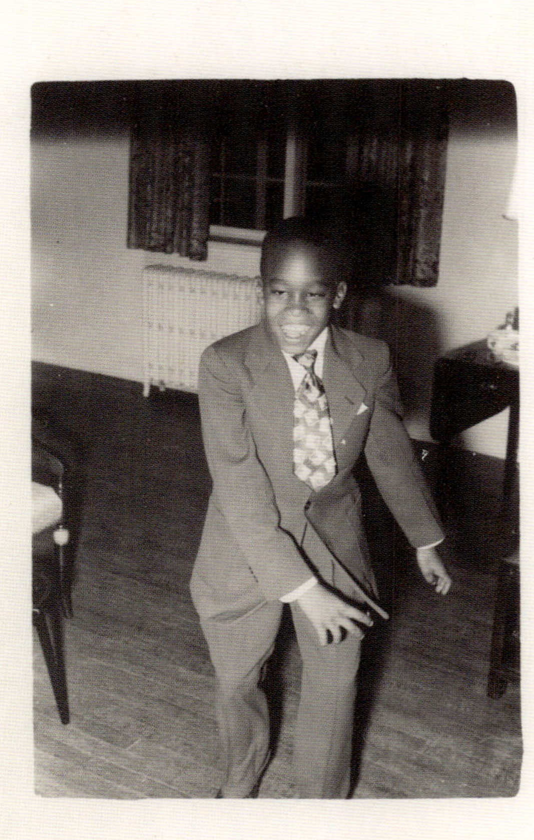
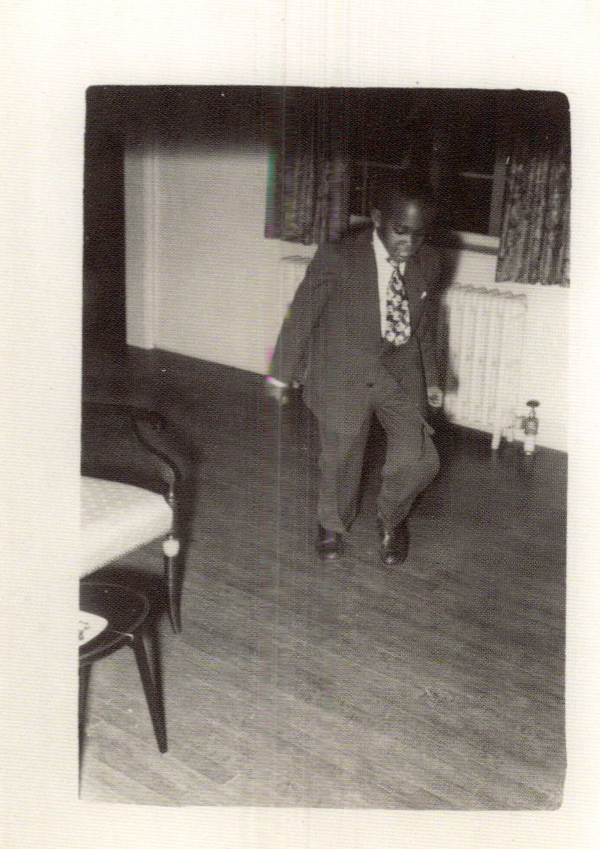
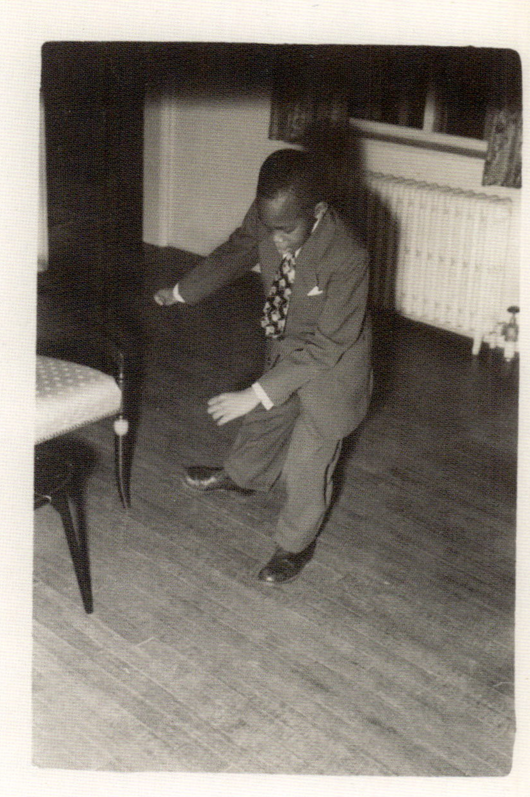
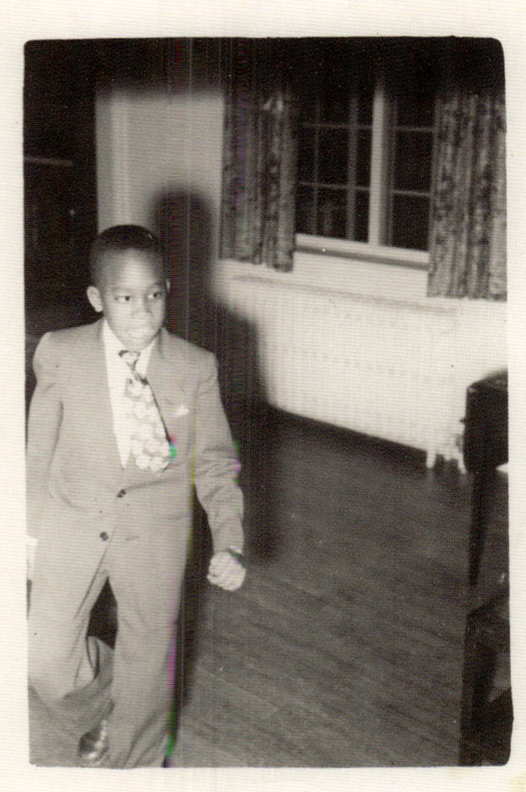

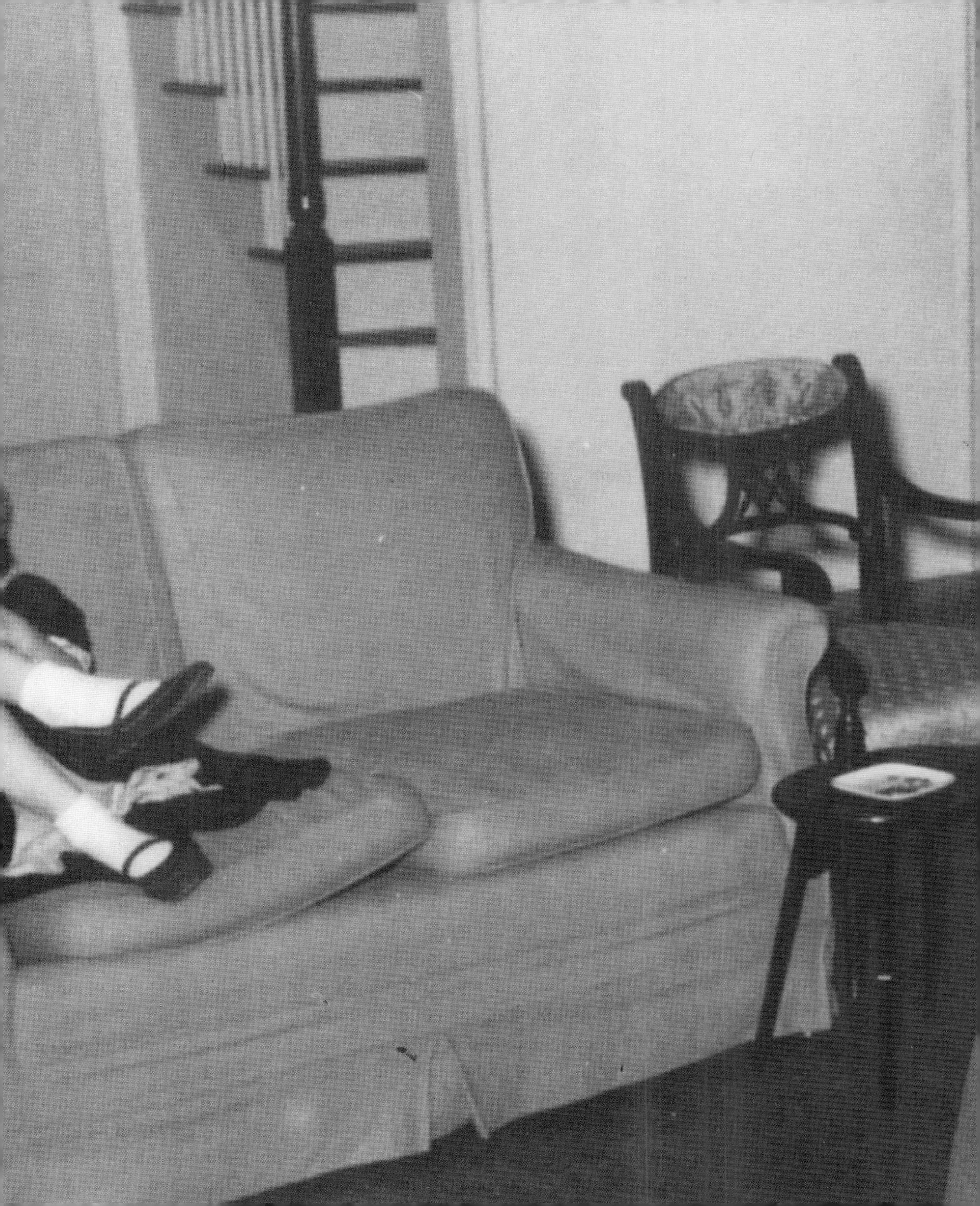

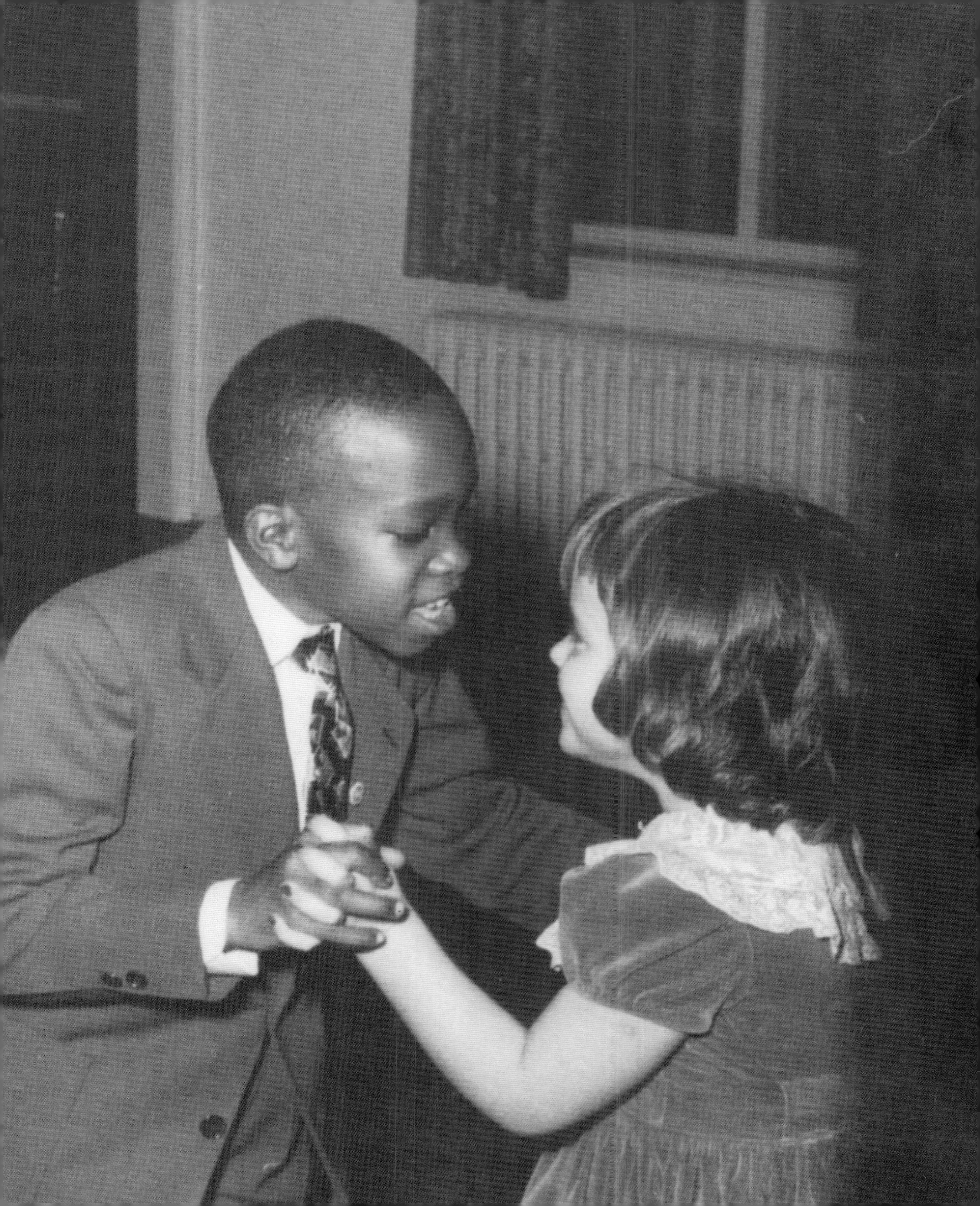

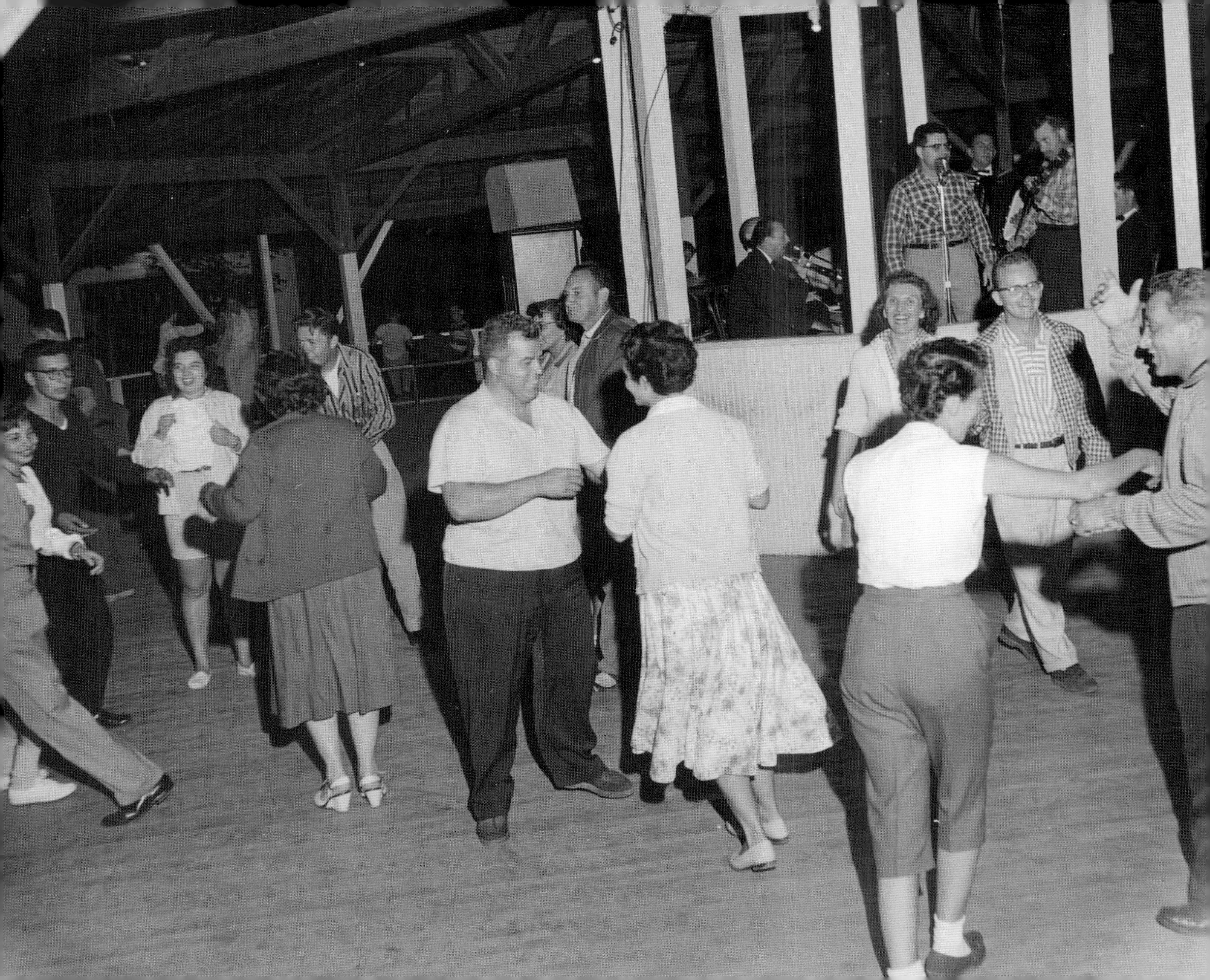

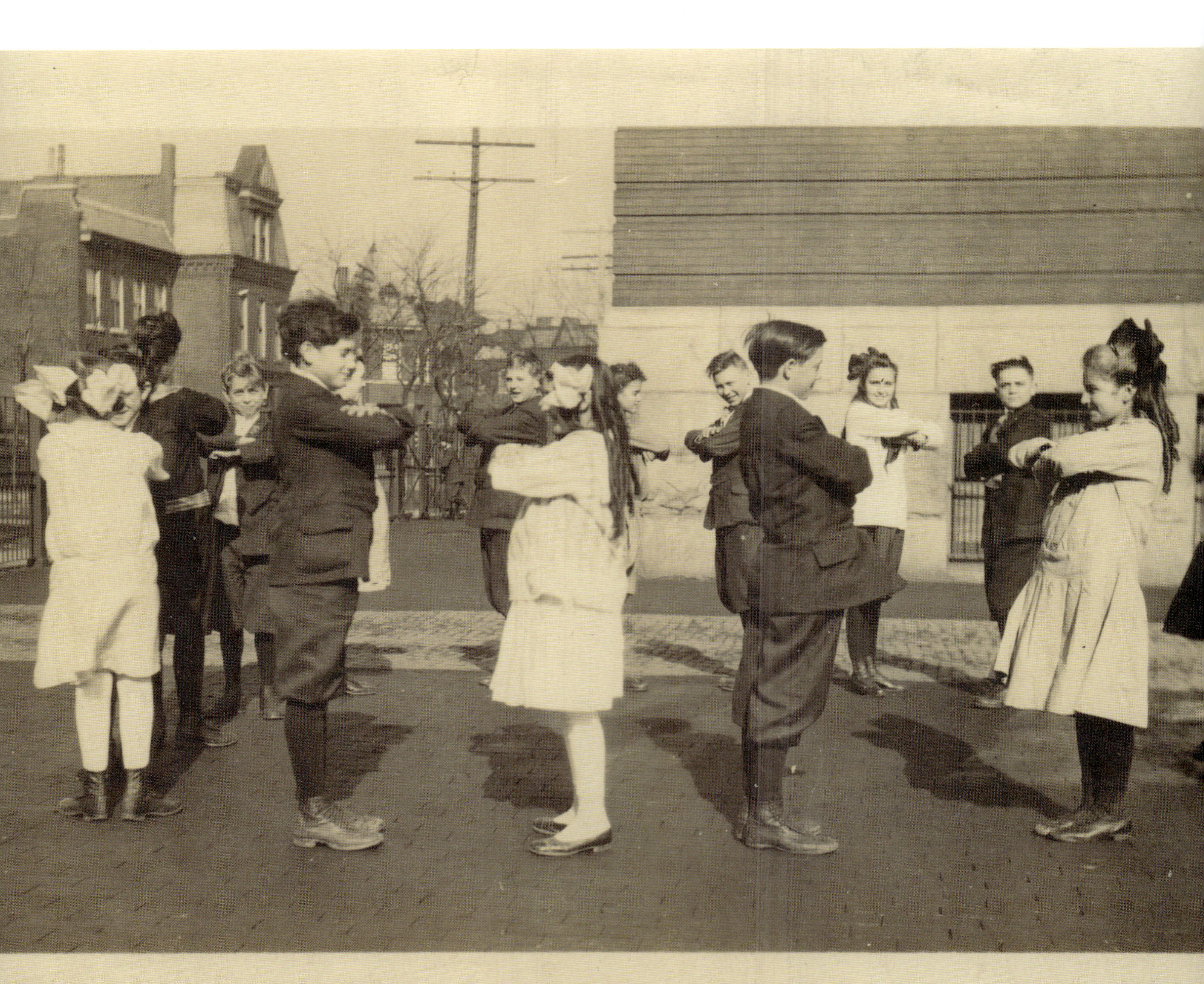

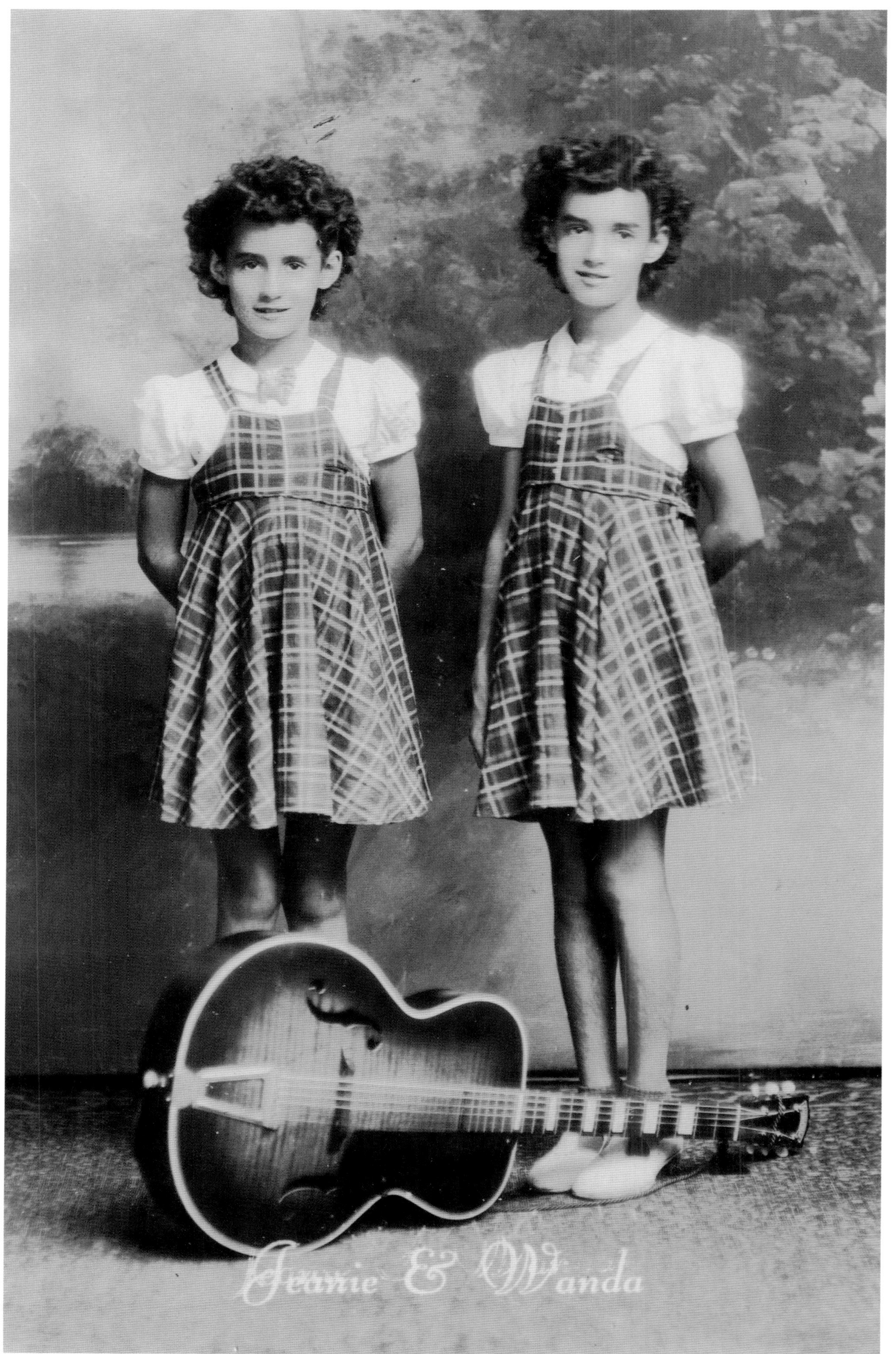
Jeanie & Wanda

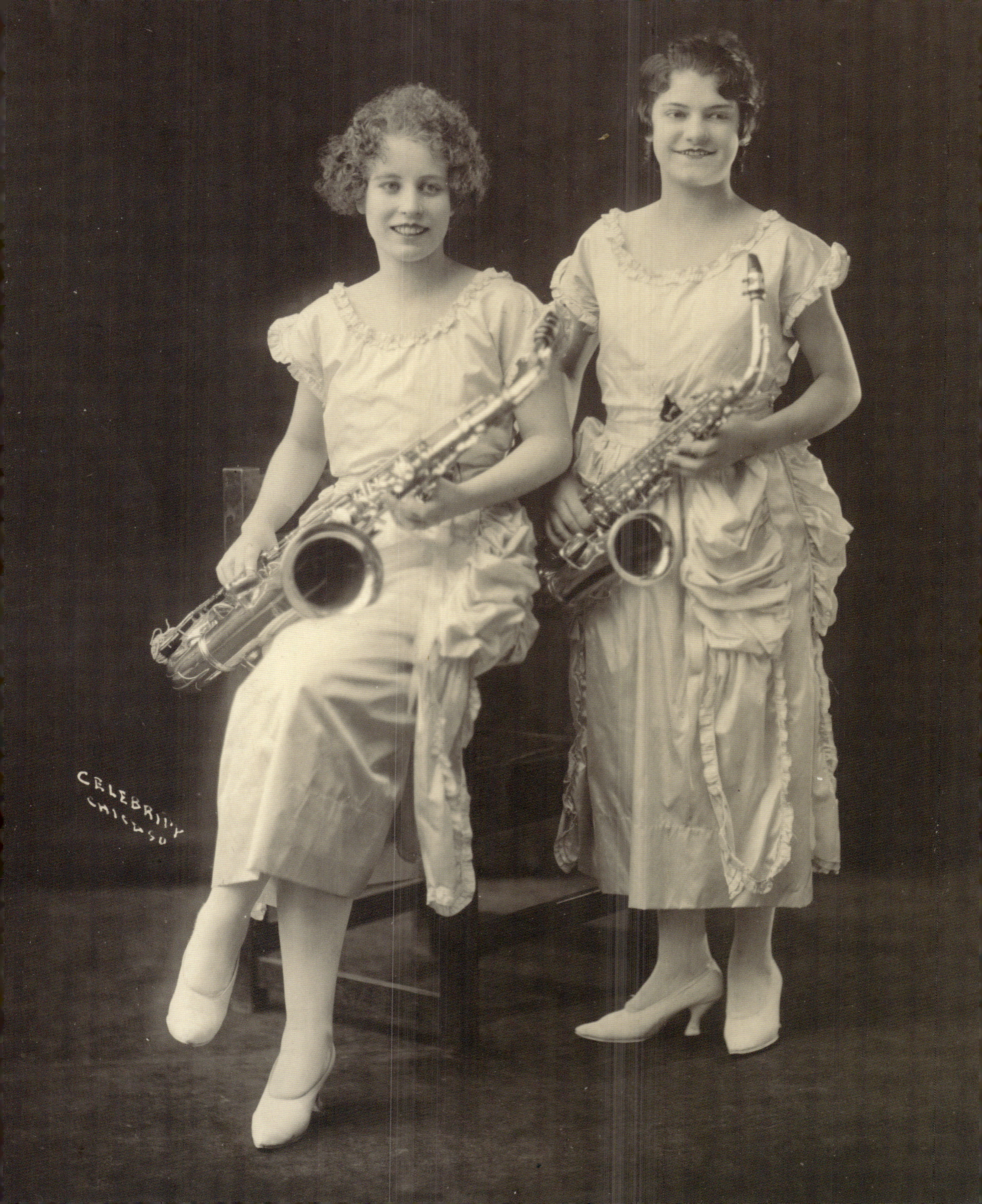
CELEBRITY
CHICAGO

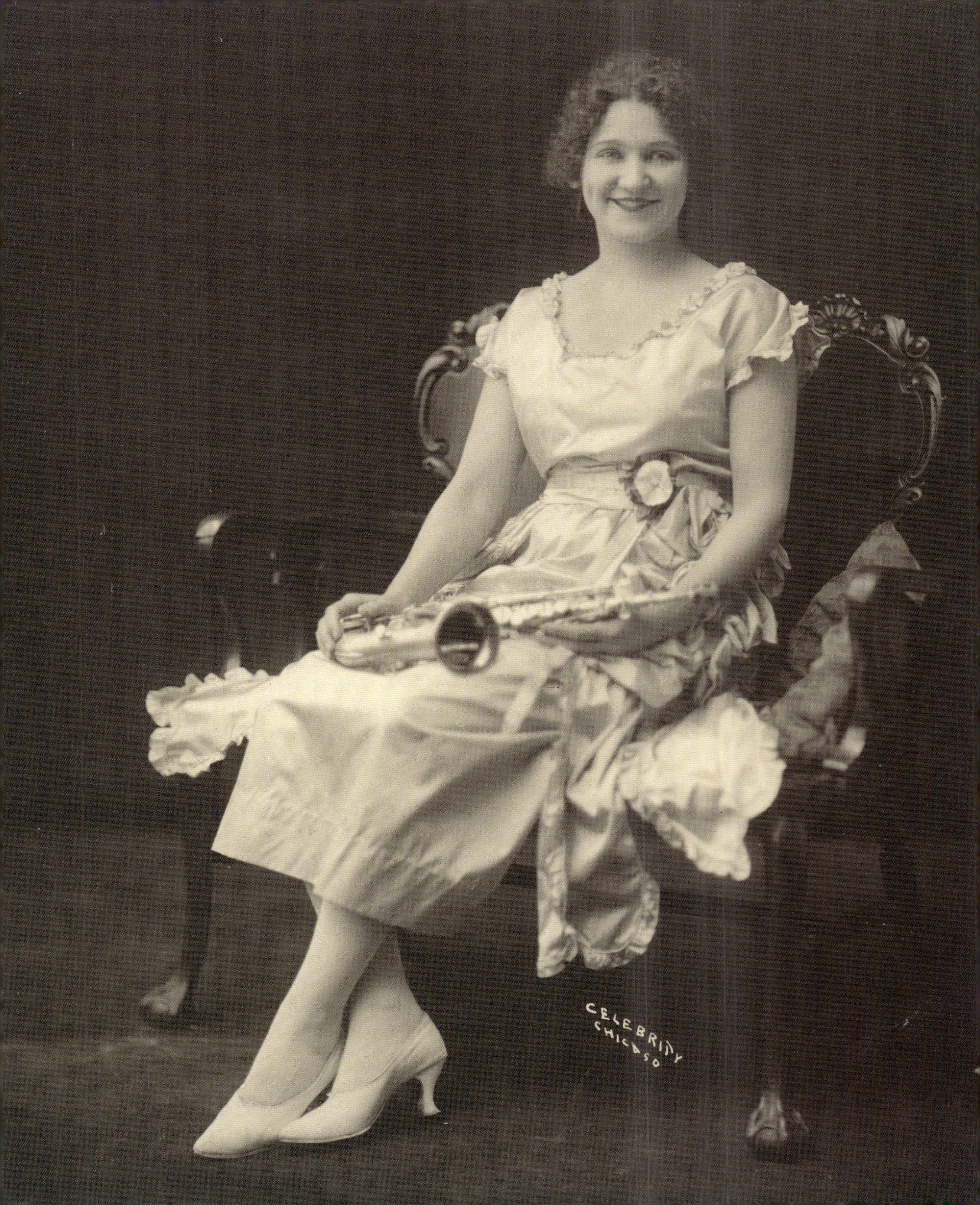
CELEBRITY
CHICAGO

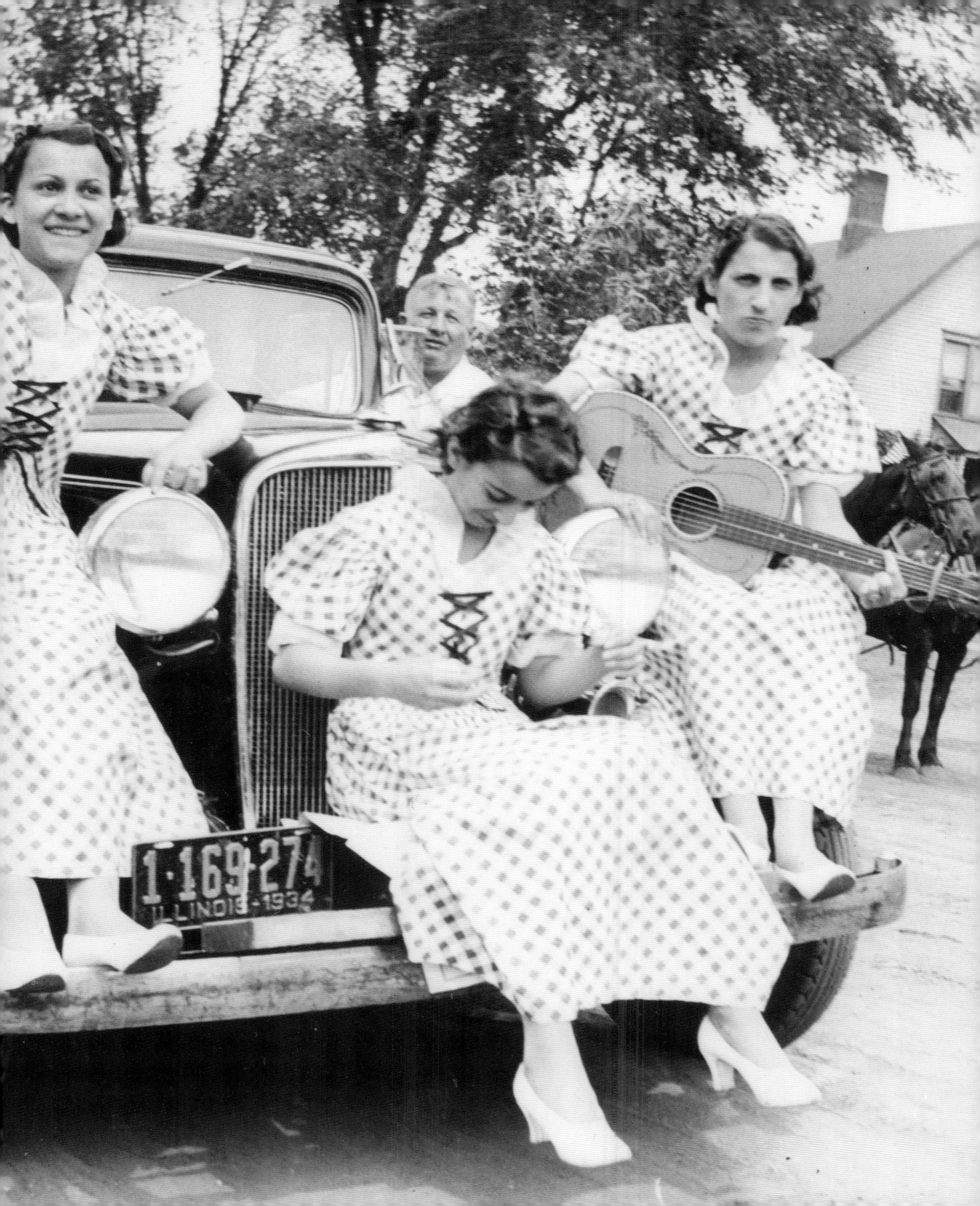
1-169-274
ILLINOIS-1934

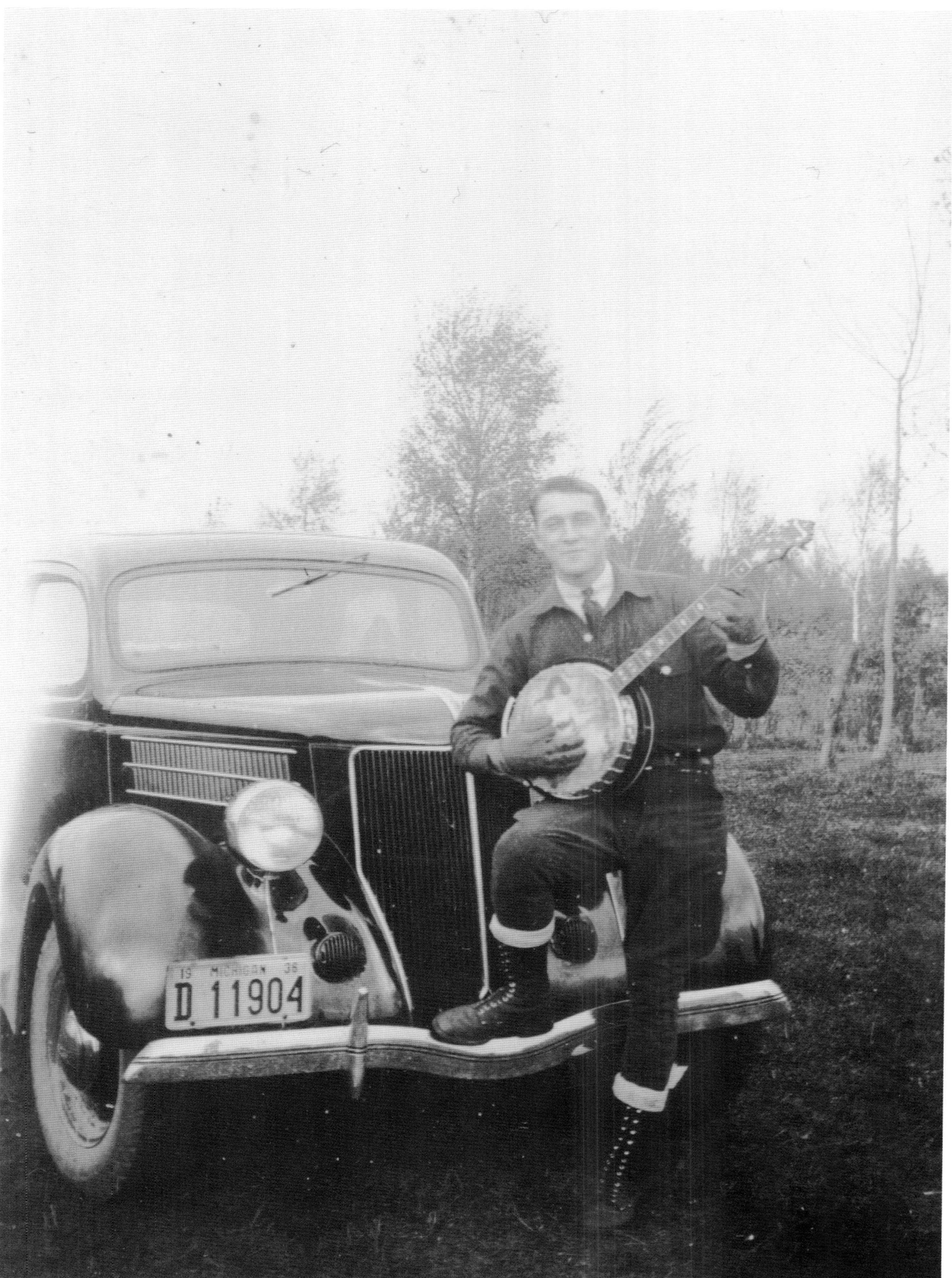
19 MICHIGAN 36
D 11904

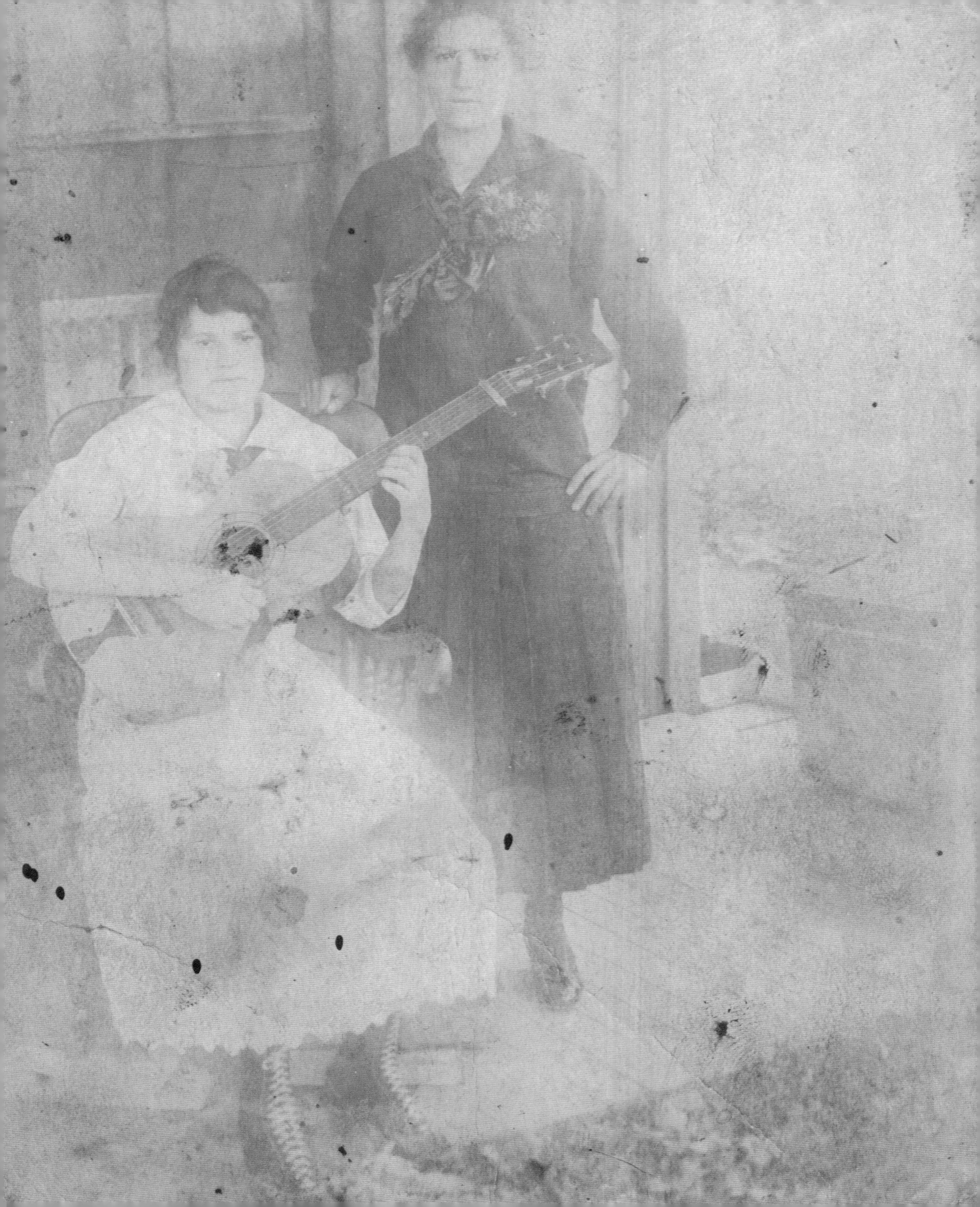

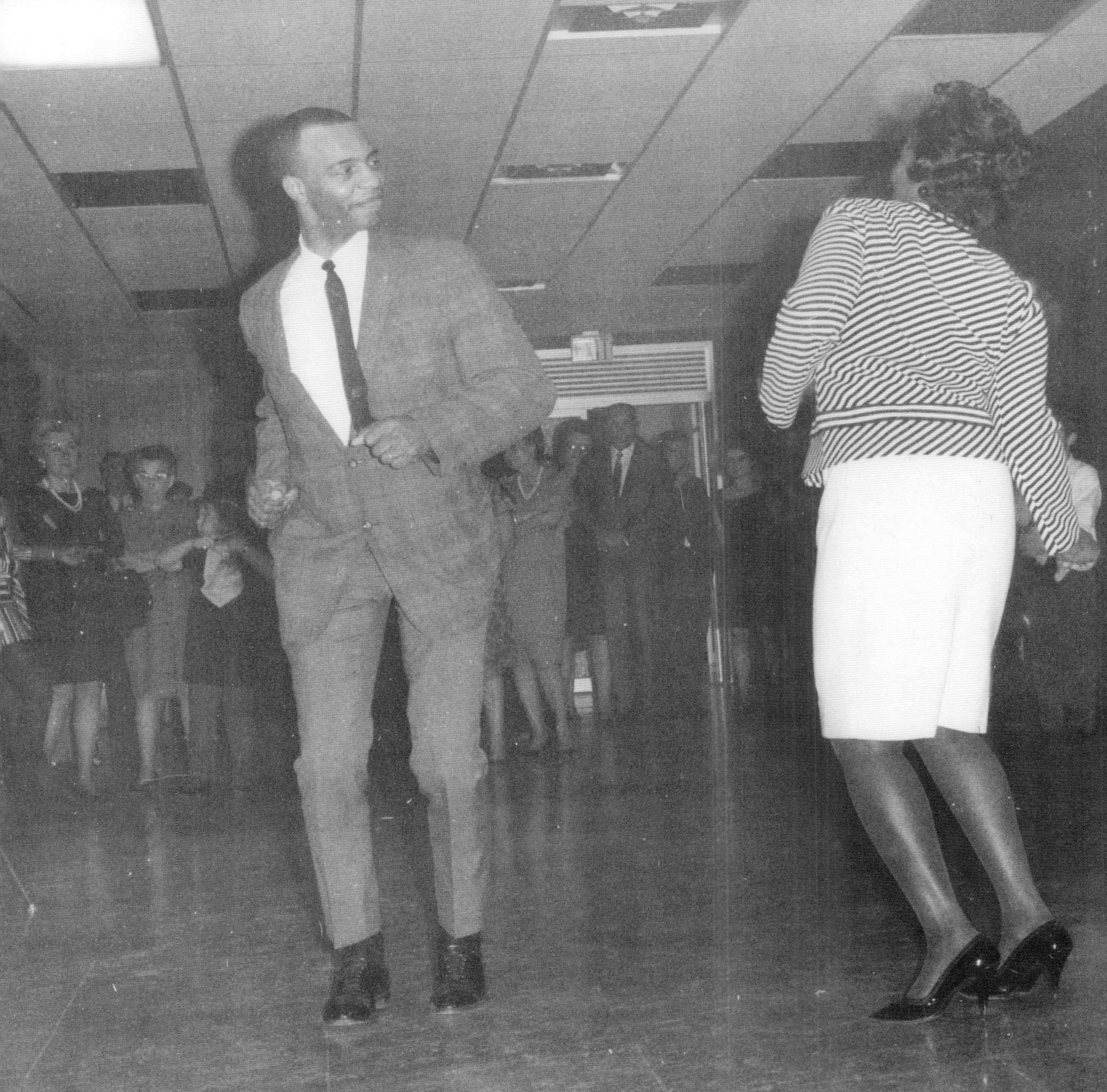

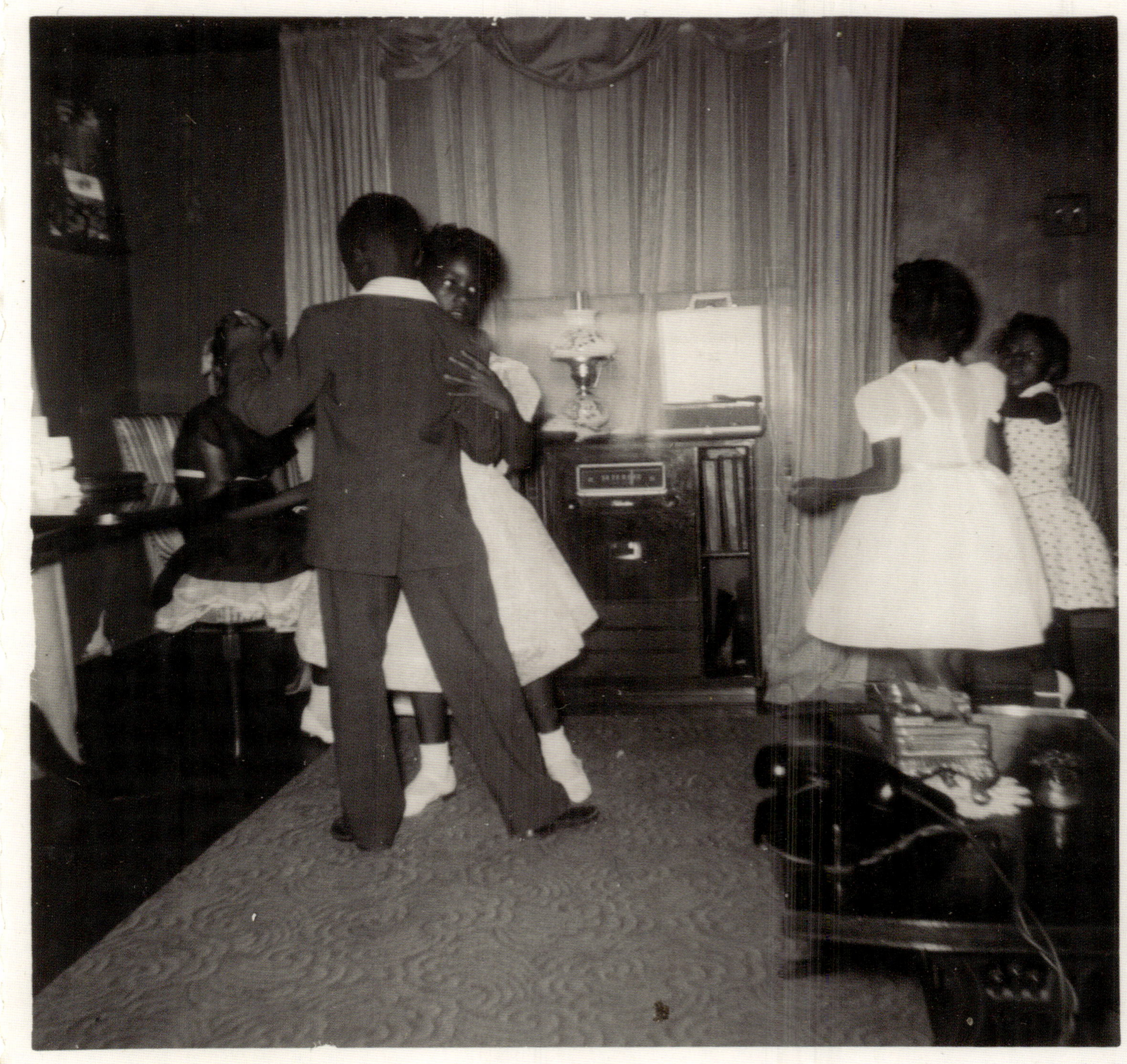
AUG • 57

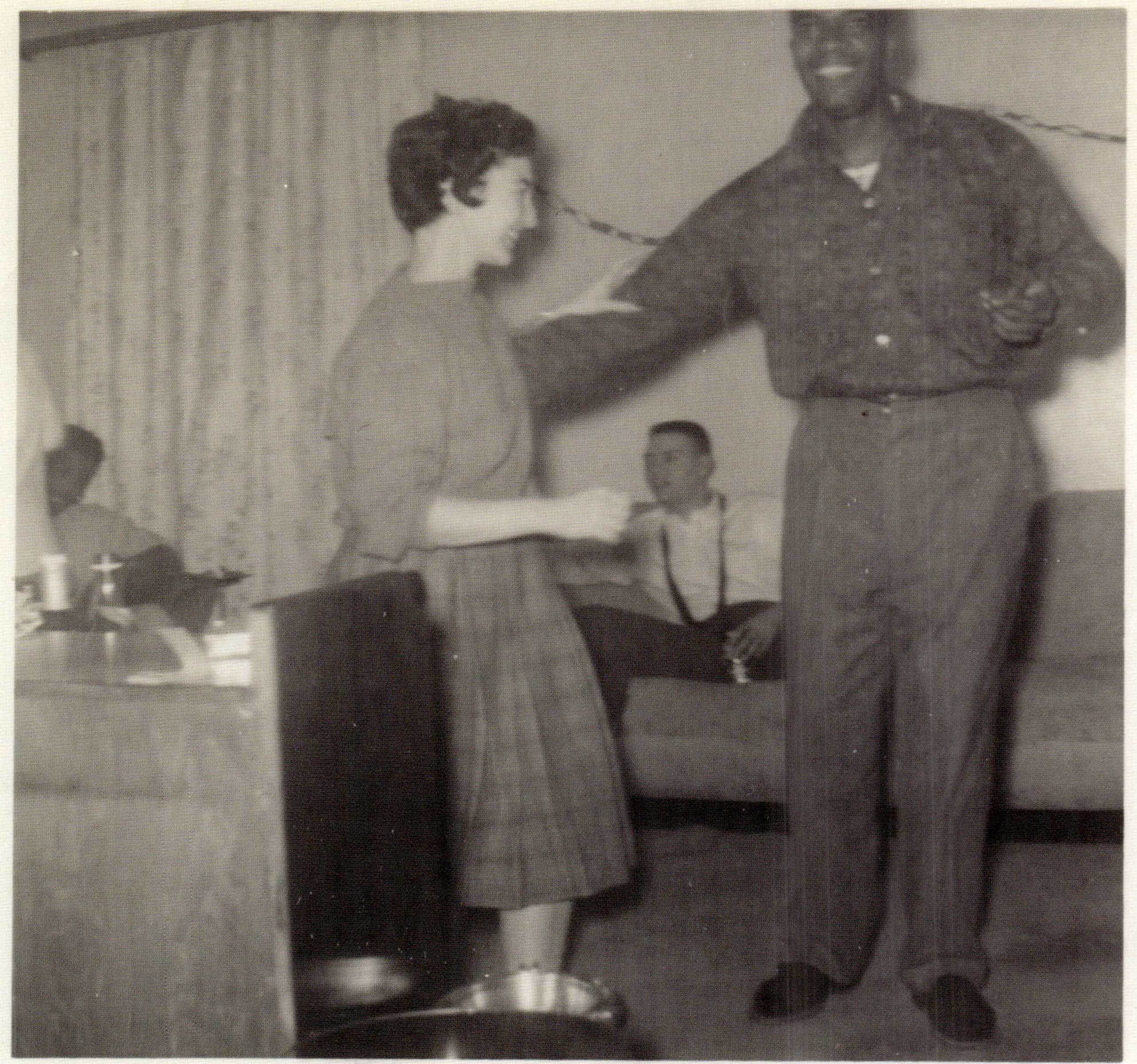

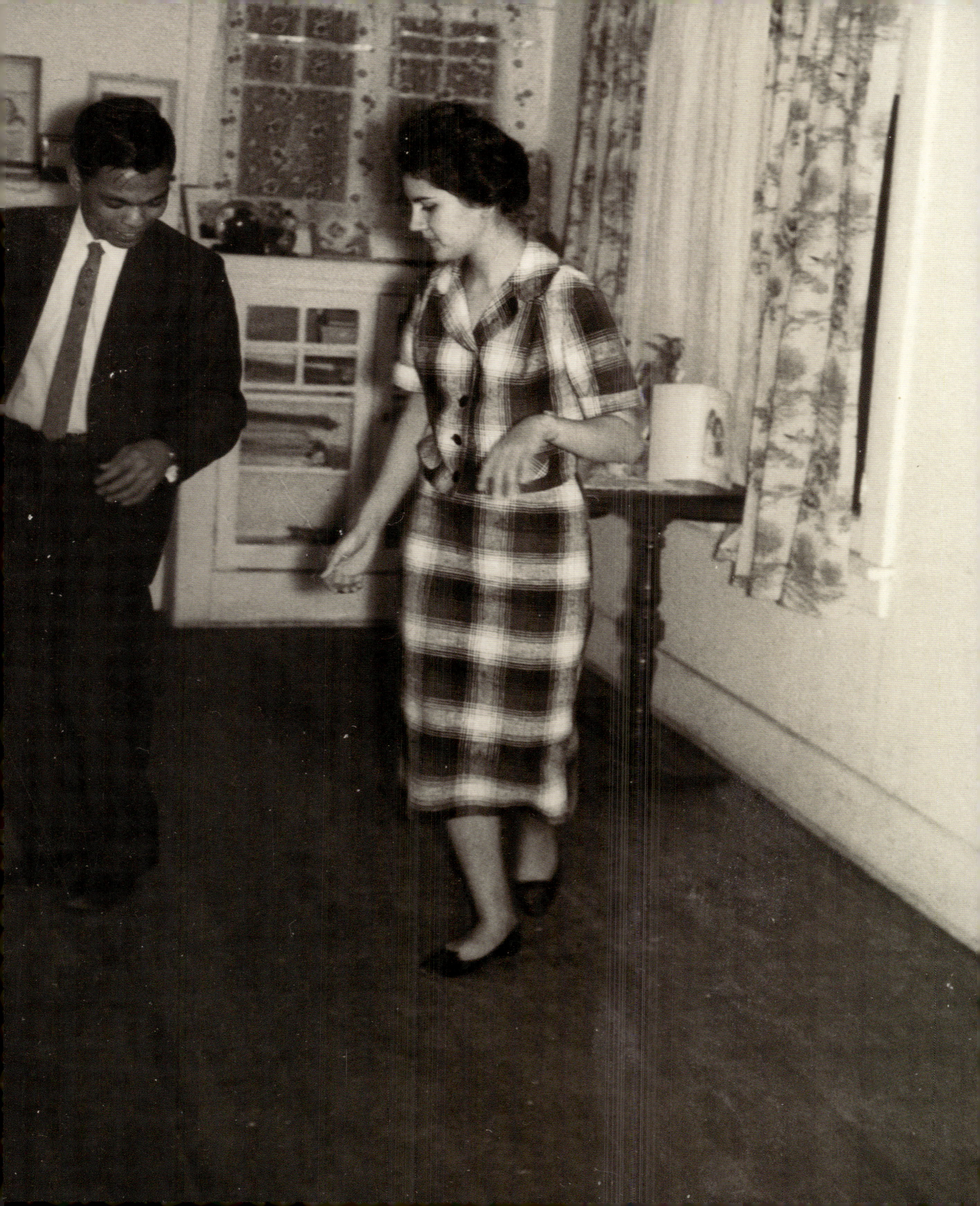

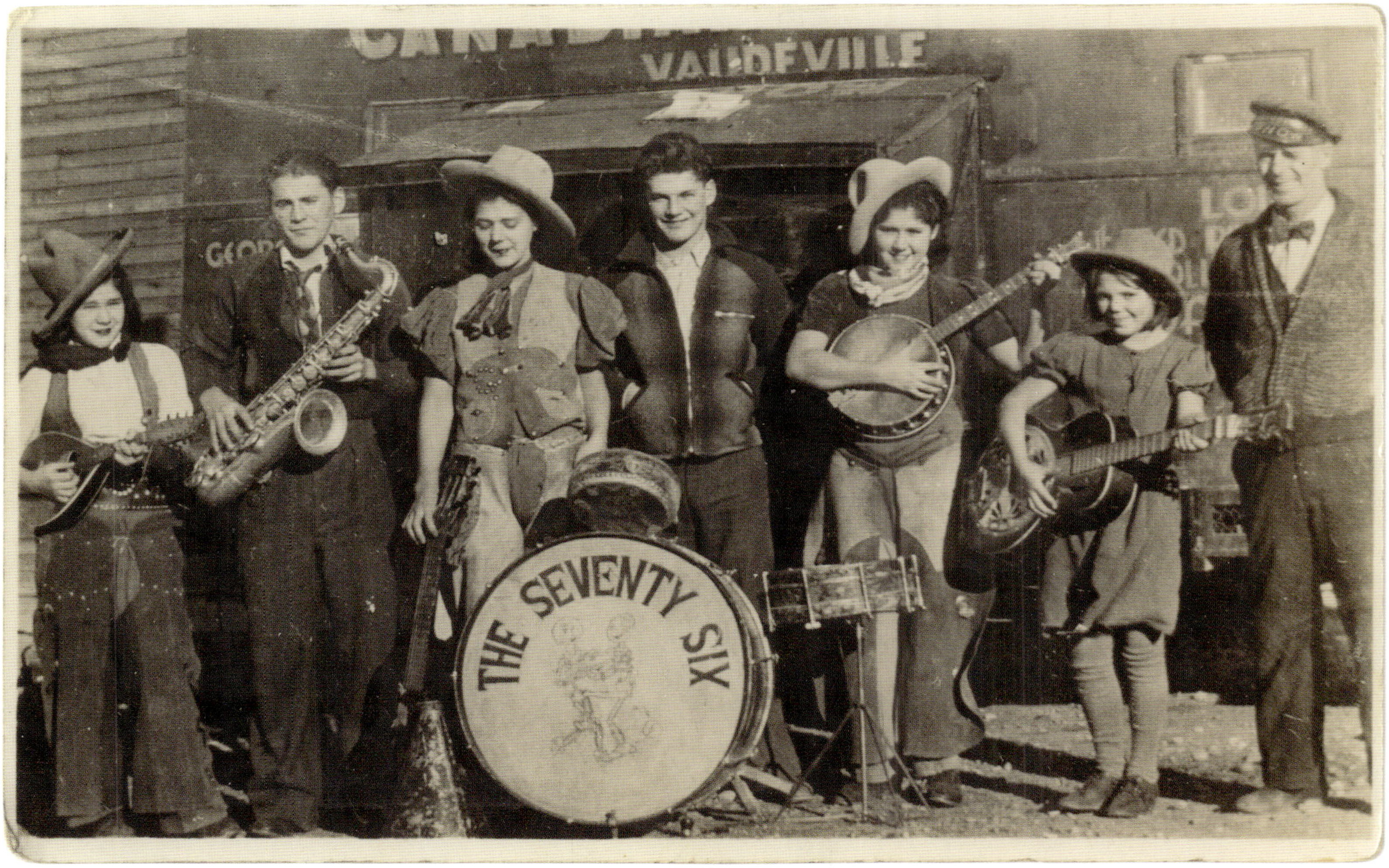

VAUDEVILLE

THE SEVENTY SIX

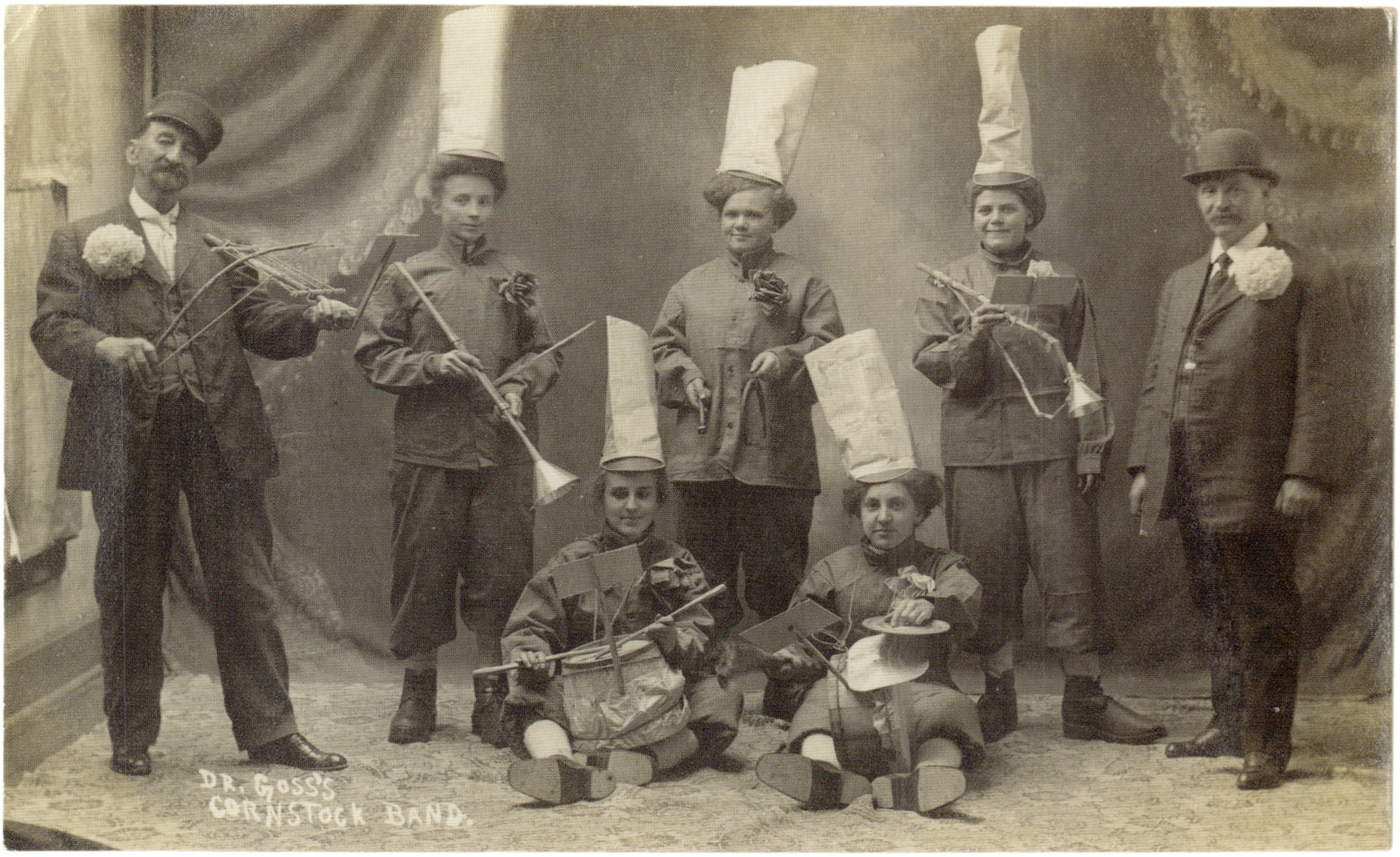

DR. GOSS'S
CORNSTOCK BAND.

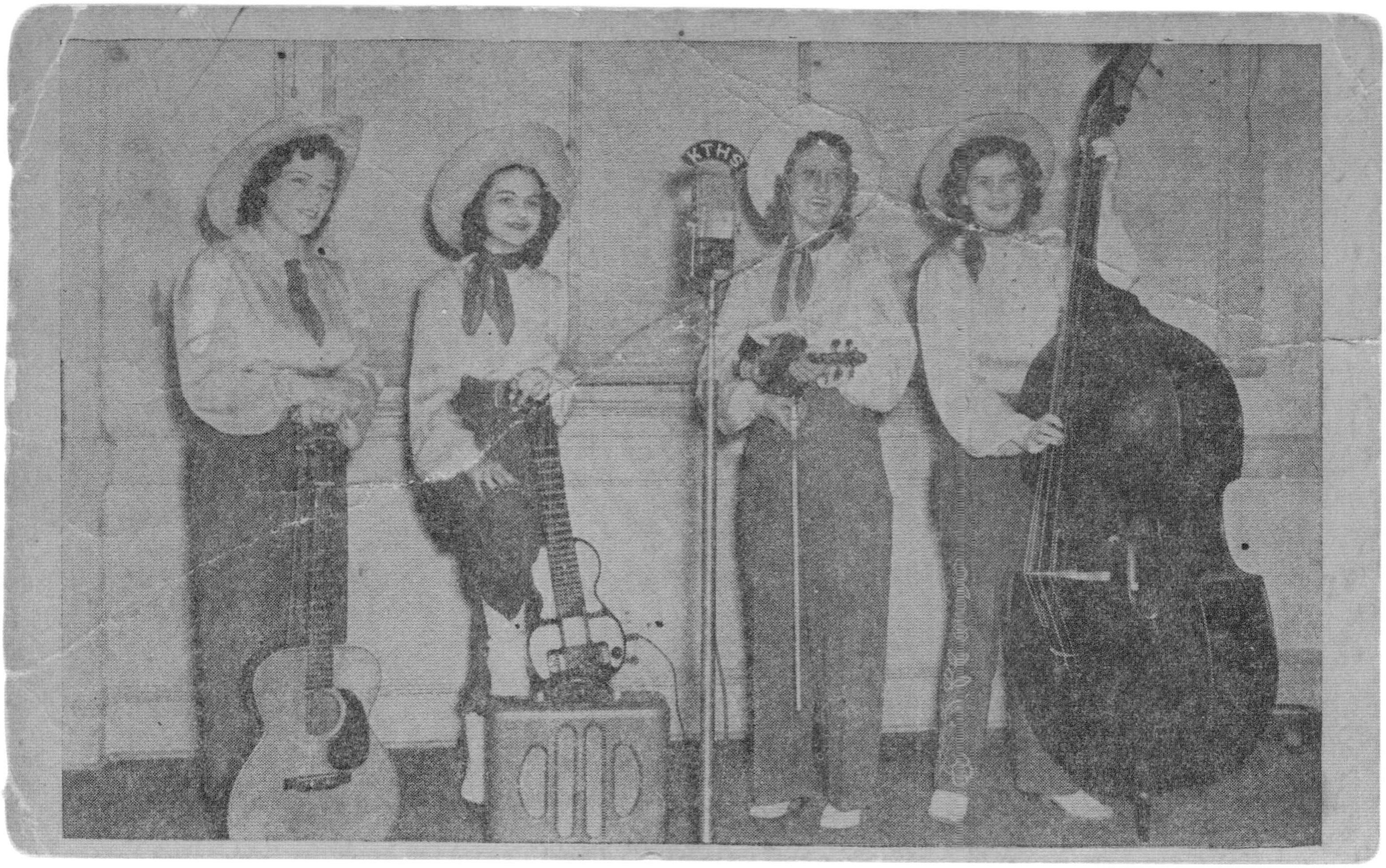

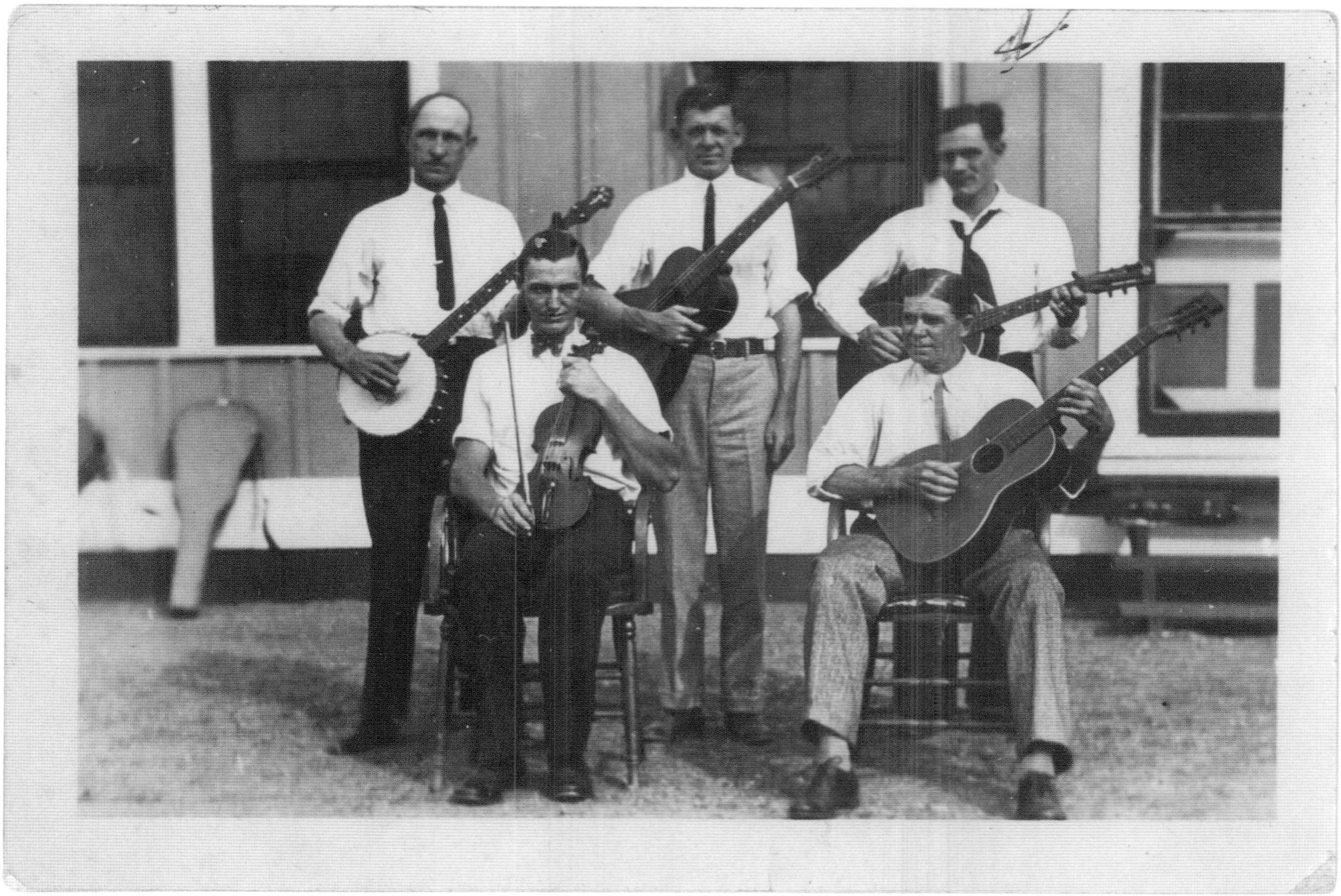

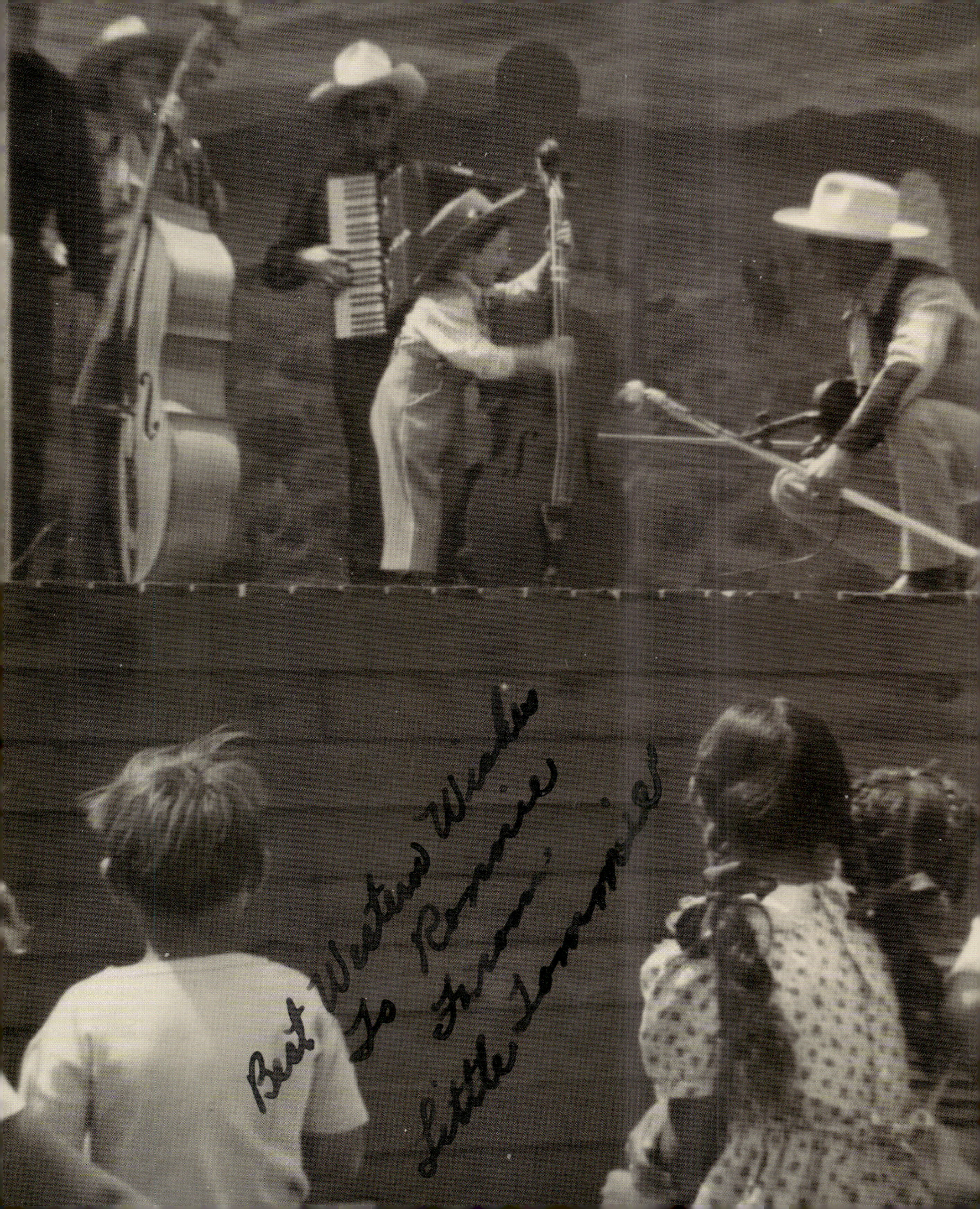
Best Western Wishes
To Ronnie
From
Little Tommie

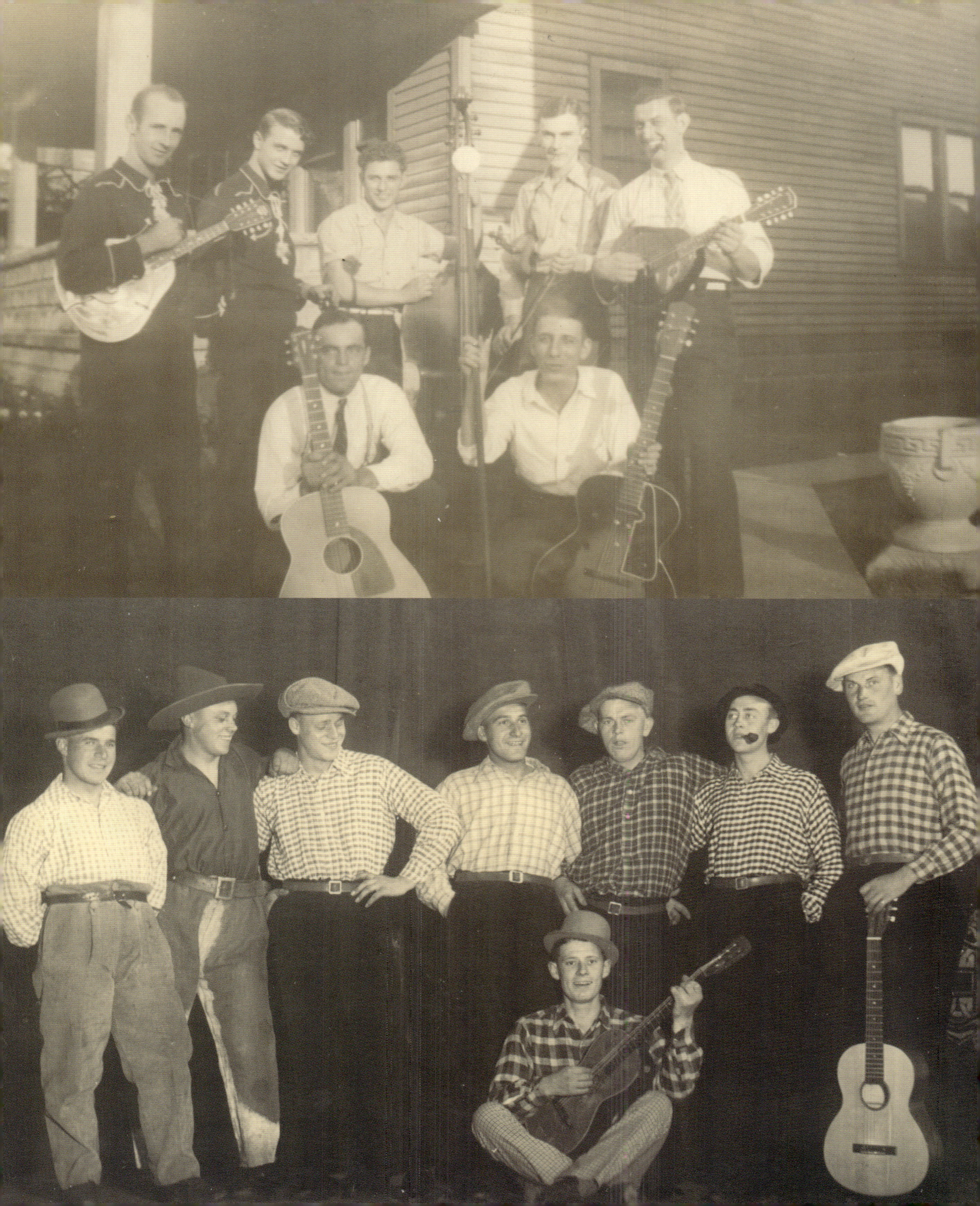

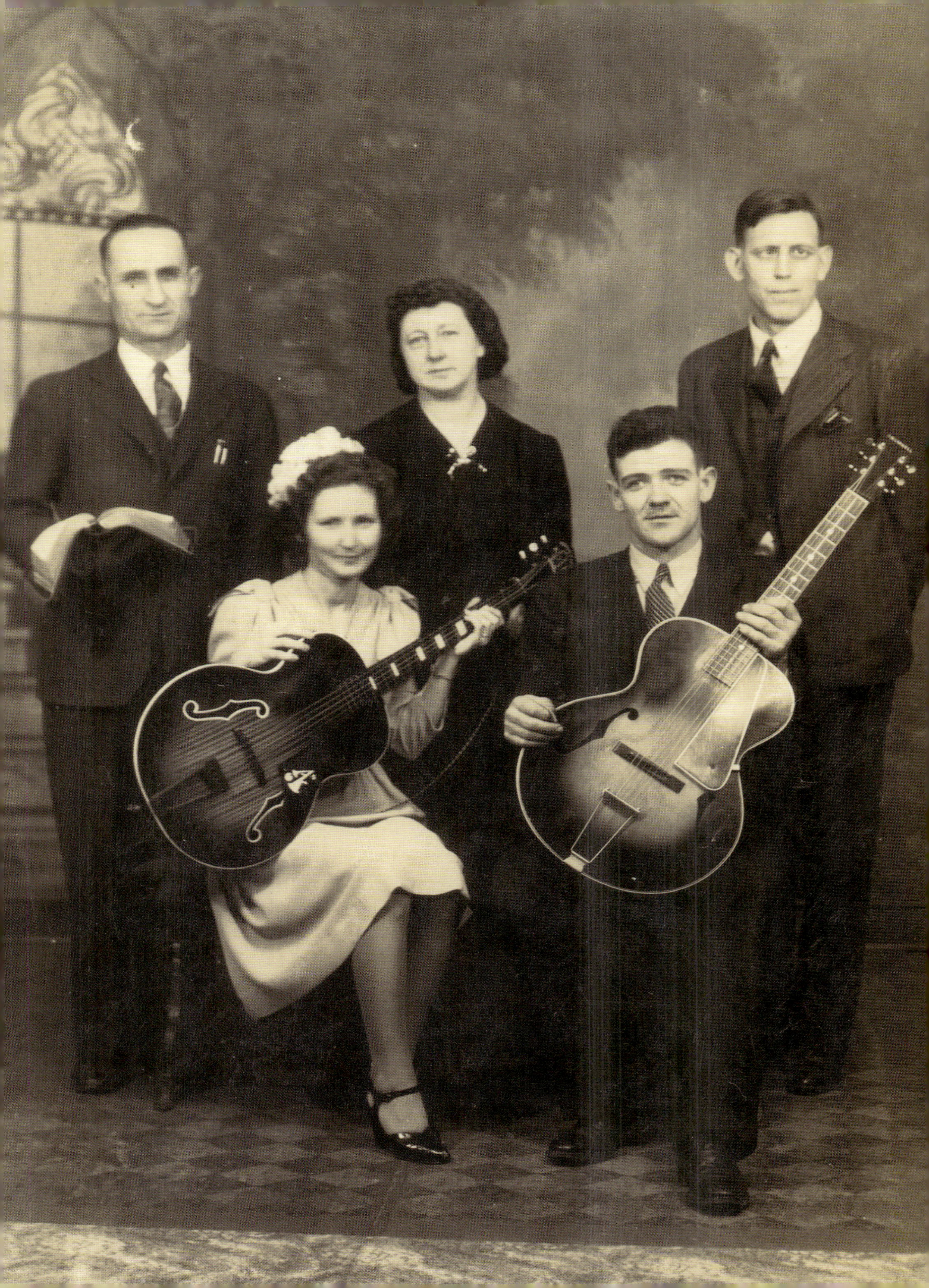

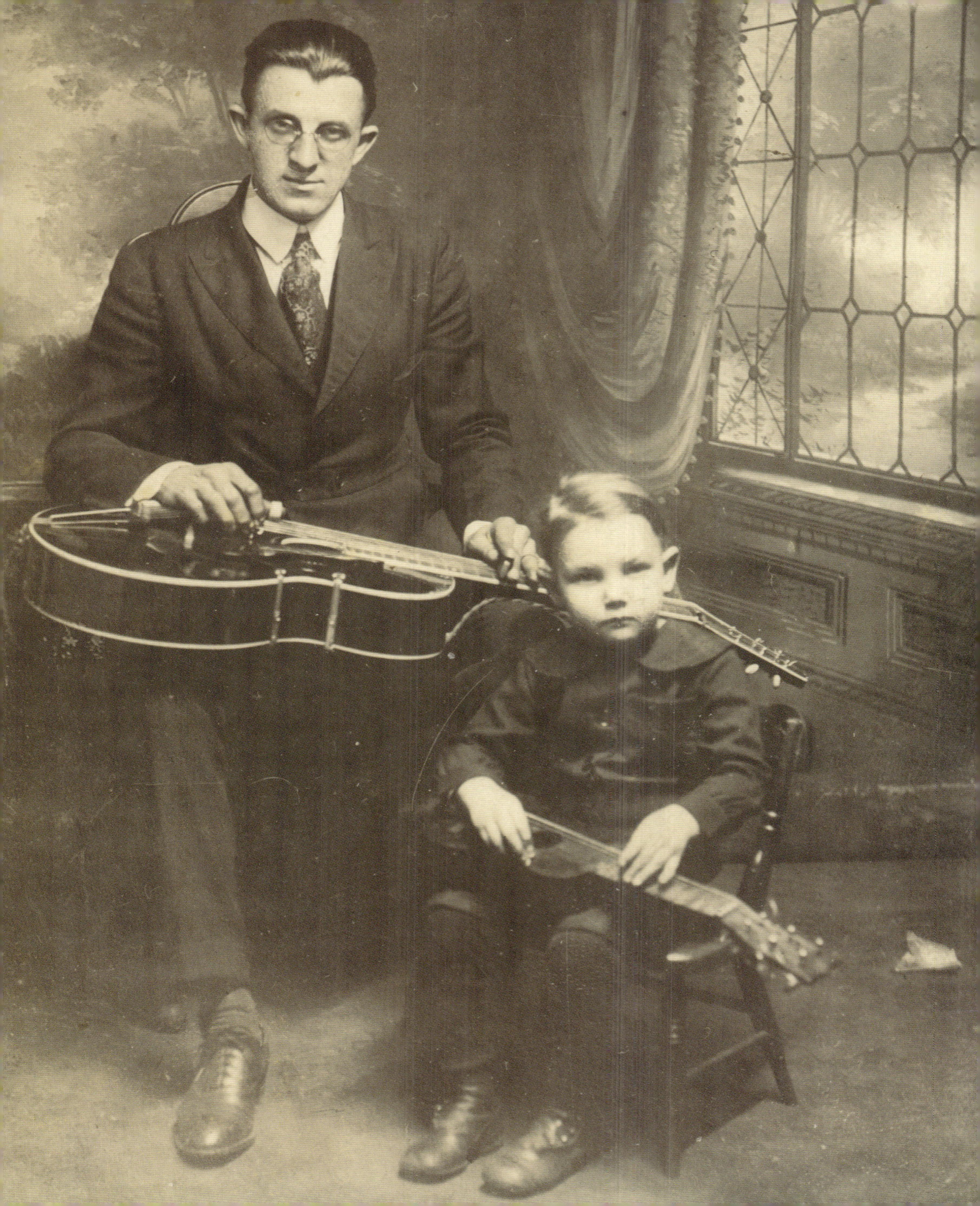

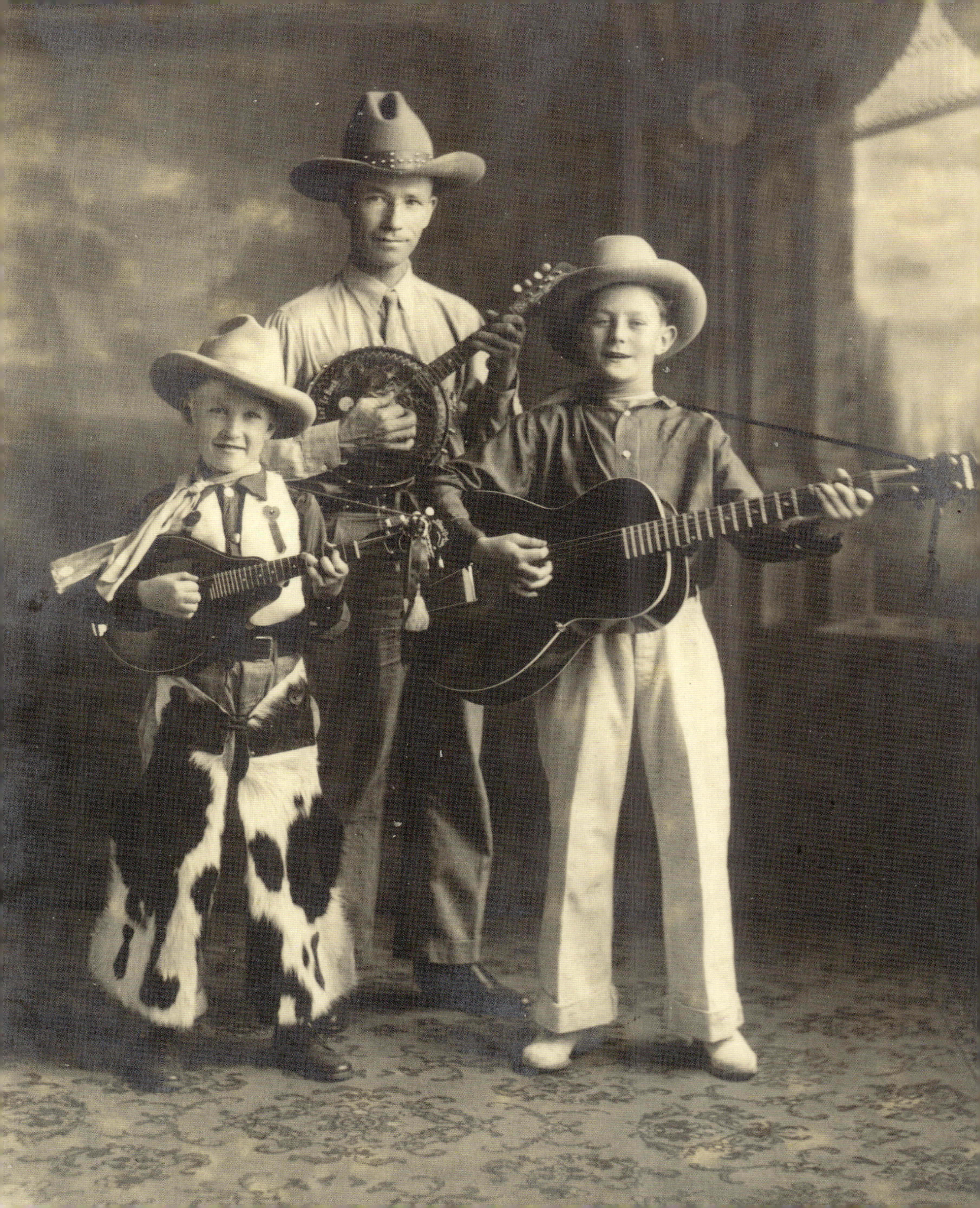

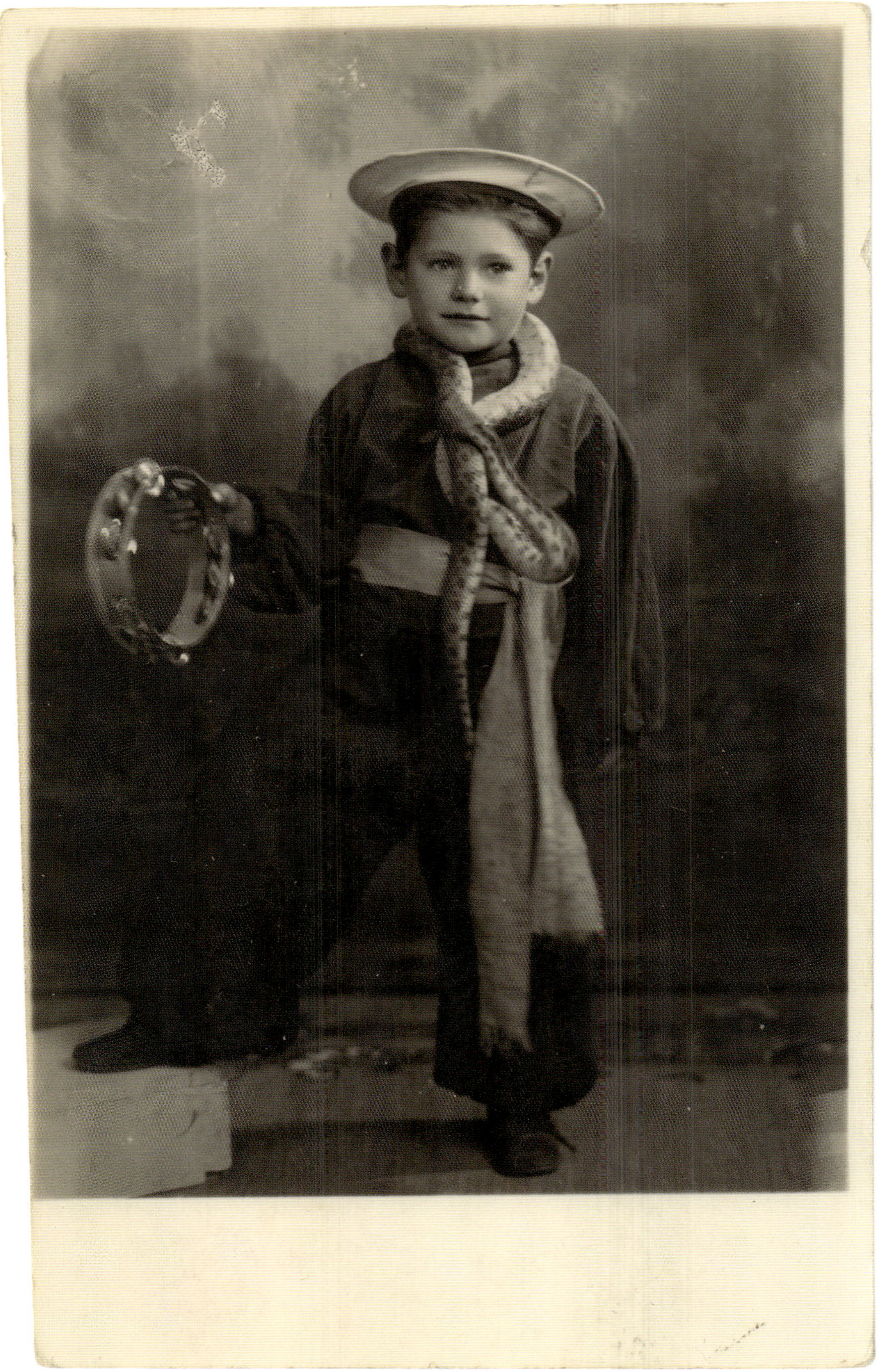

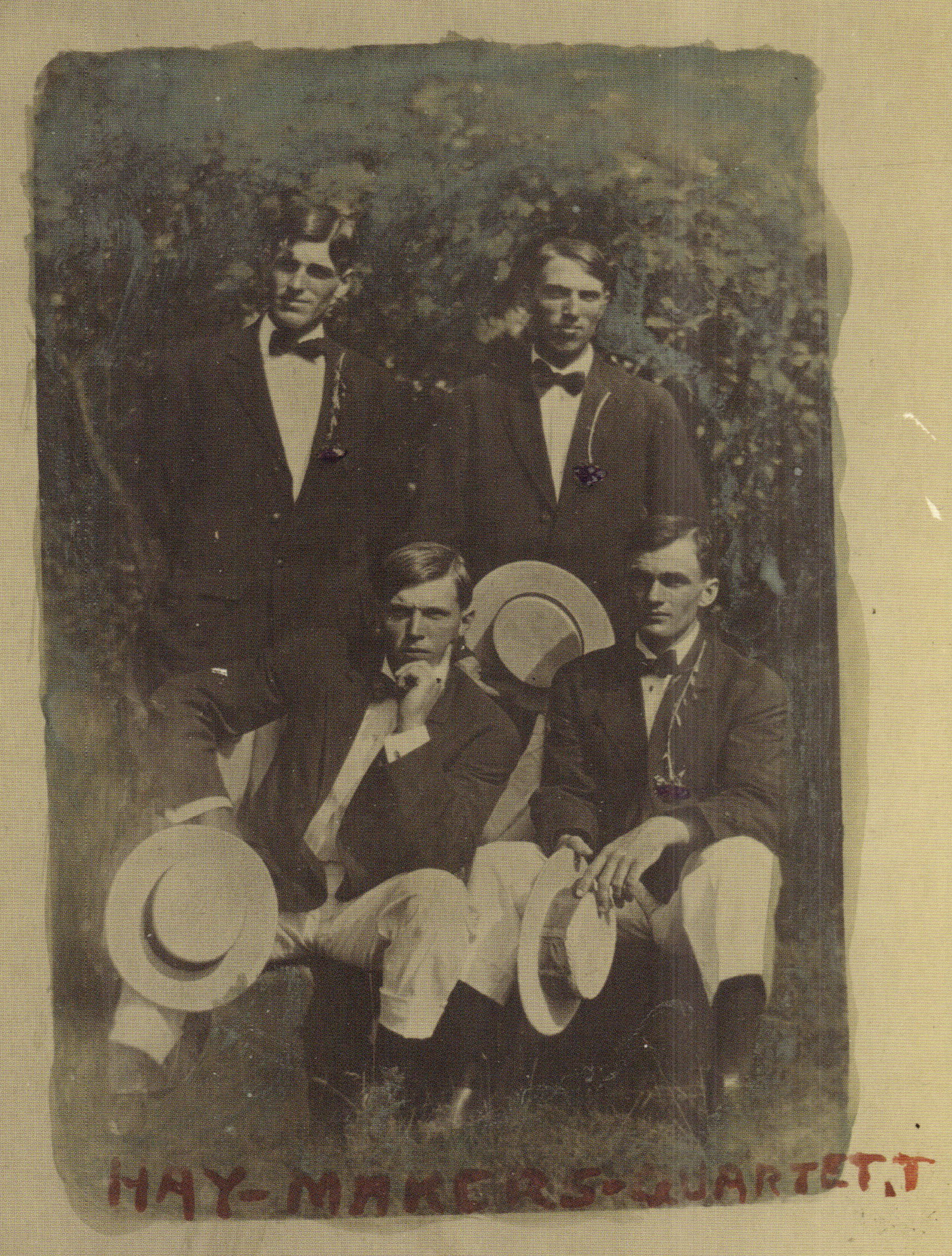
HAY-MAKERS-QUARTET.T

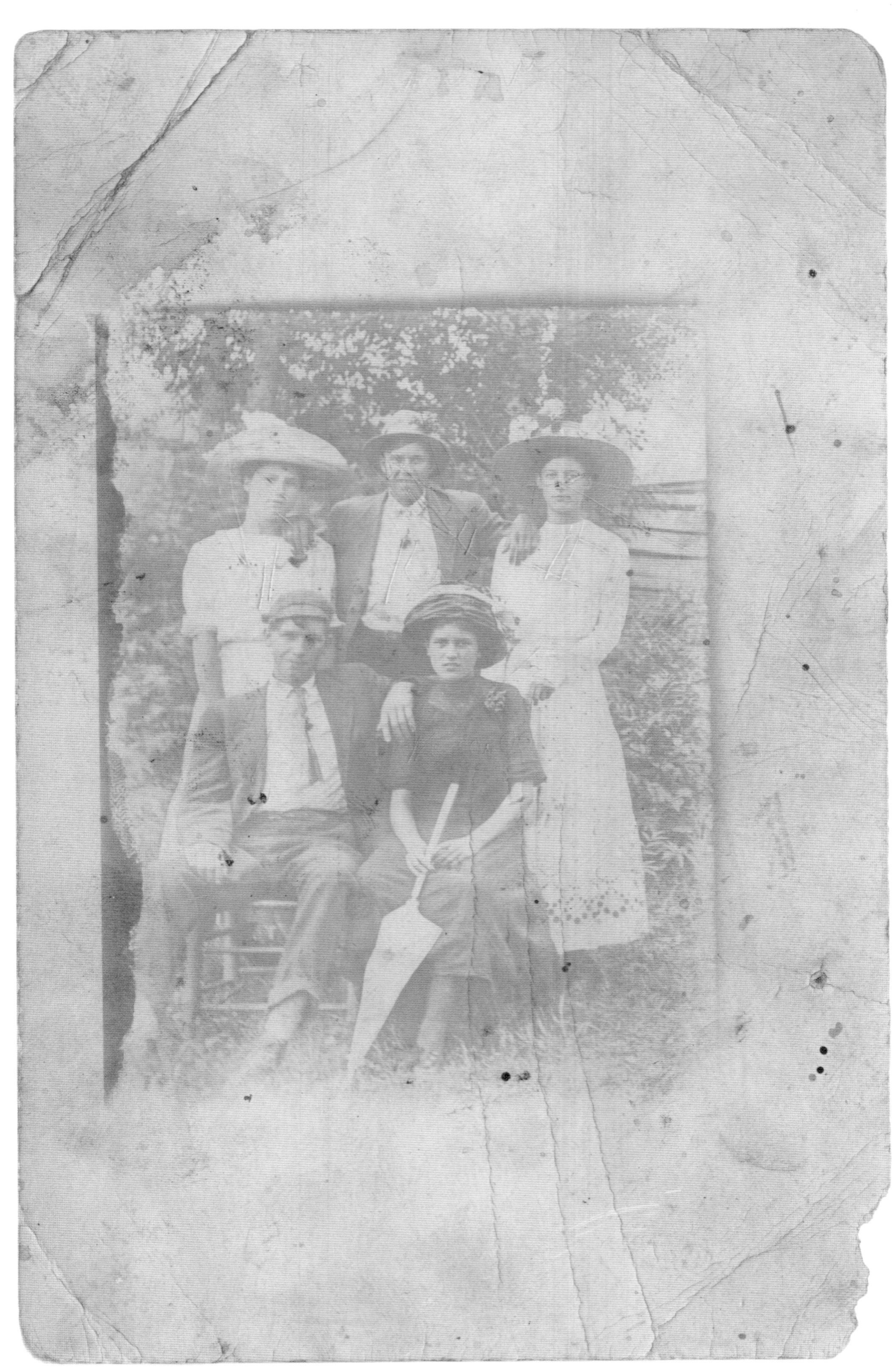

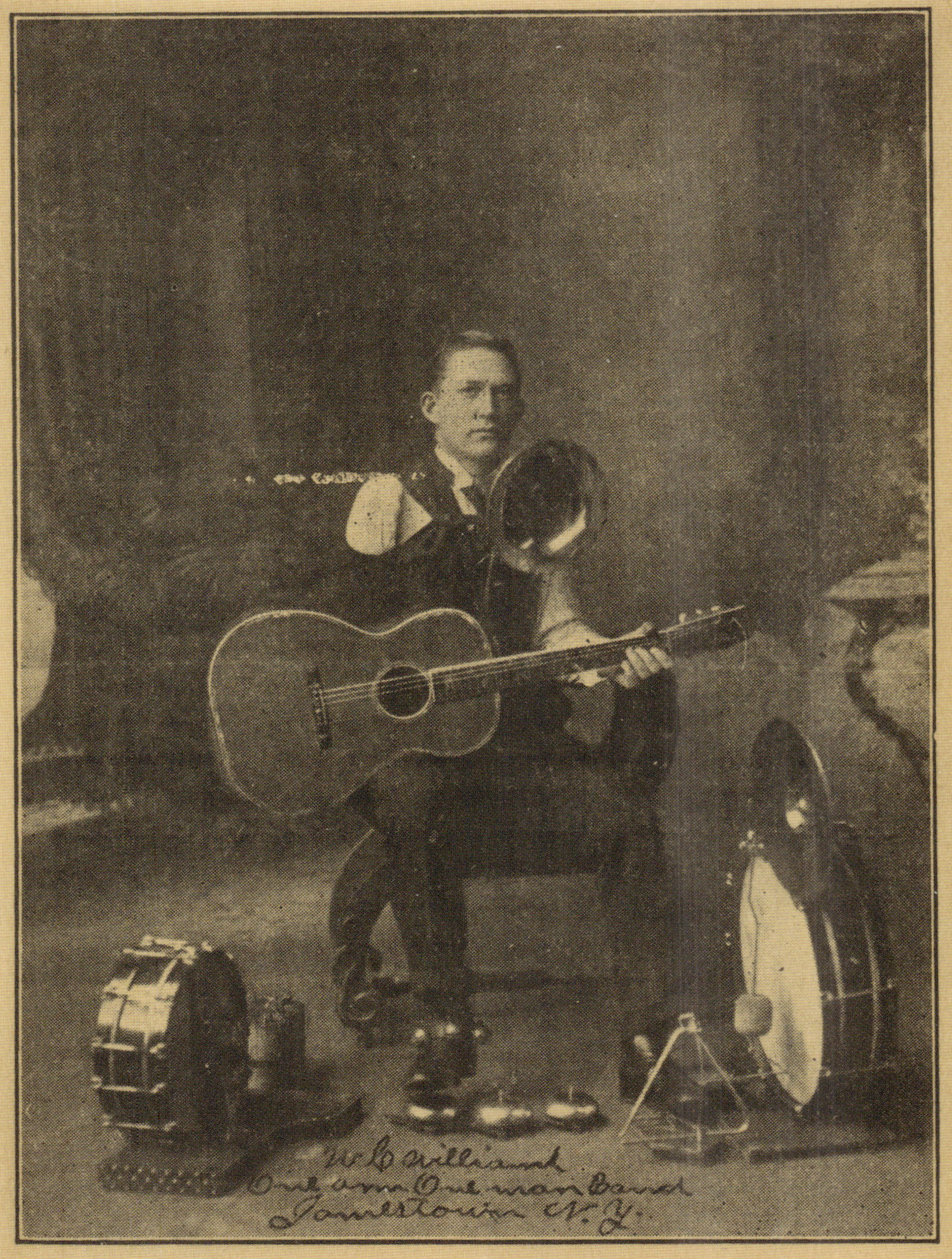

W. C. WILLIAMS
One Man Band
234 Sprague Street, Jamestown, N. Y.

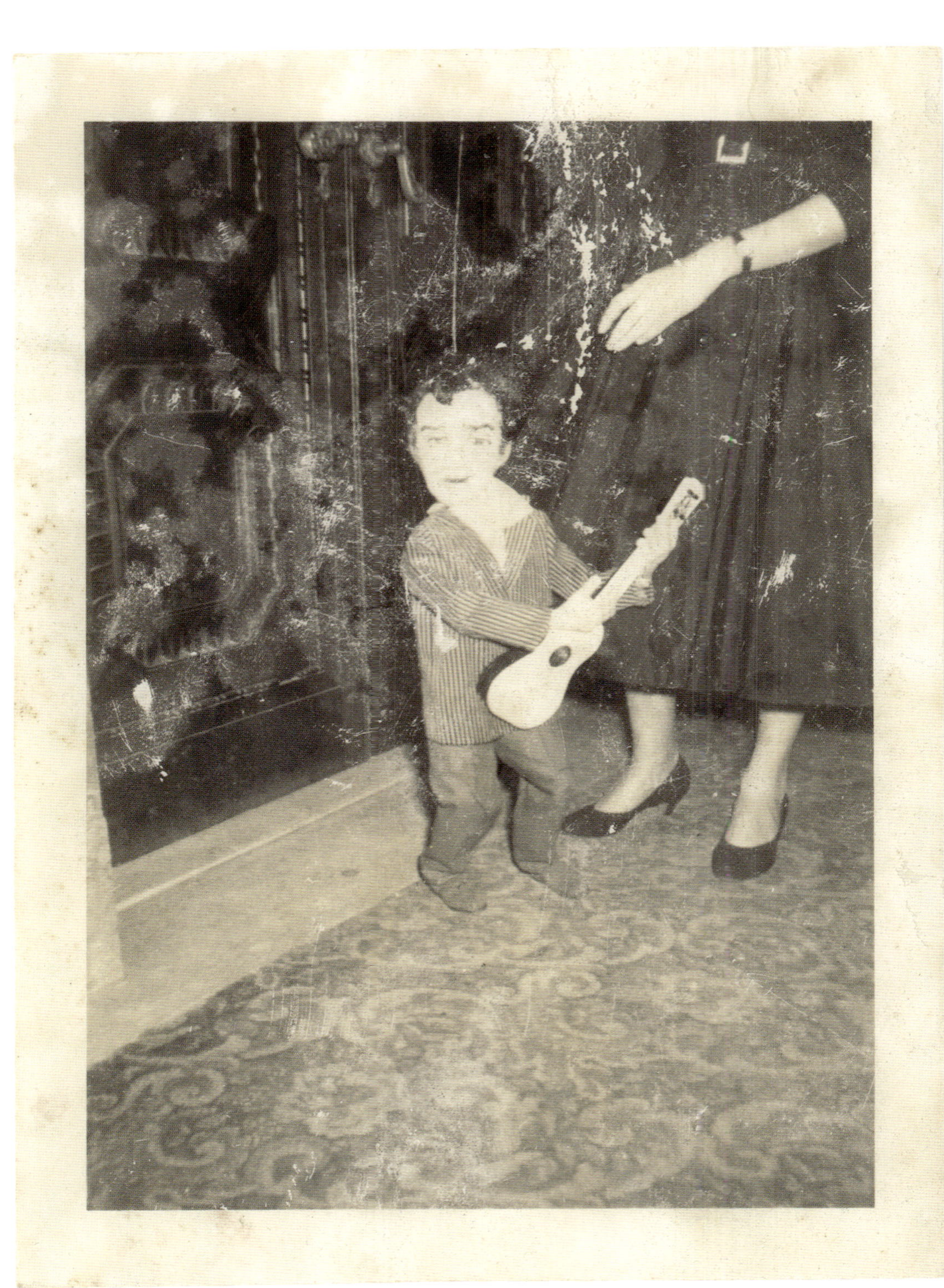

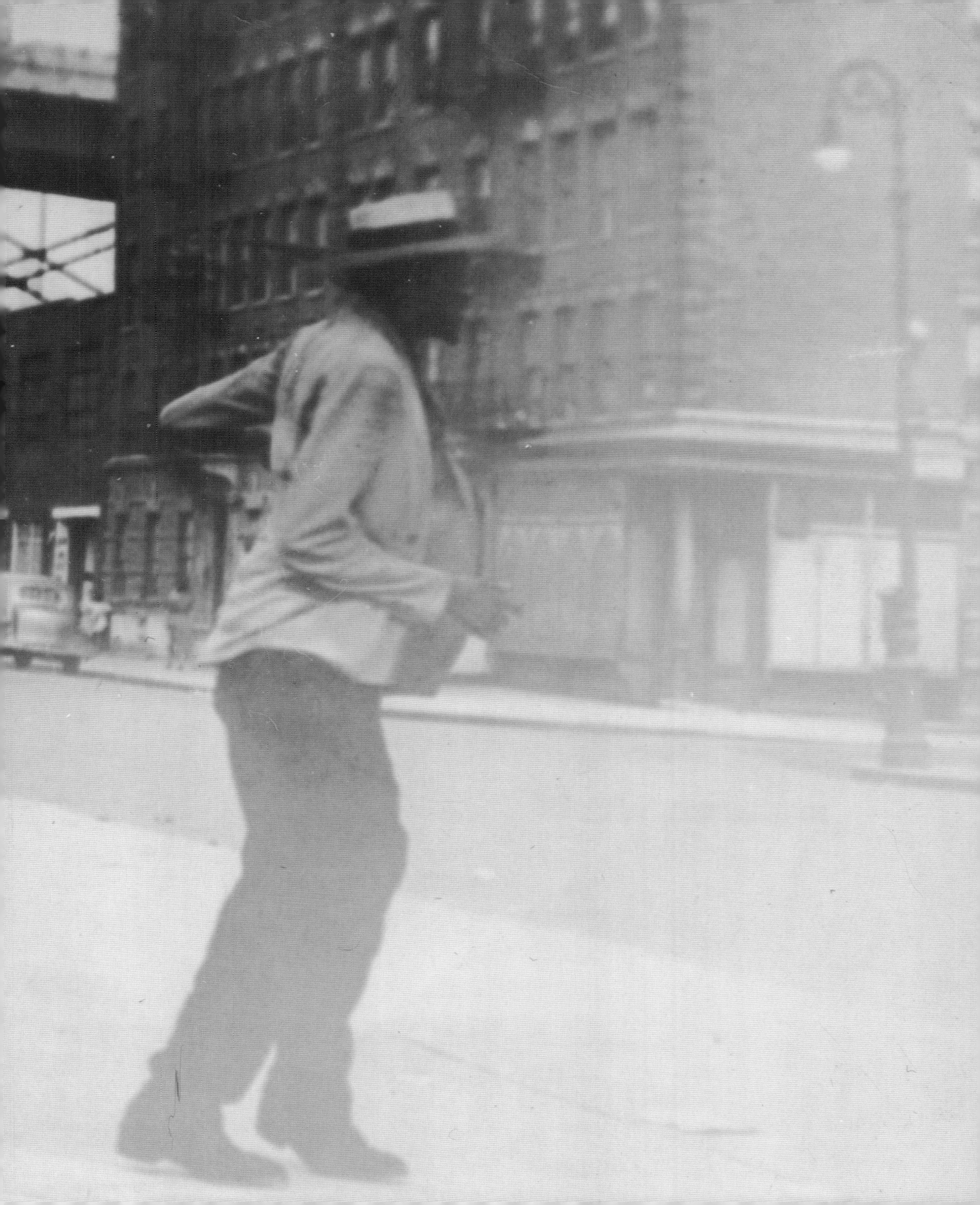

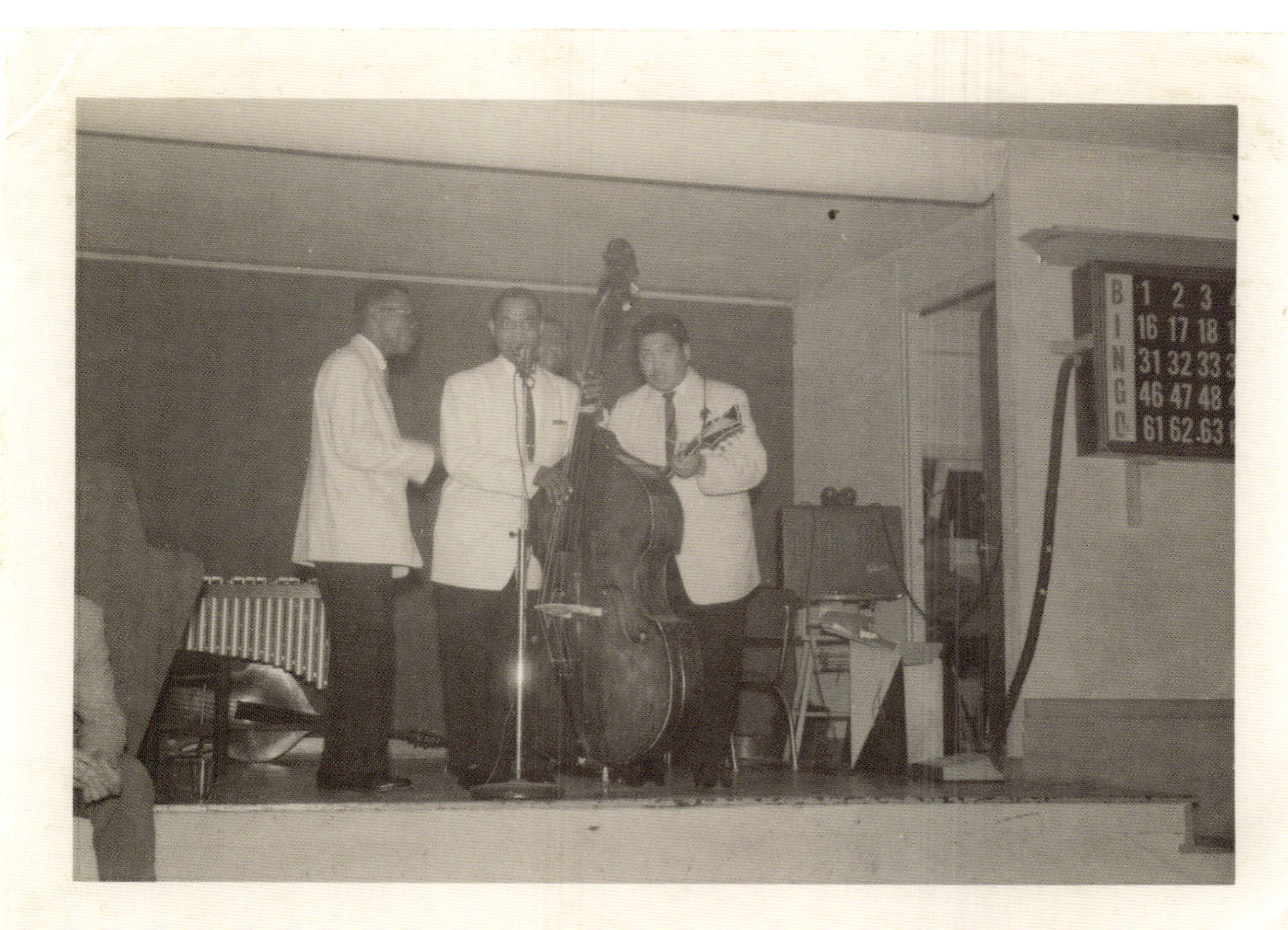
BINGO
1 2 3
16 17 18
31 32 33
46 47 48
61 62 63

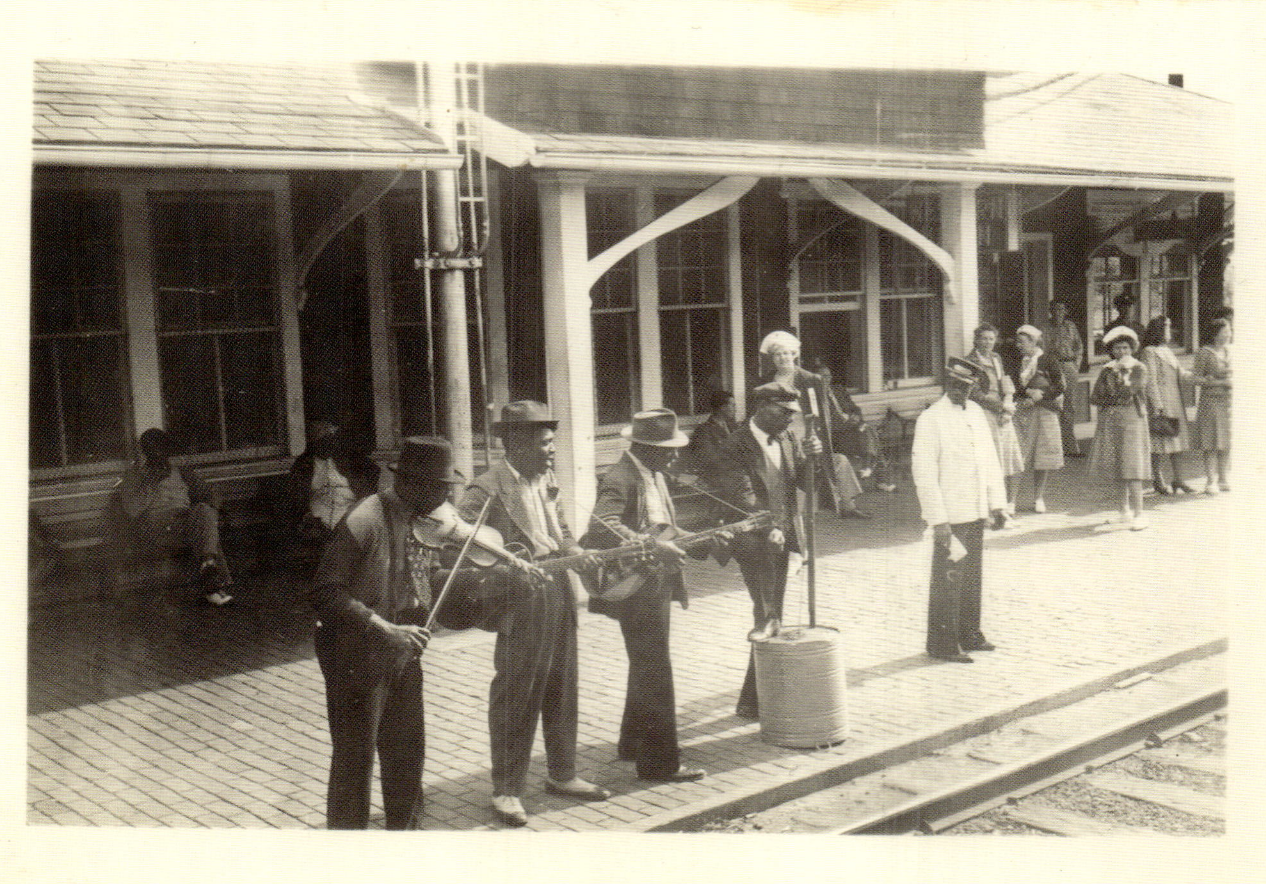

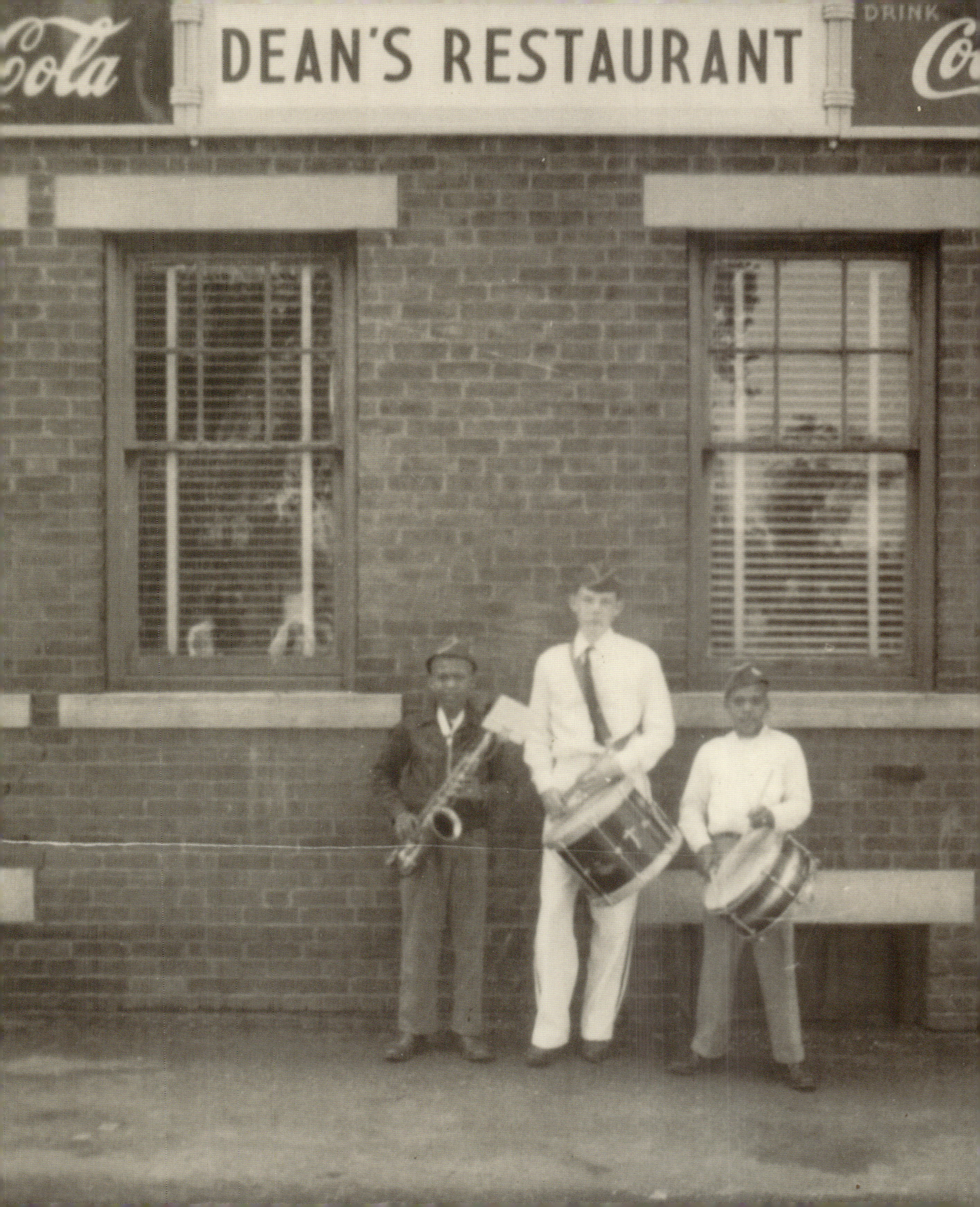

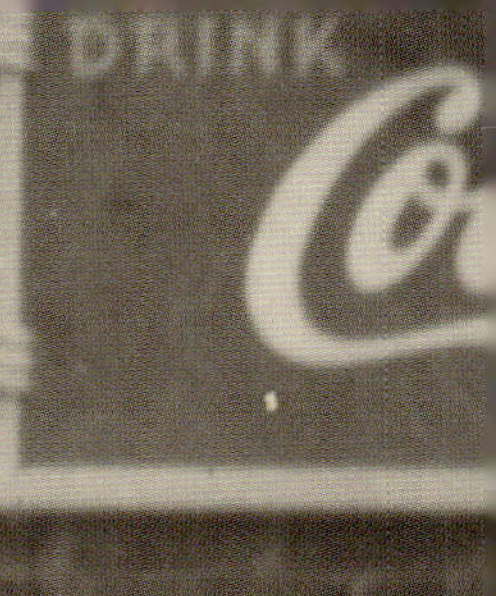
Cola
DEAN'S RESTAURANT
DRINK

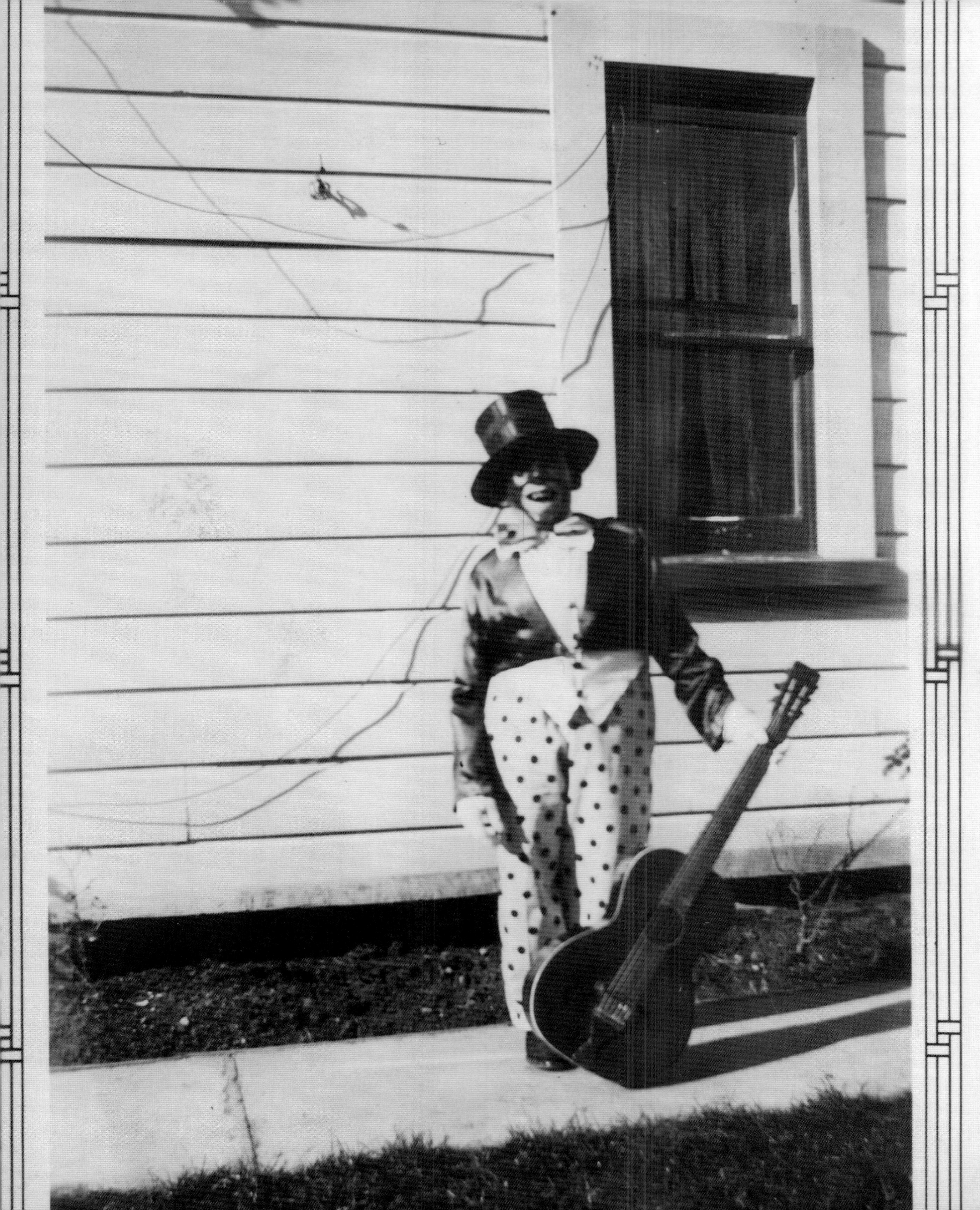

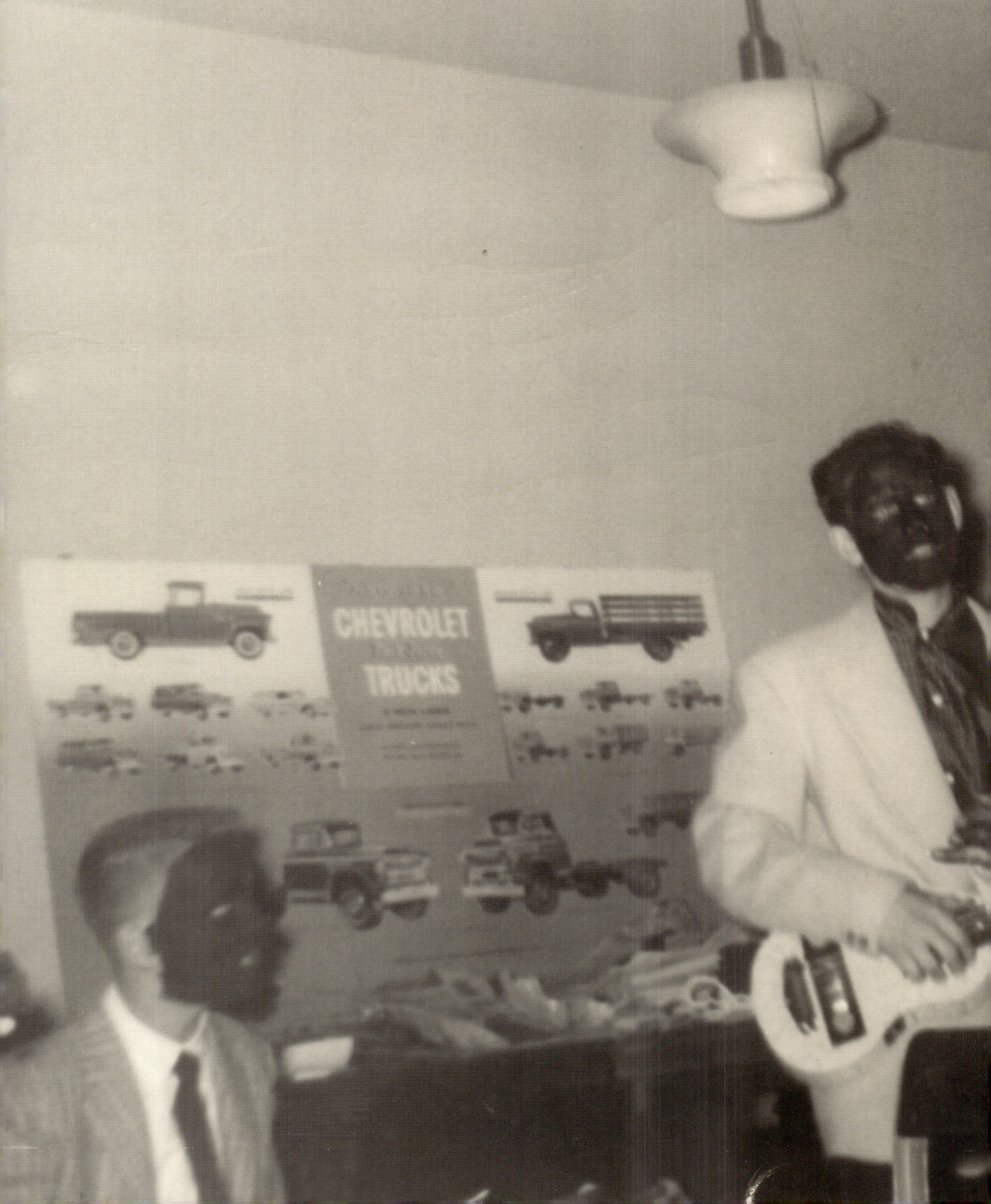
CHEVROLET
TRUCKS

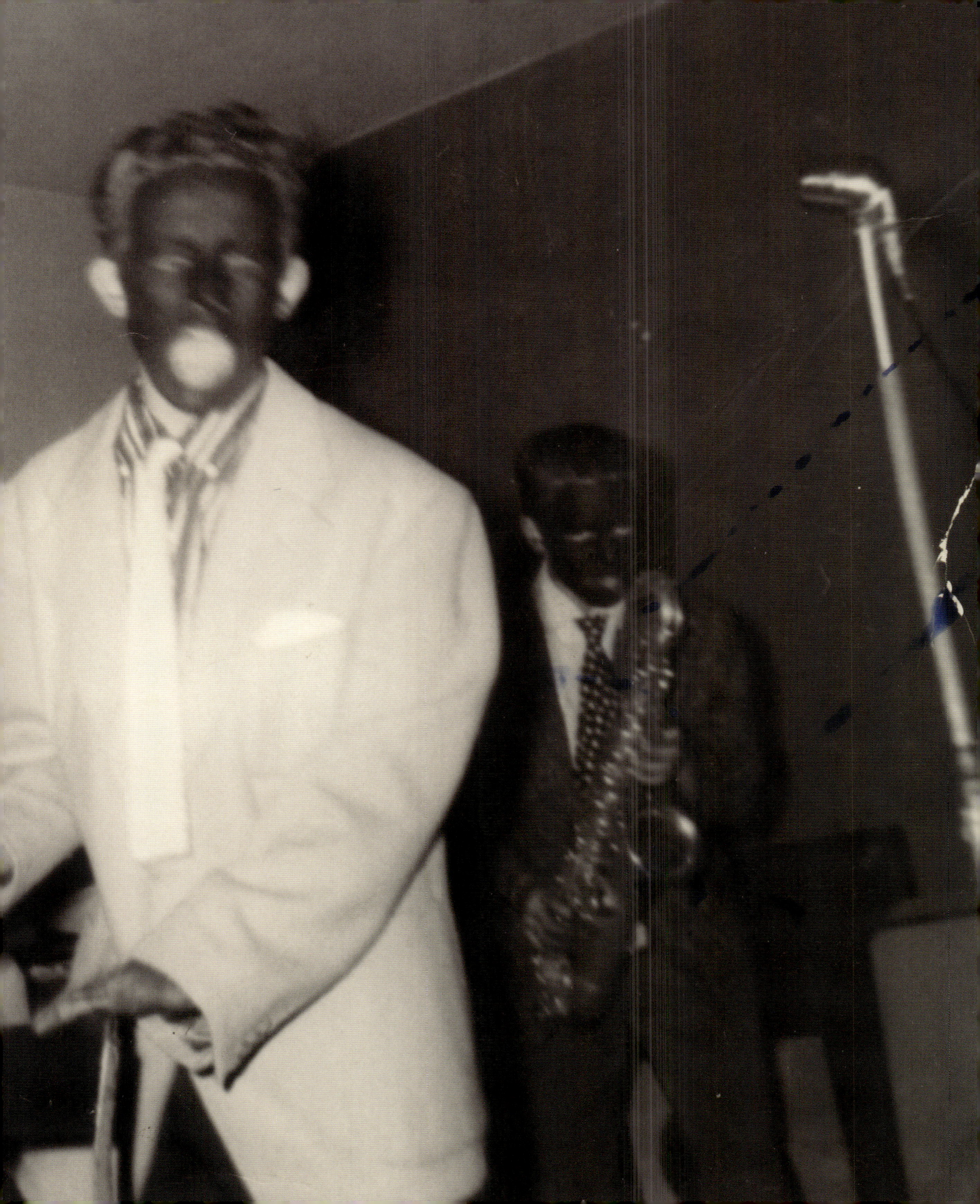

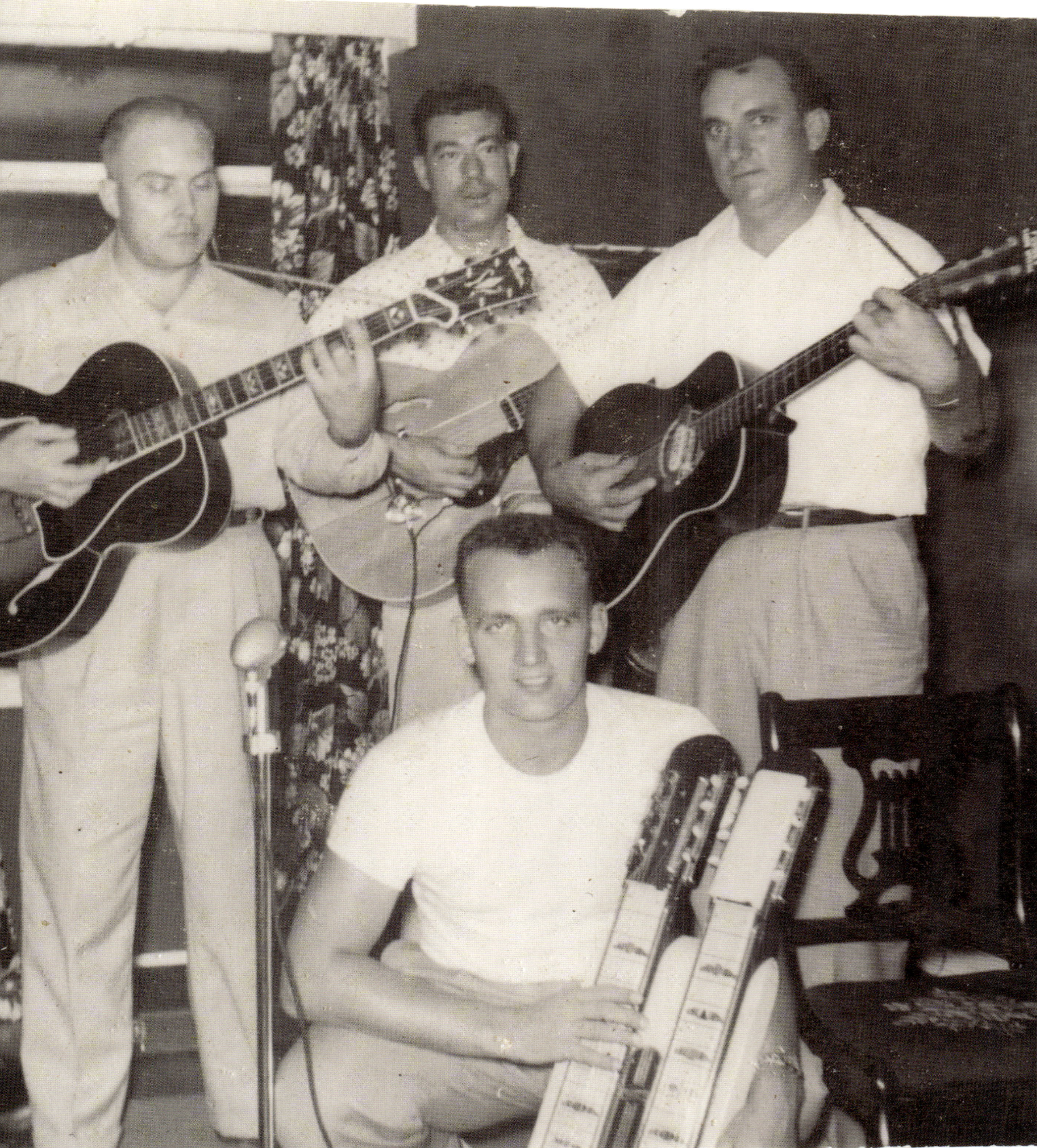

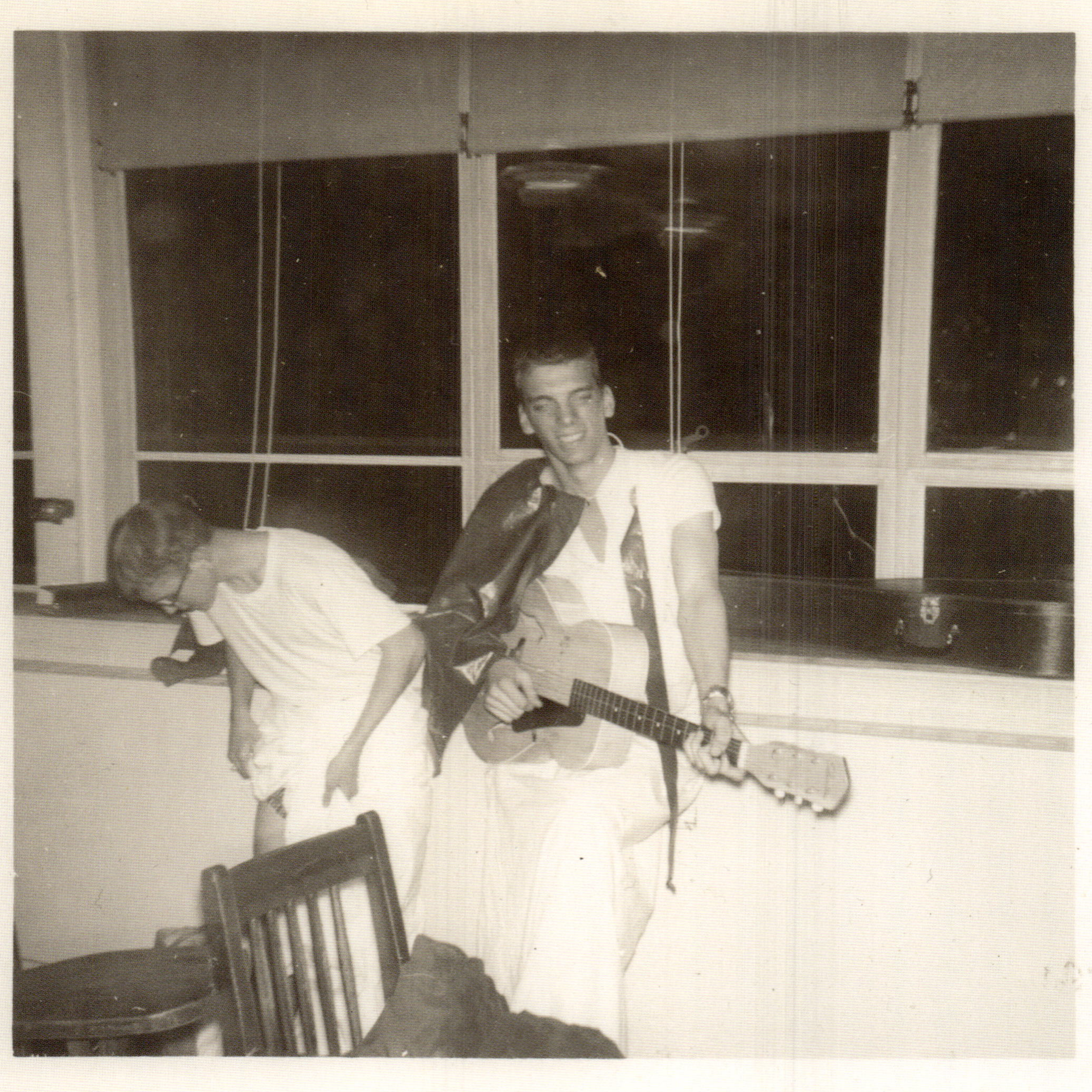
MAY

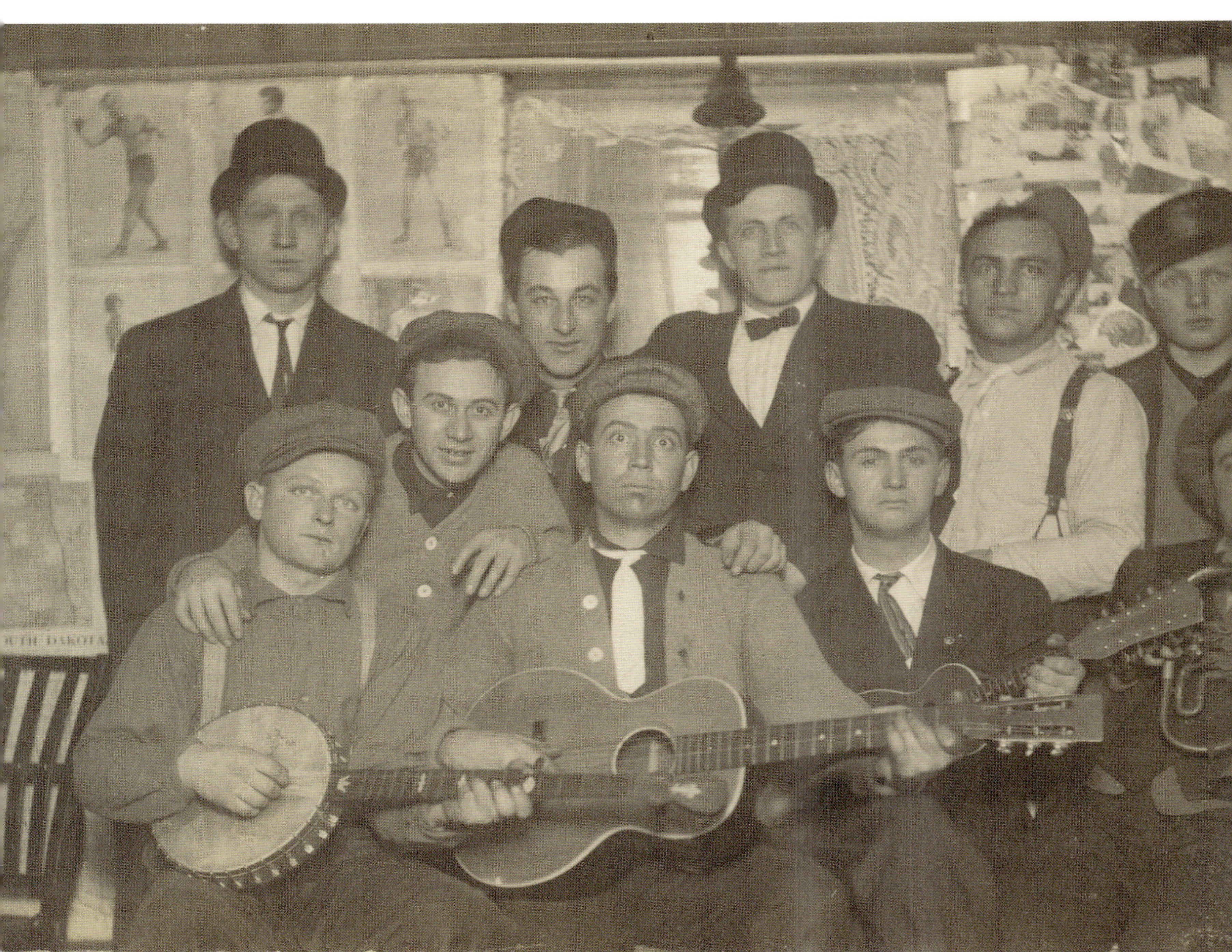

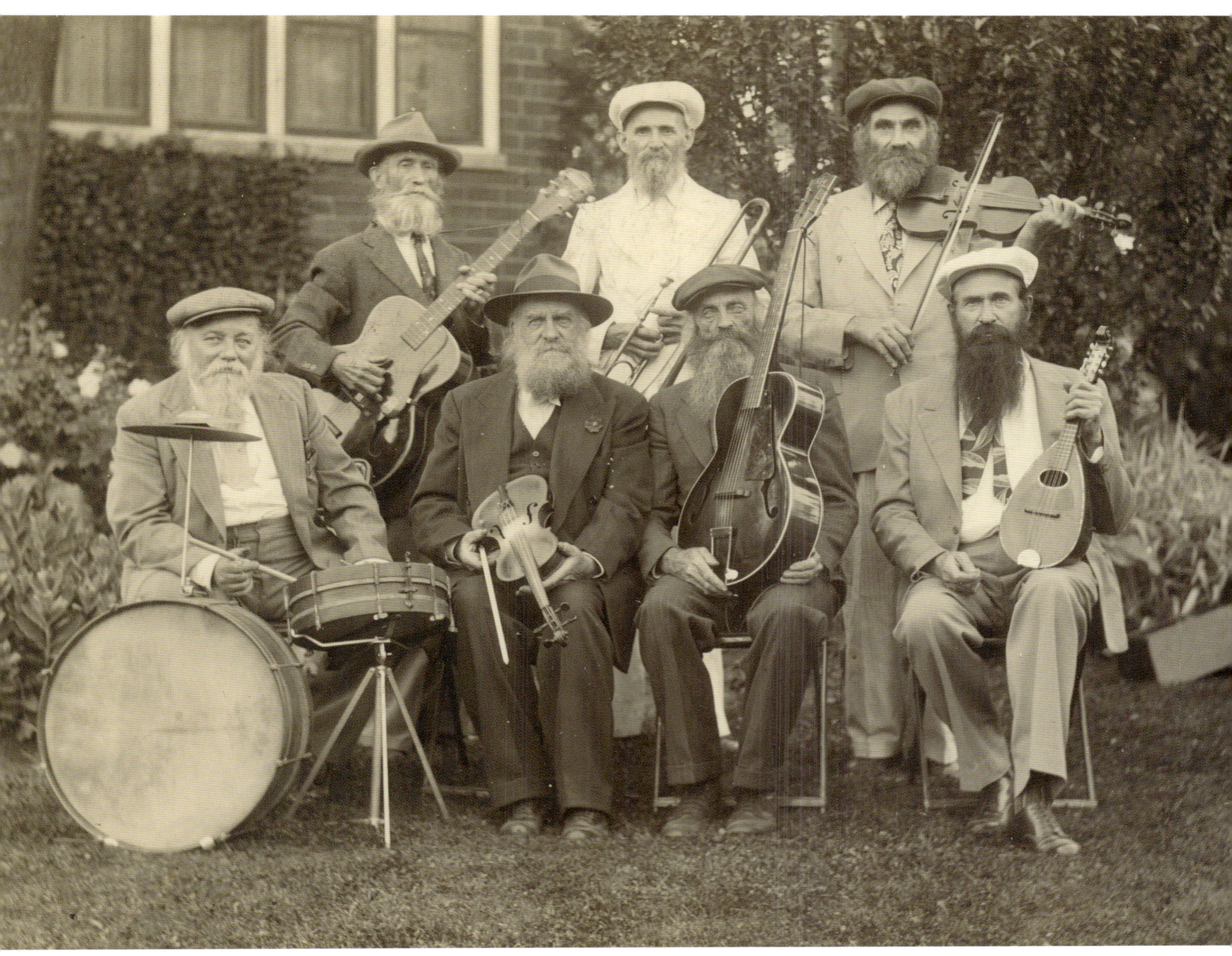

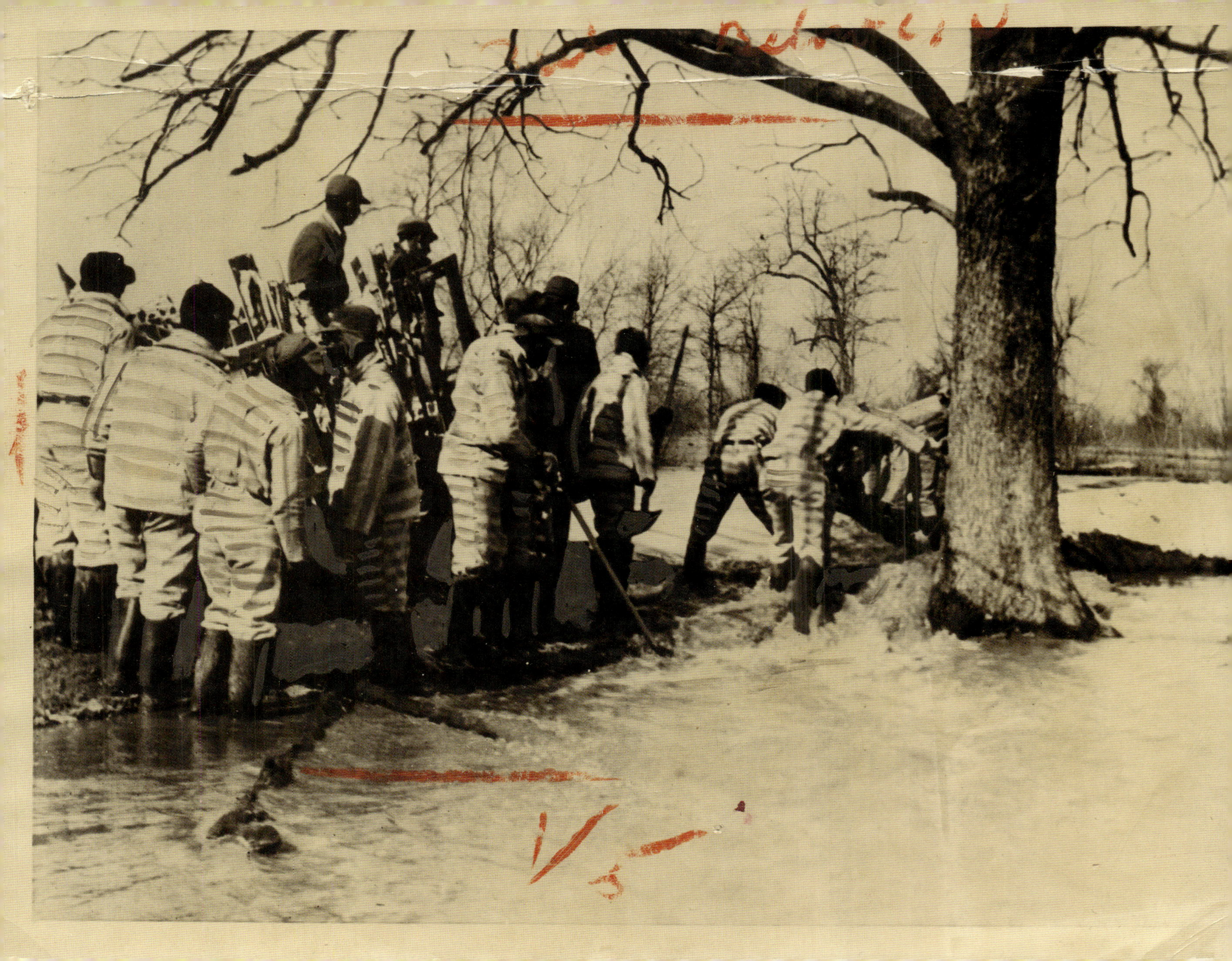

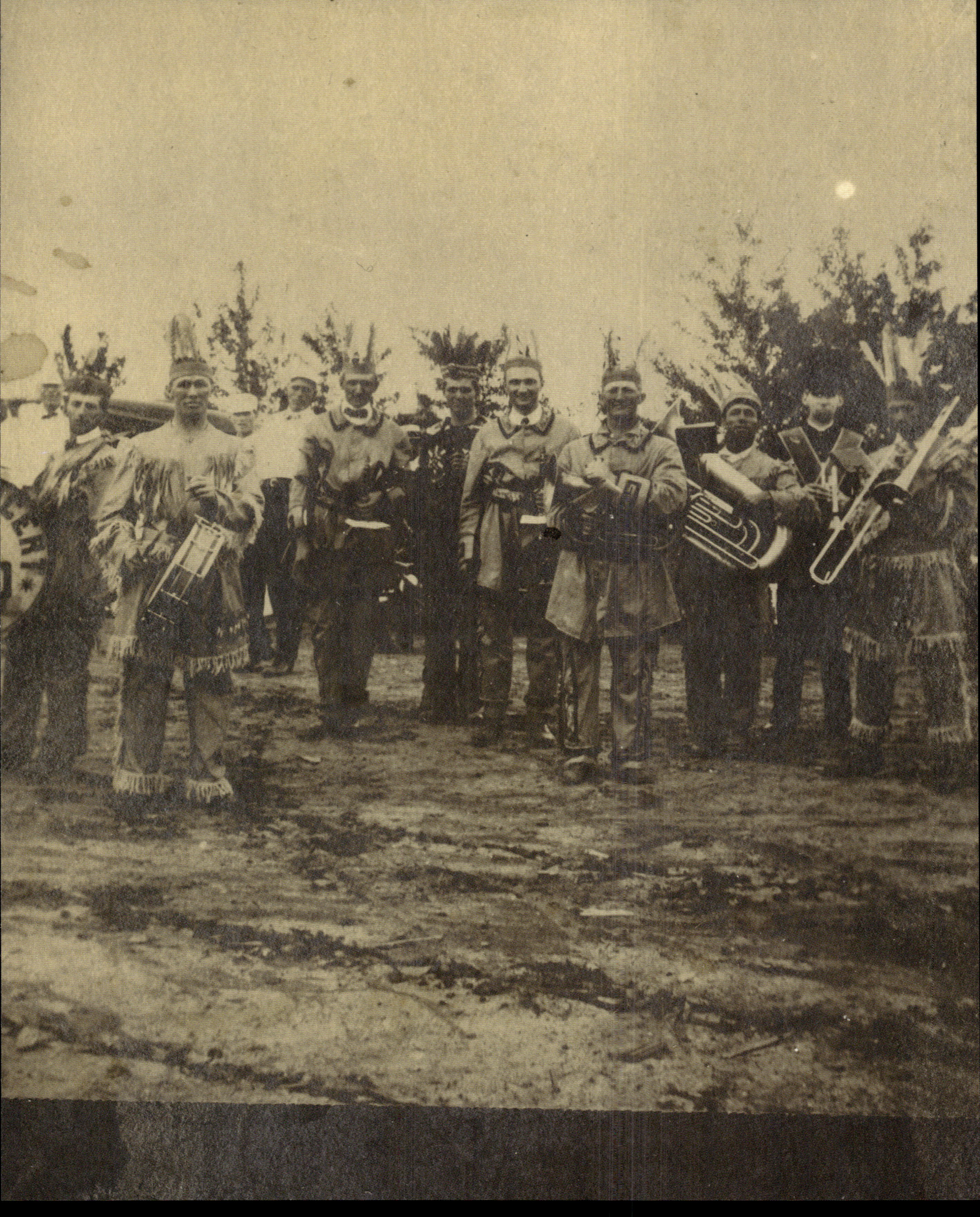

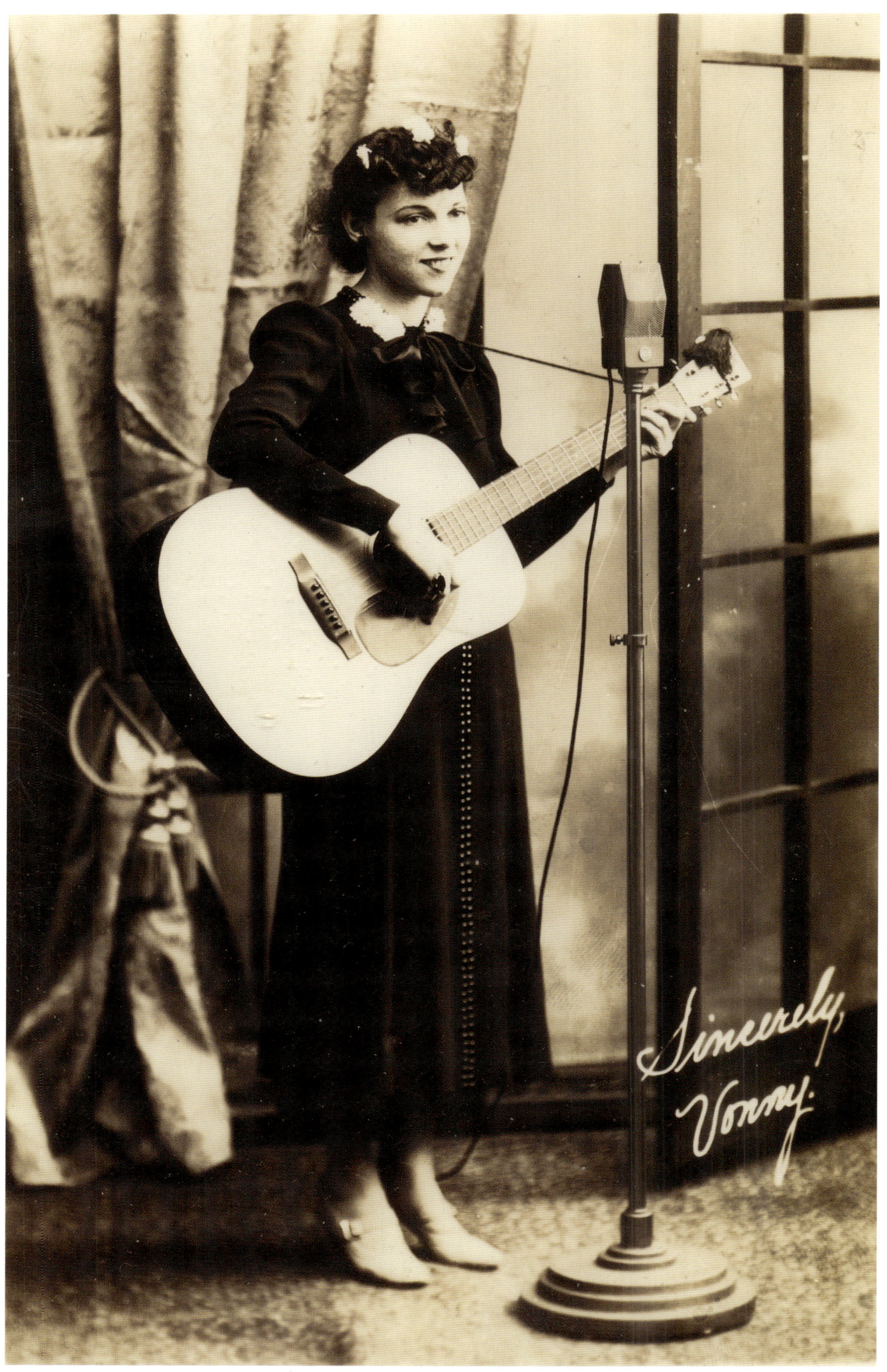
Sincerely,
Vonny.

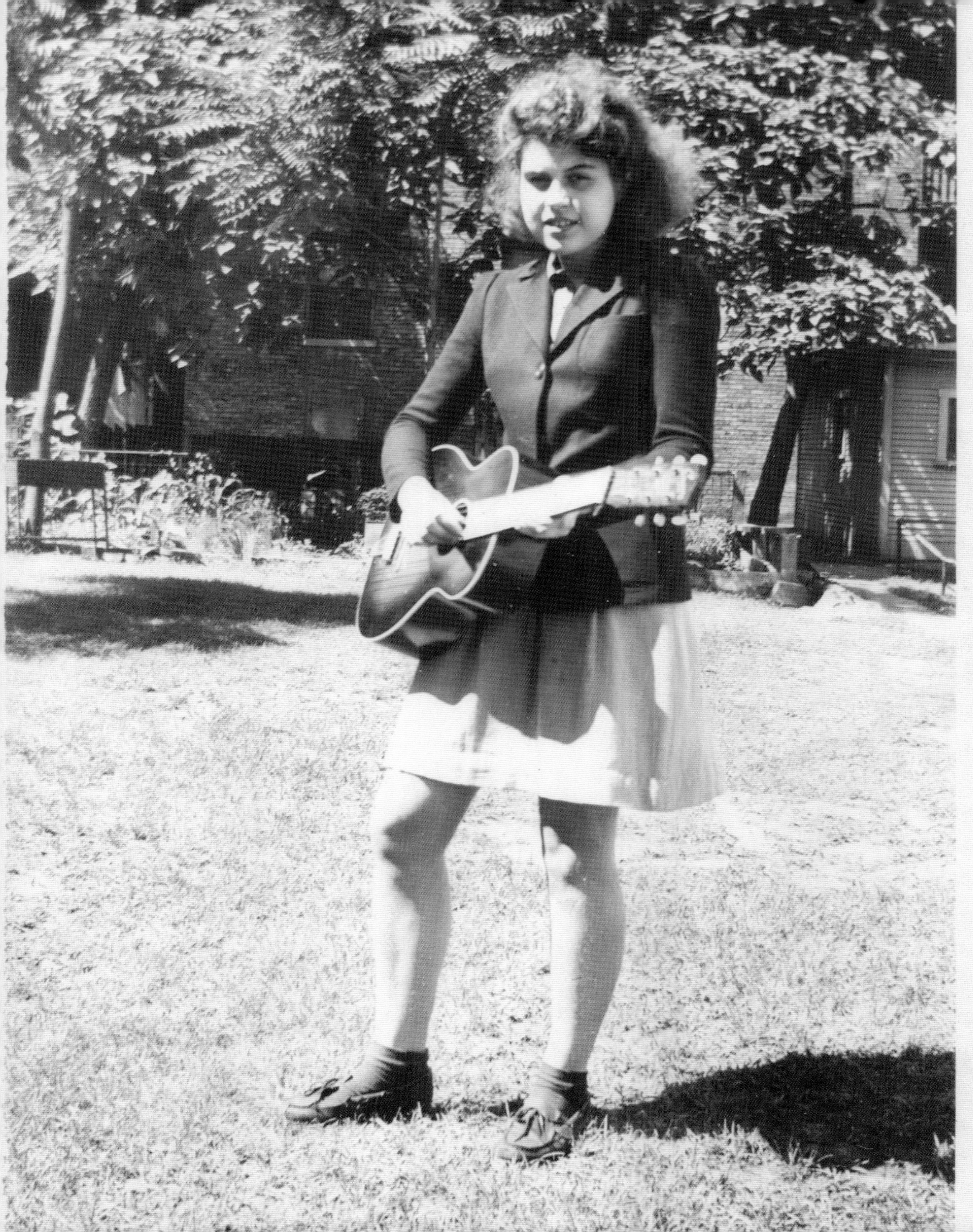

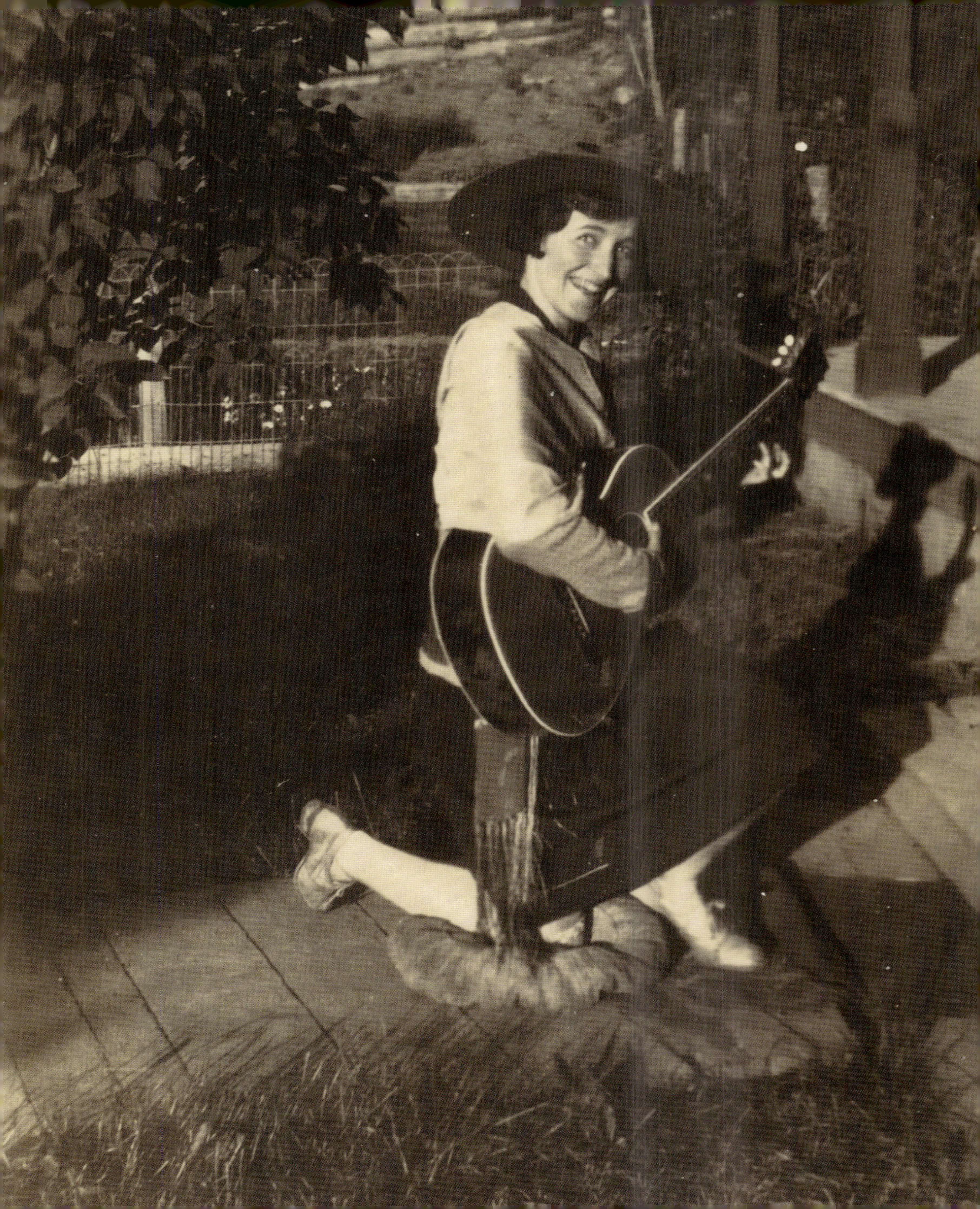

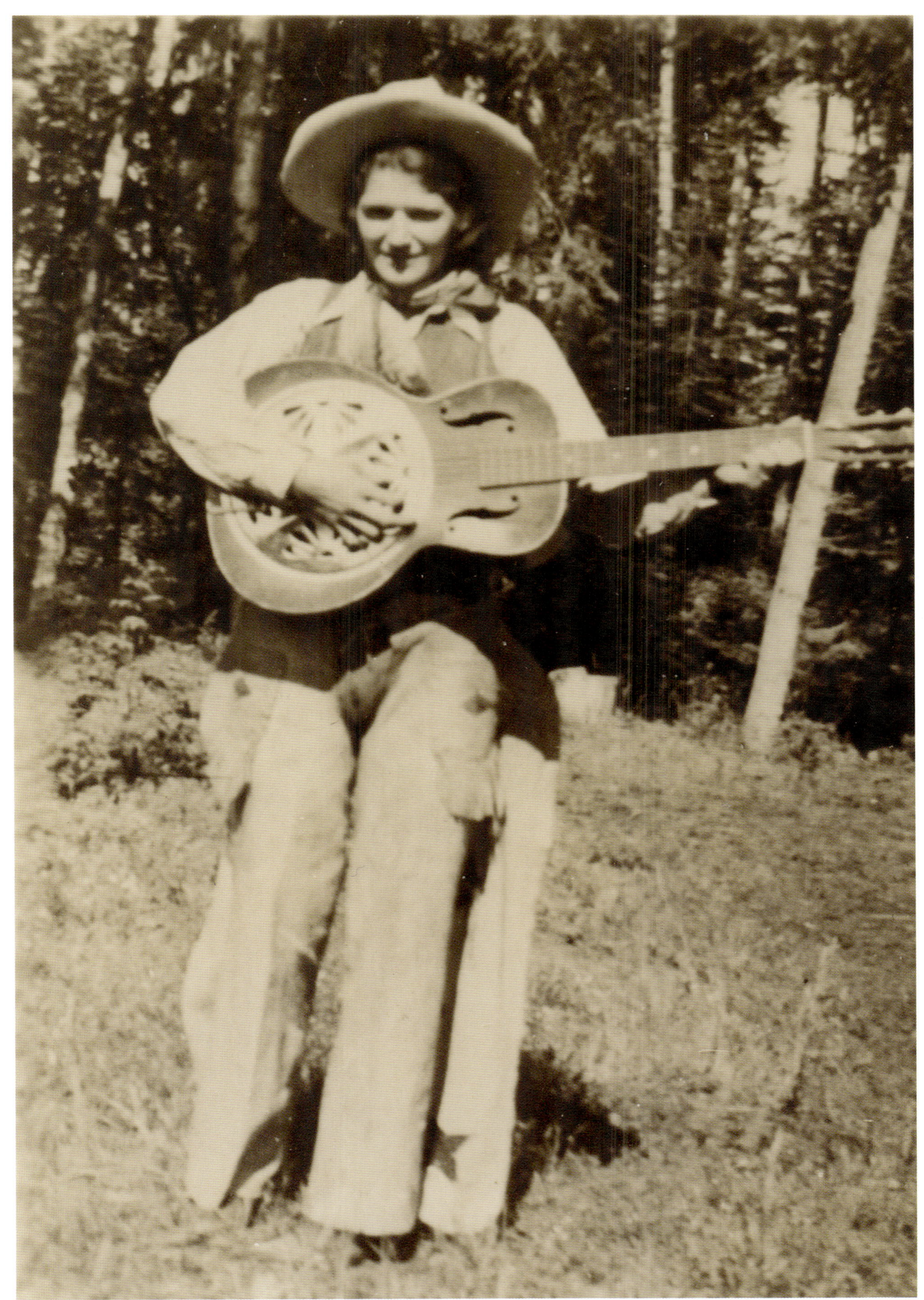

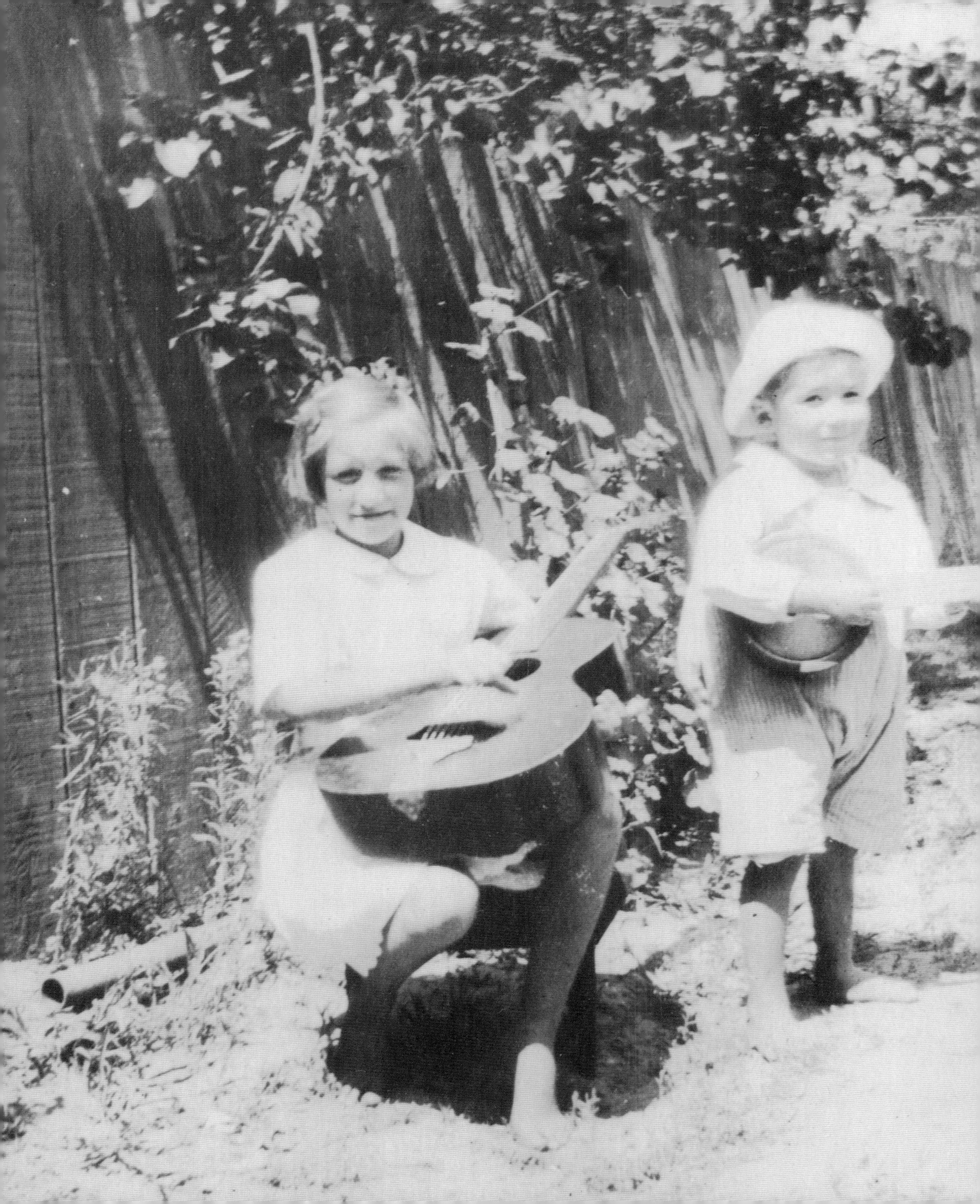

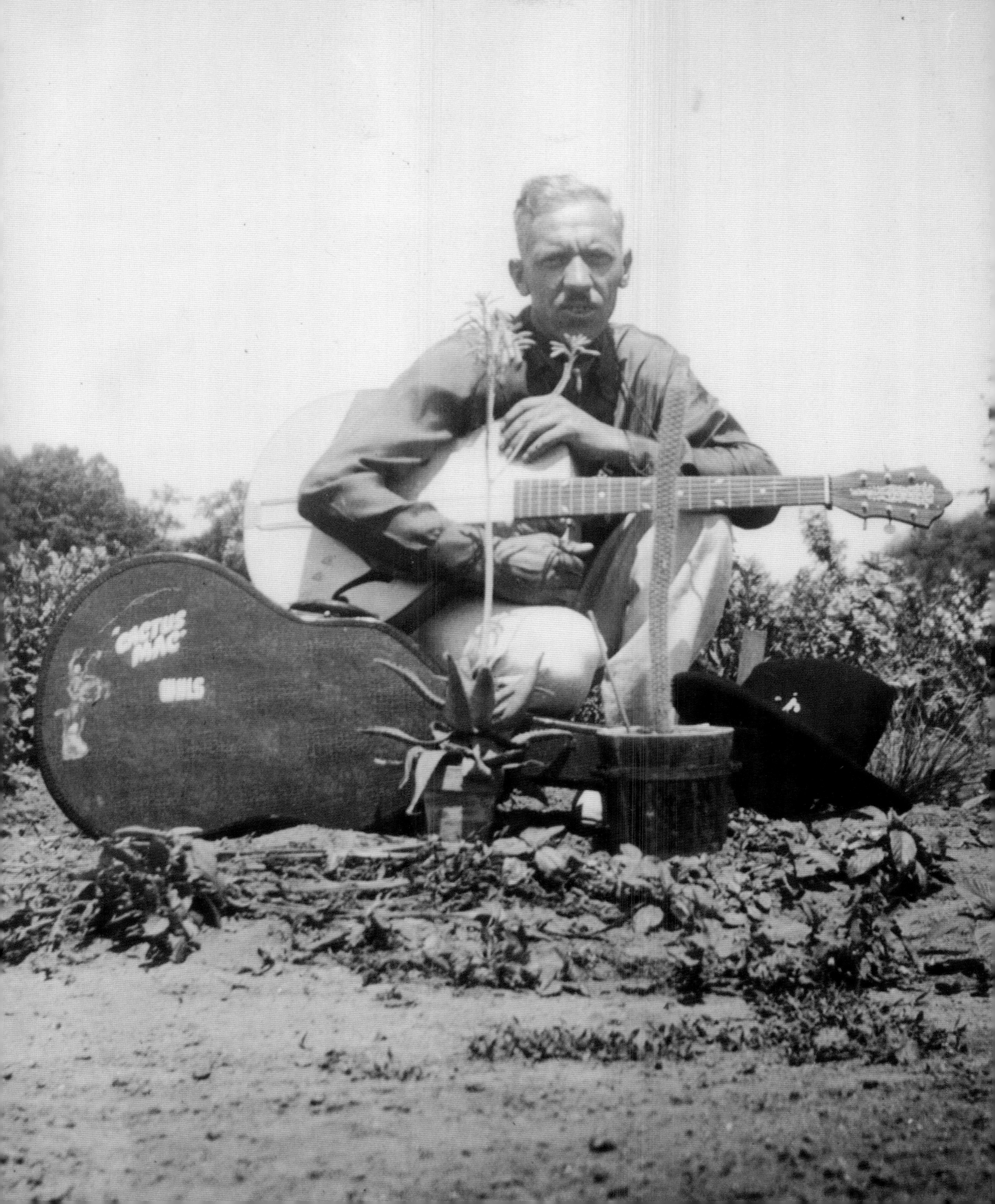
"CACTUS MAC"

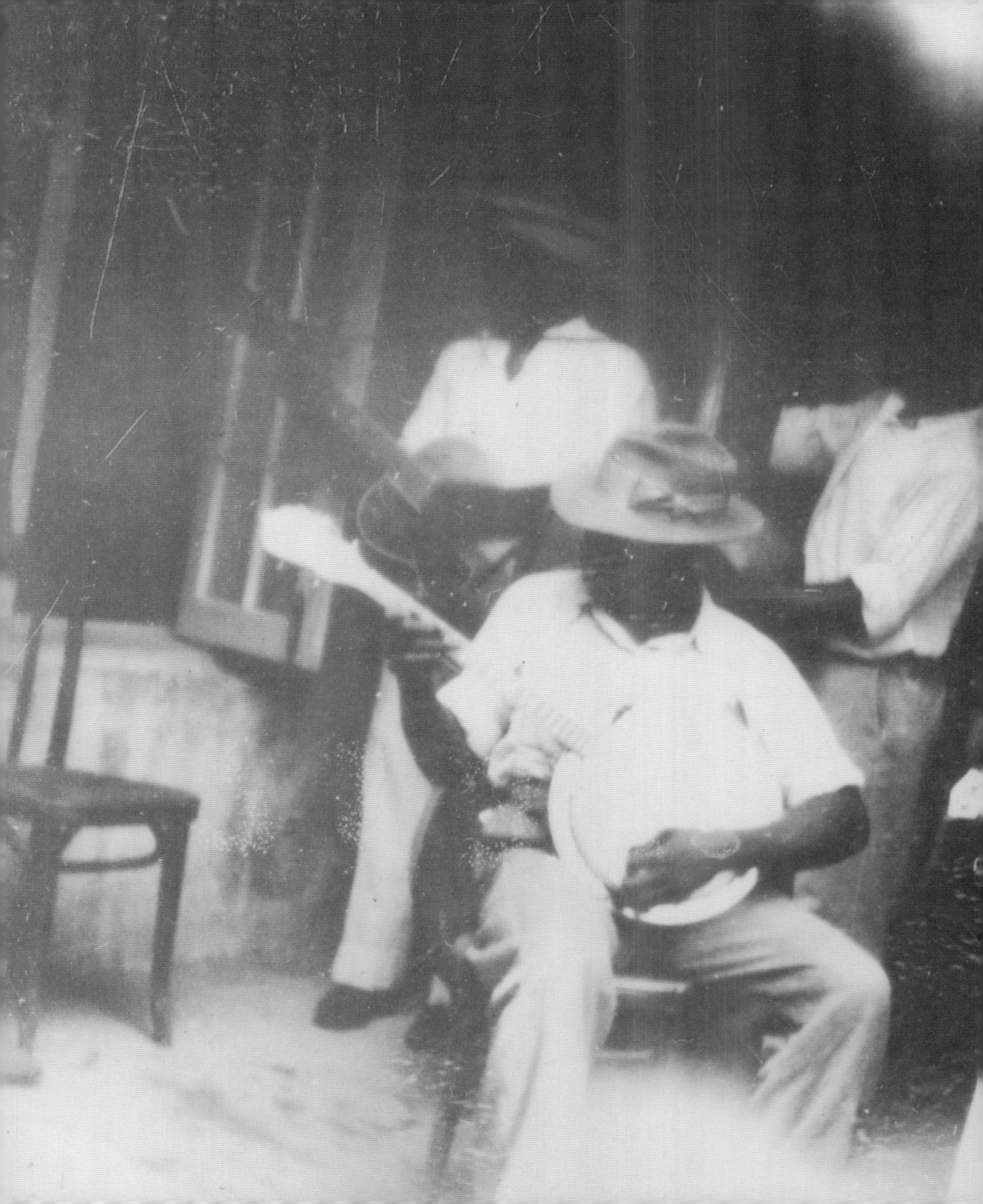

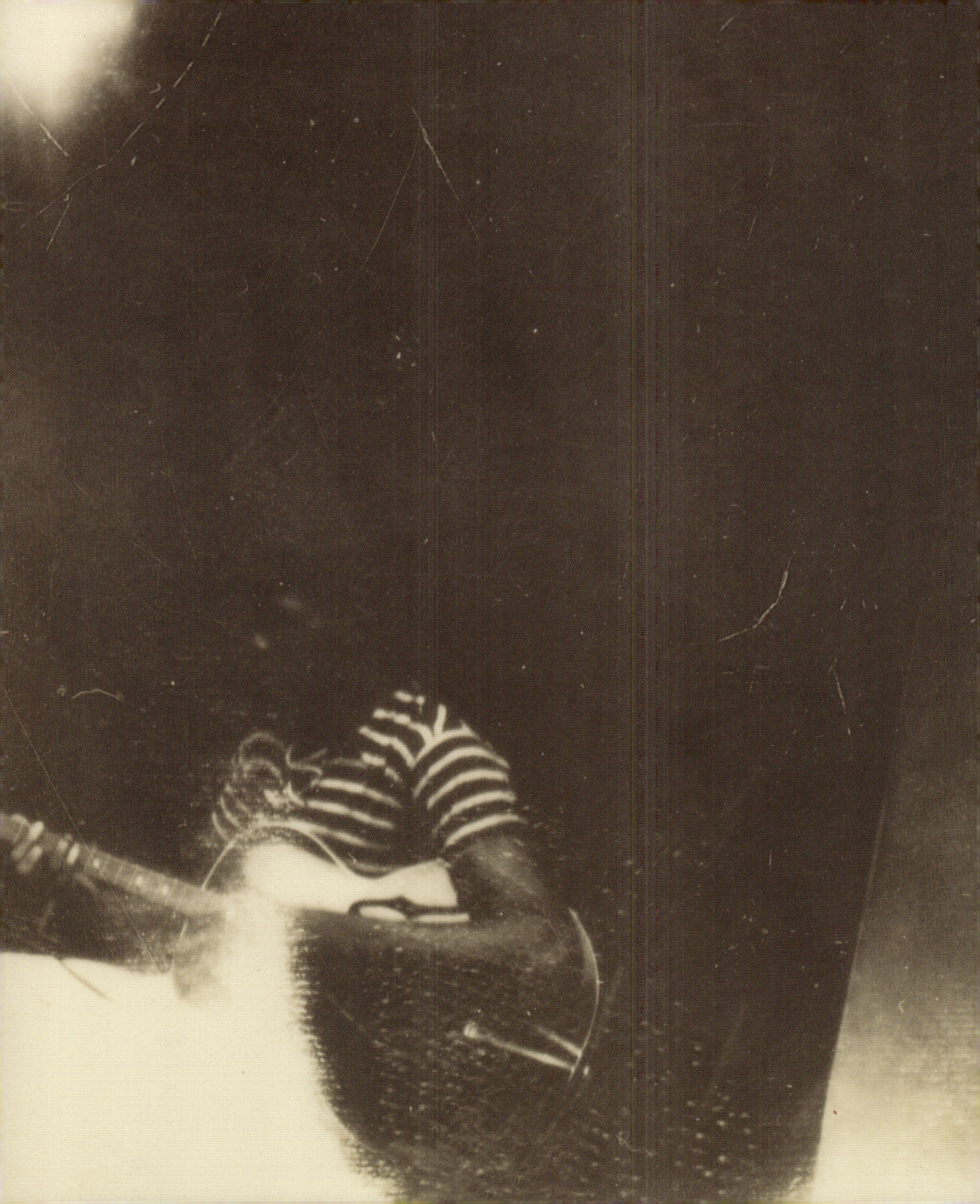

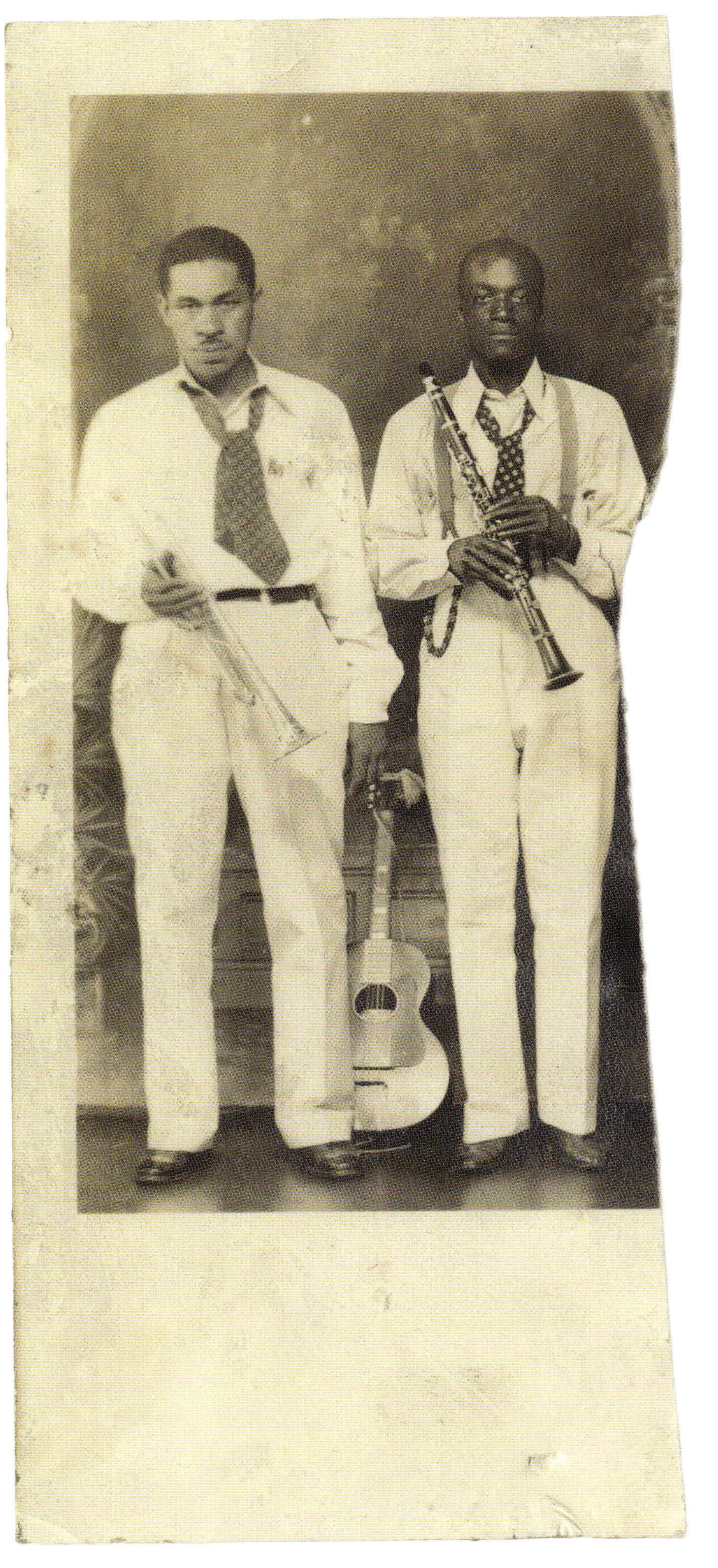

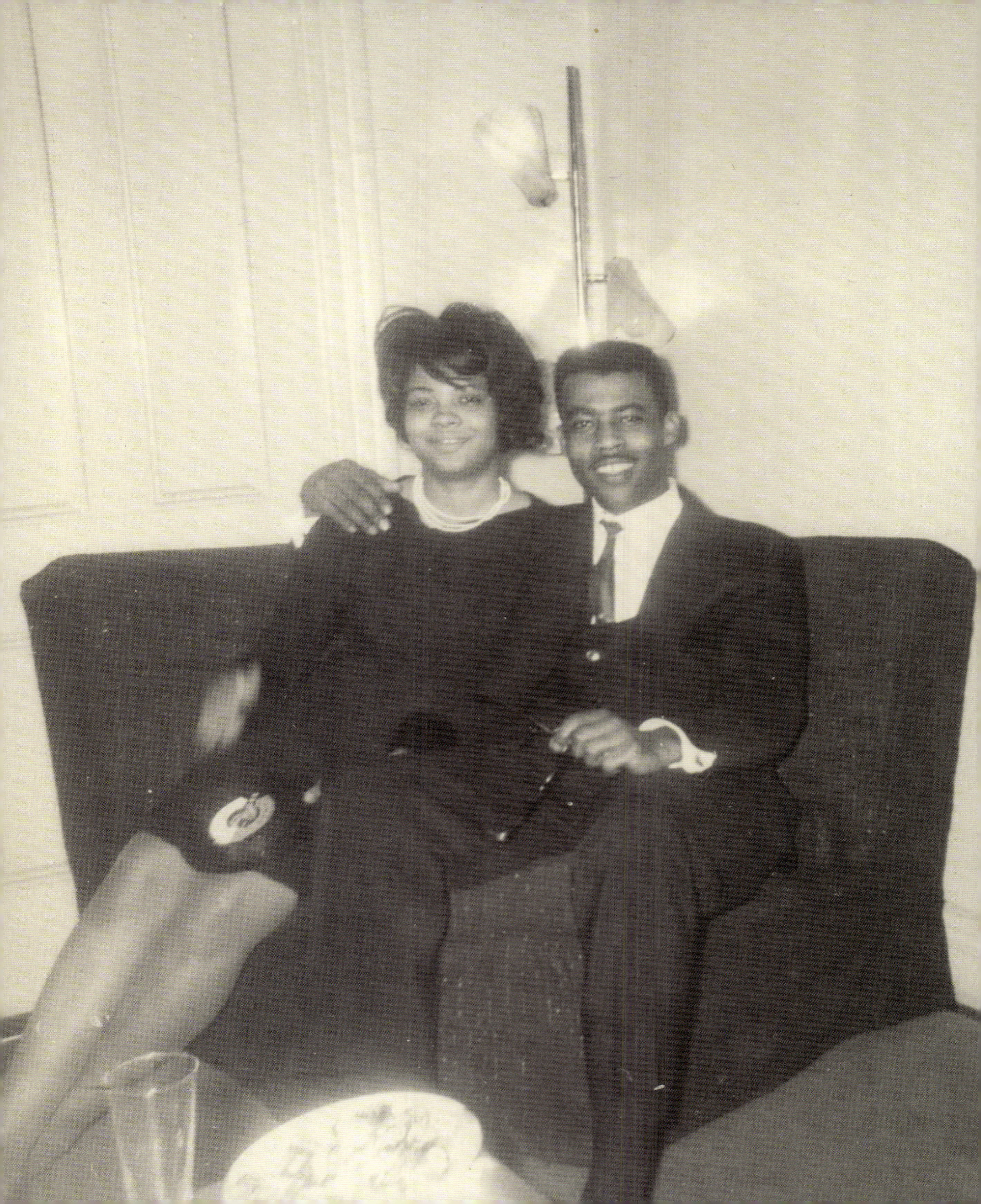

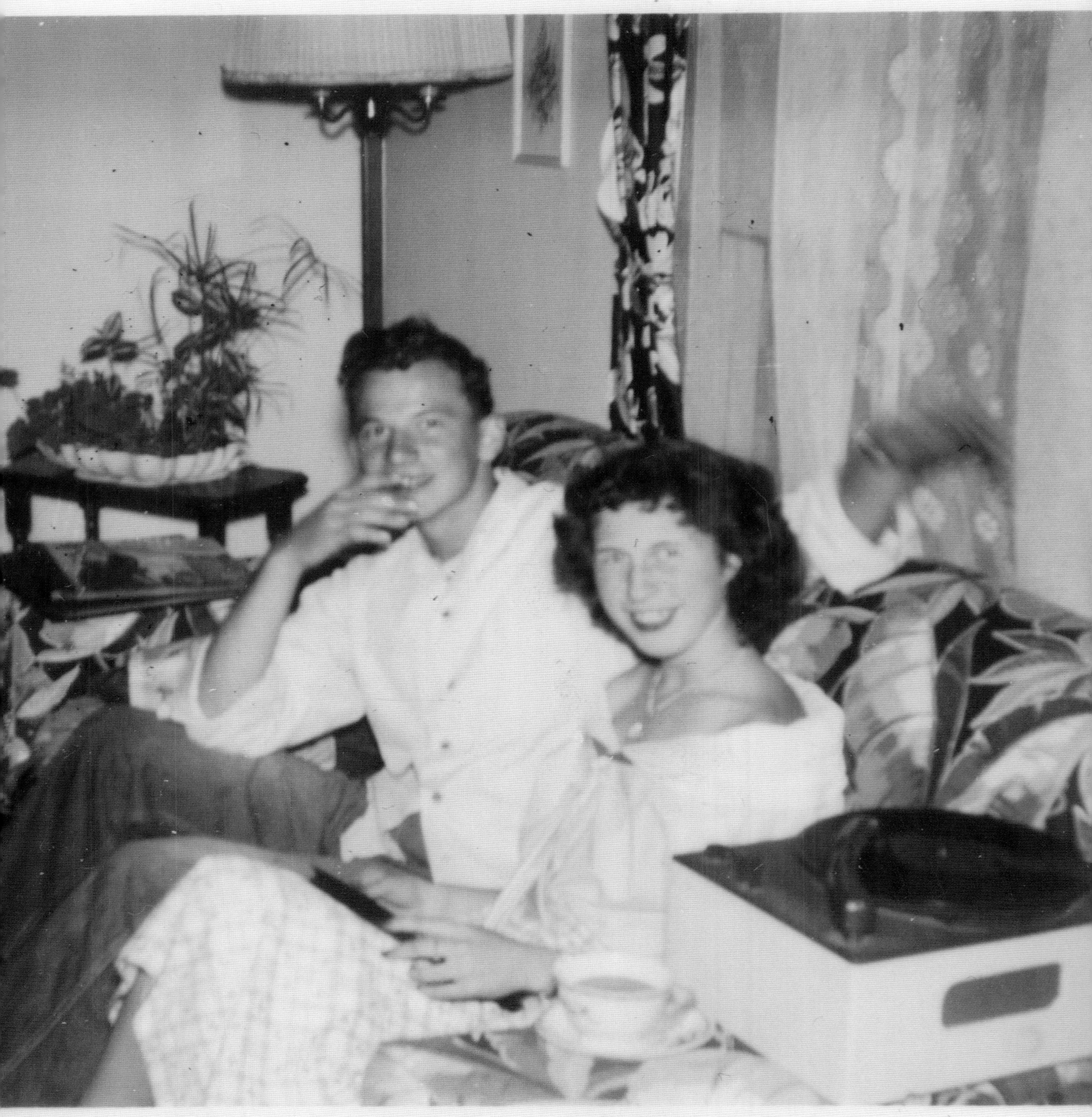

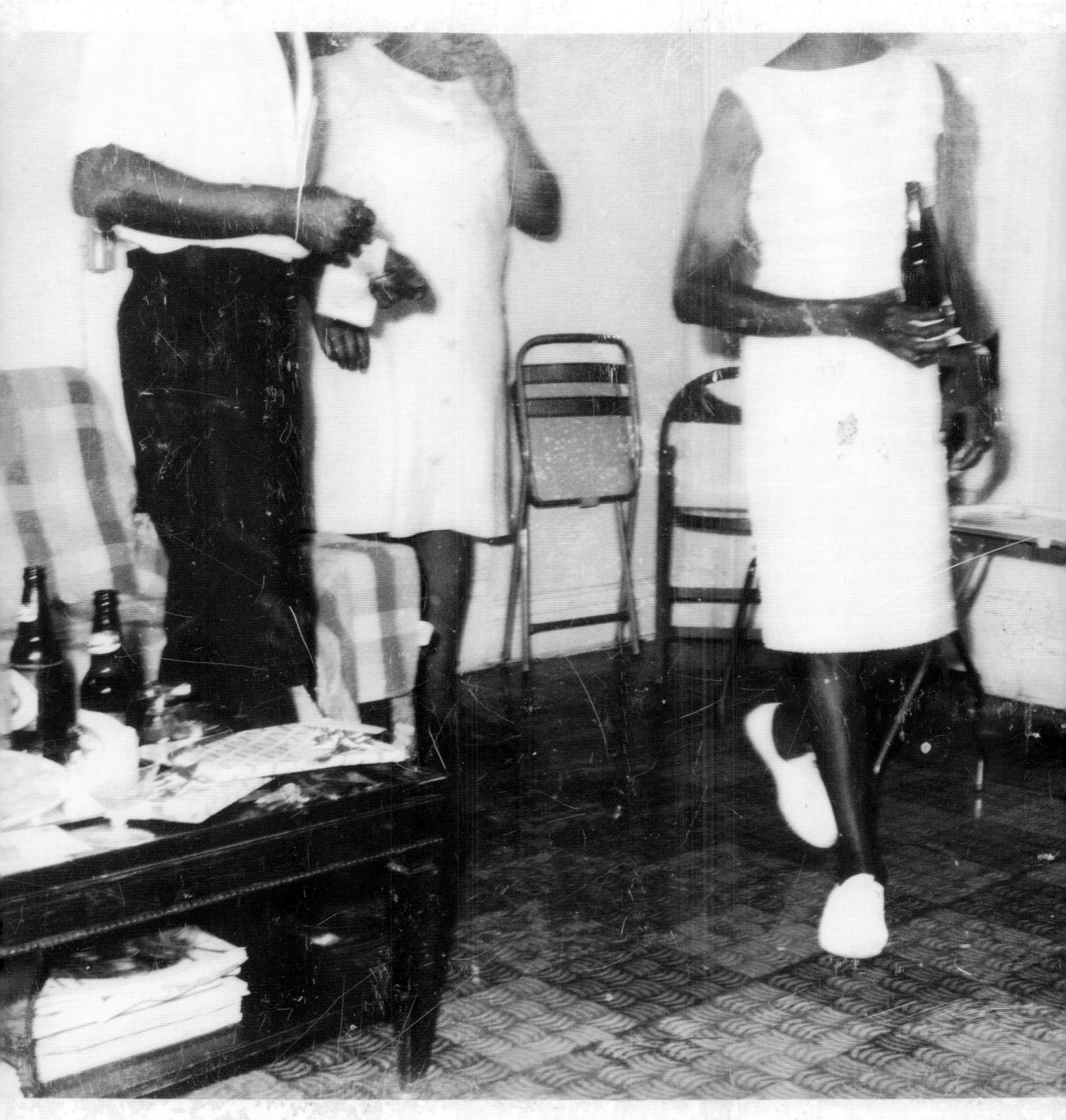

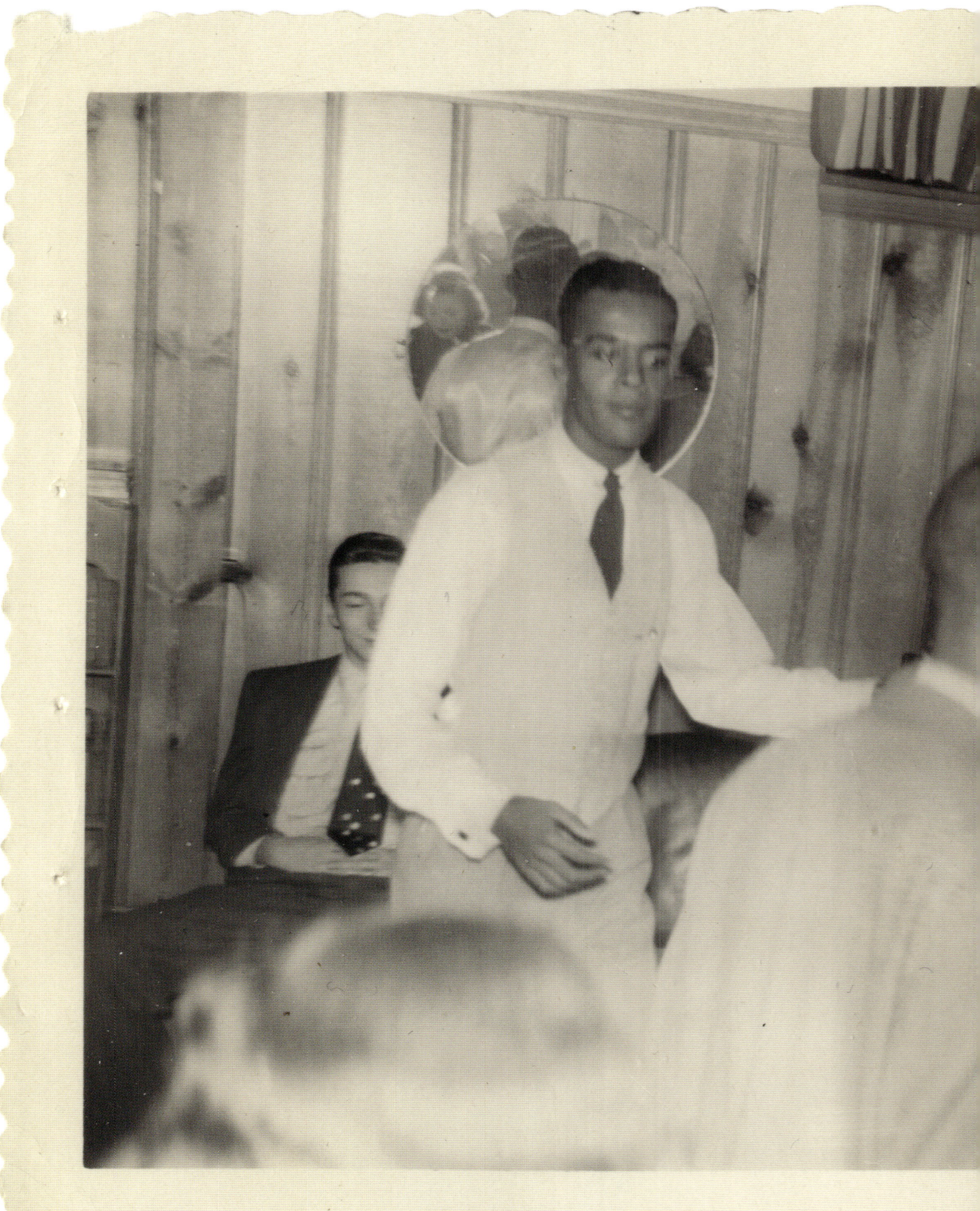

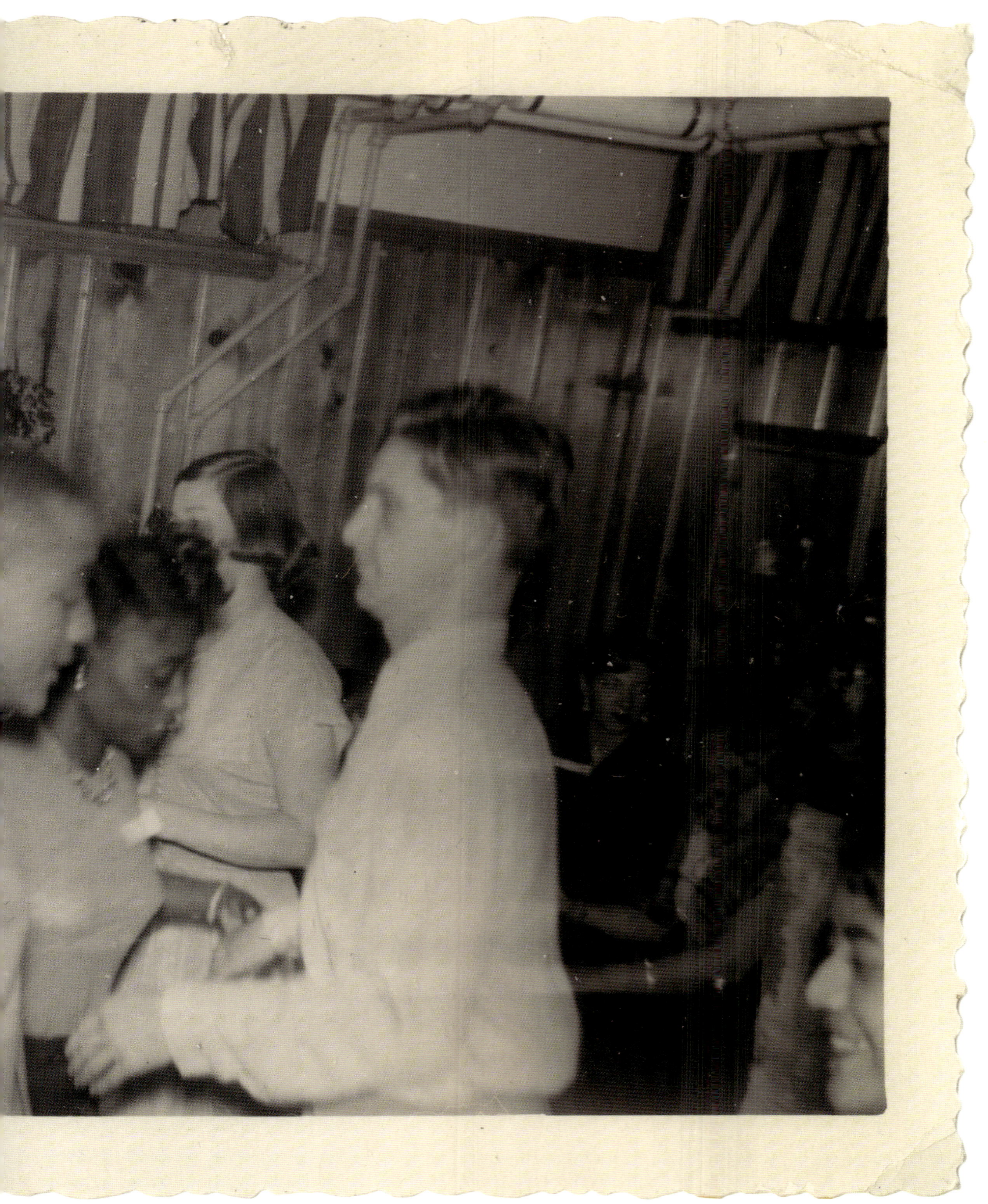

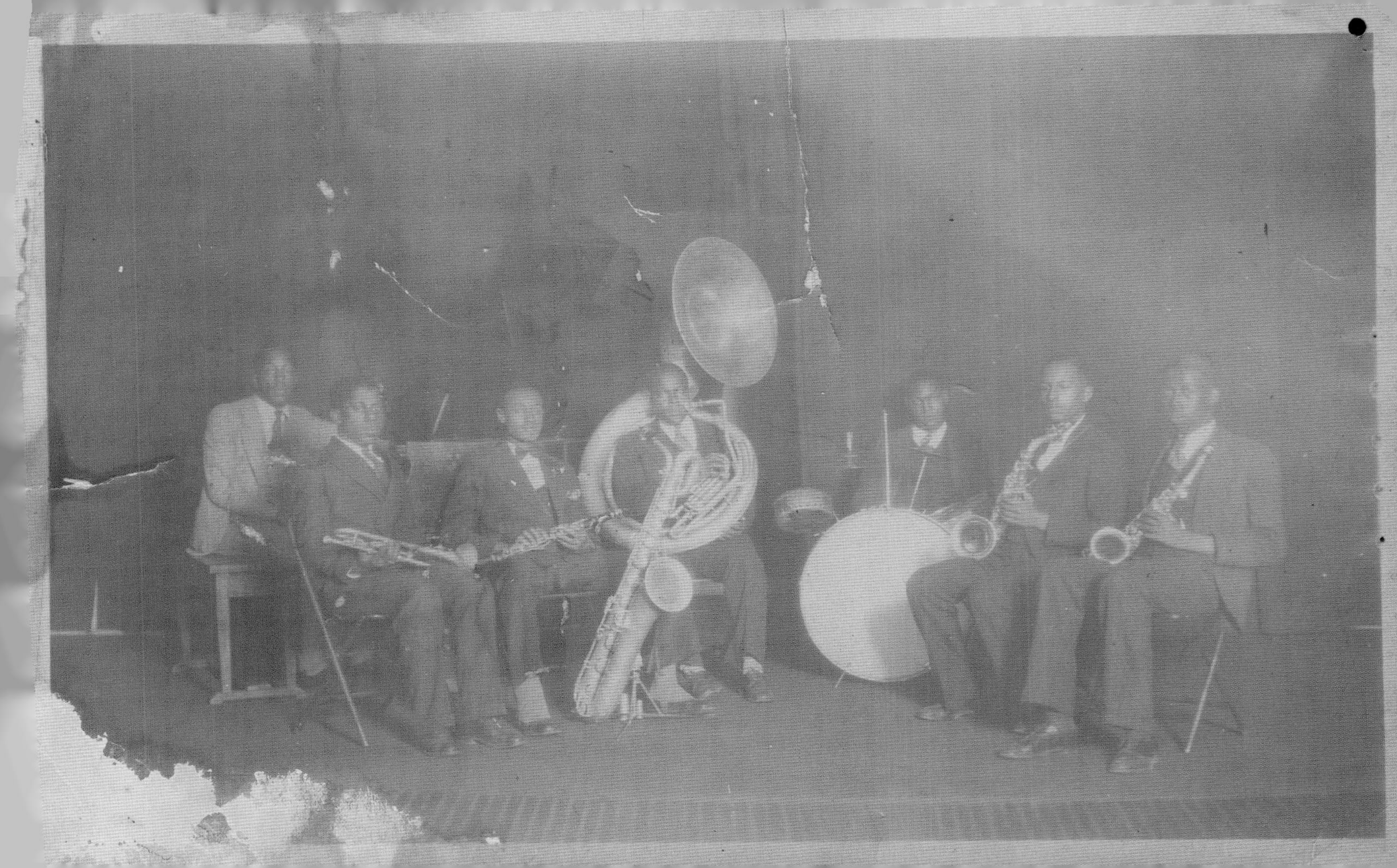

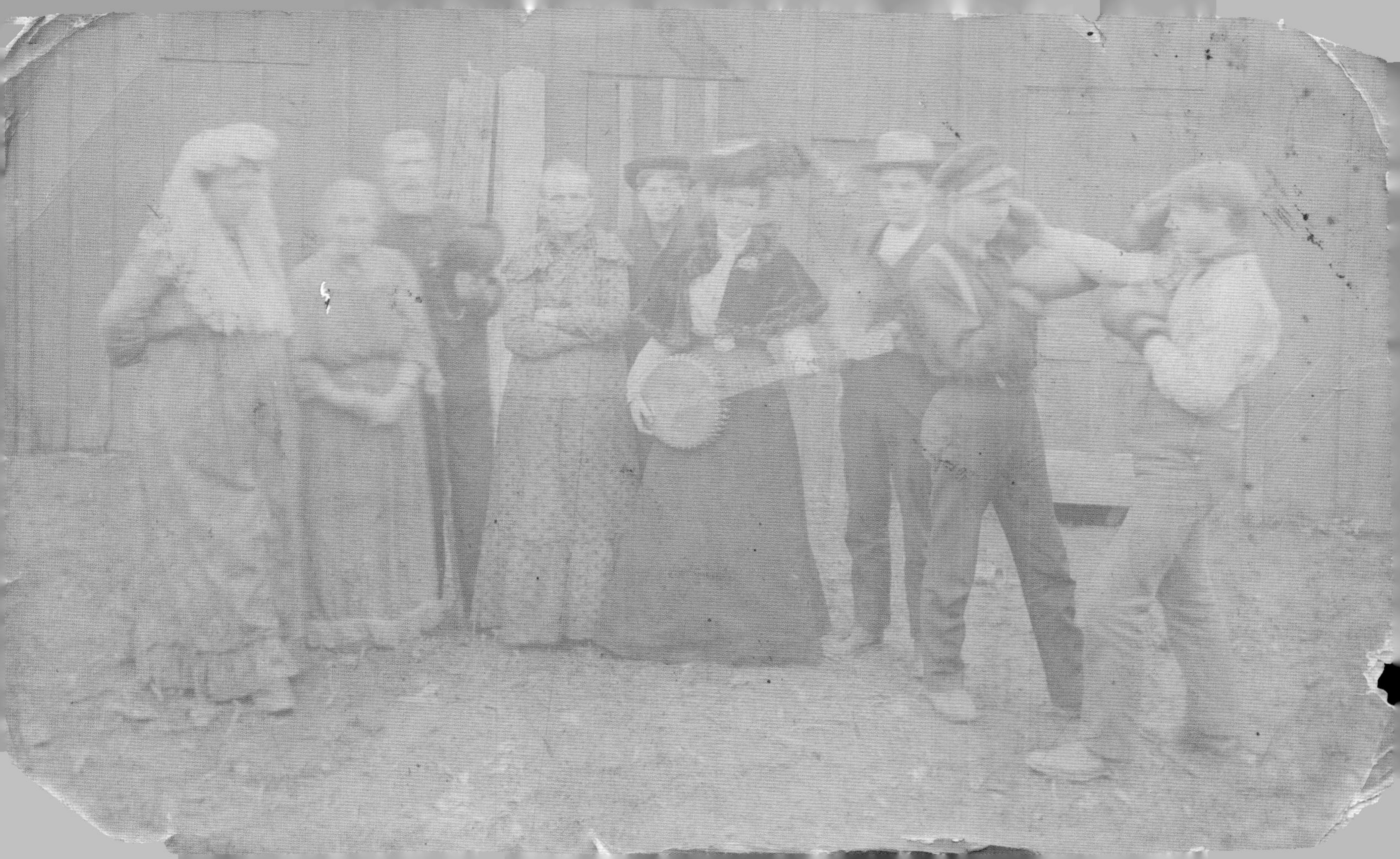

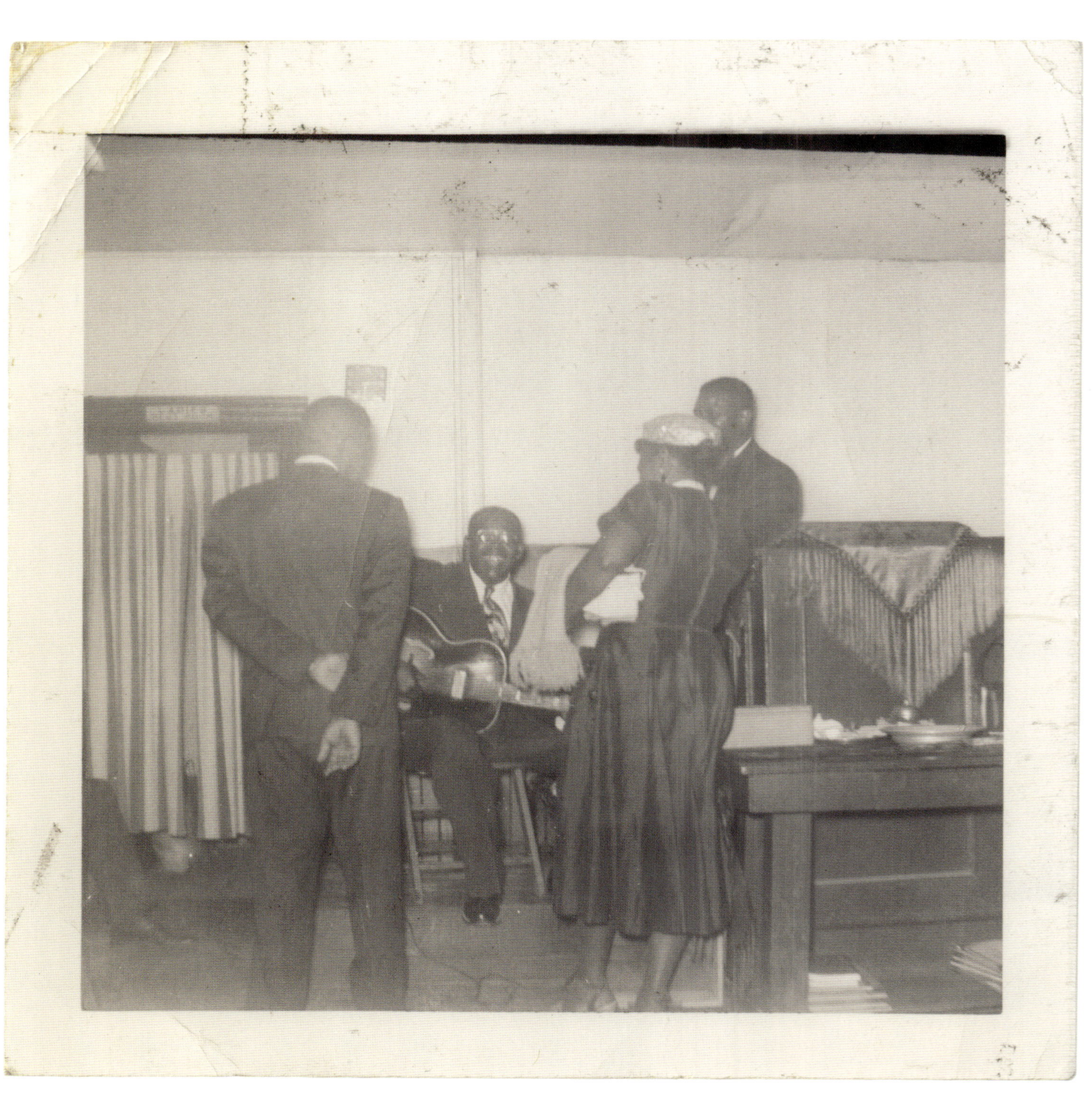

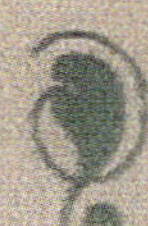

MICHIGAN'S MOST POPULAR PLAYHOUSE

PALACE THEATRE

THE SAFEST THEATRE IN THE WORLD

Monroe and Library Avenues, Detroit, Mich.

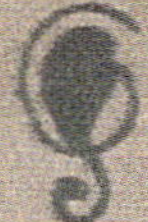

EXECUTIVE STAFF

BERT R. WILLIAMS........................Managing Director
W. M. HEINES................................Stage Manager
C. BAYER and ED. BELLMAN..................Musical Directors

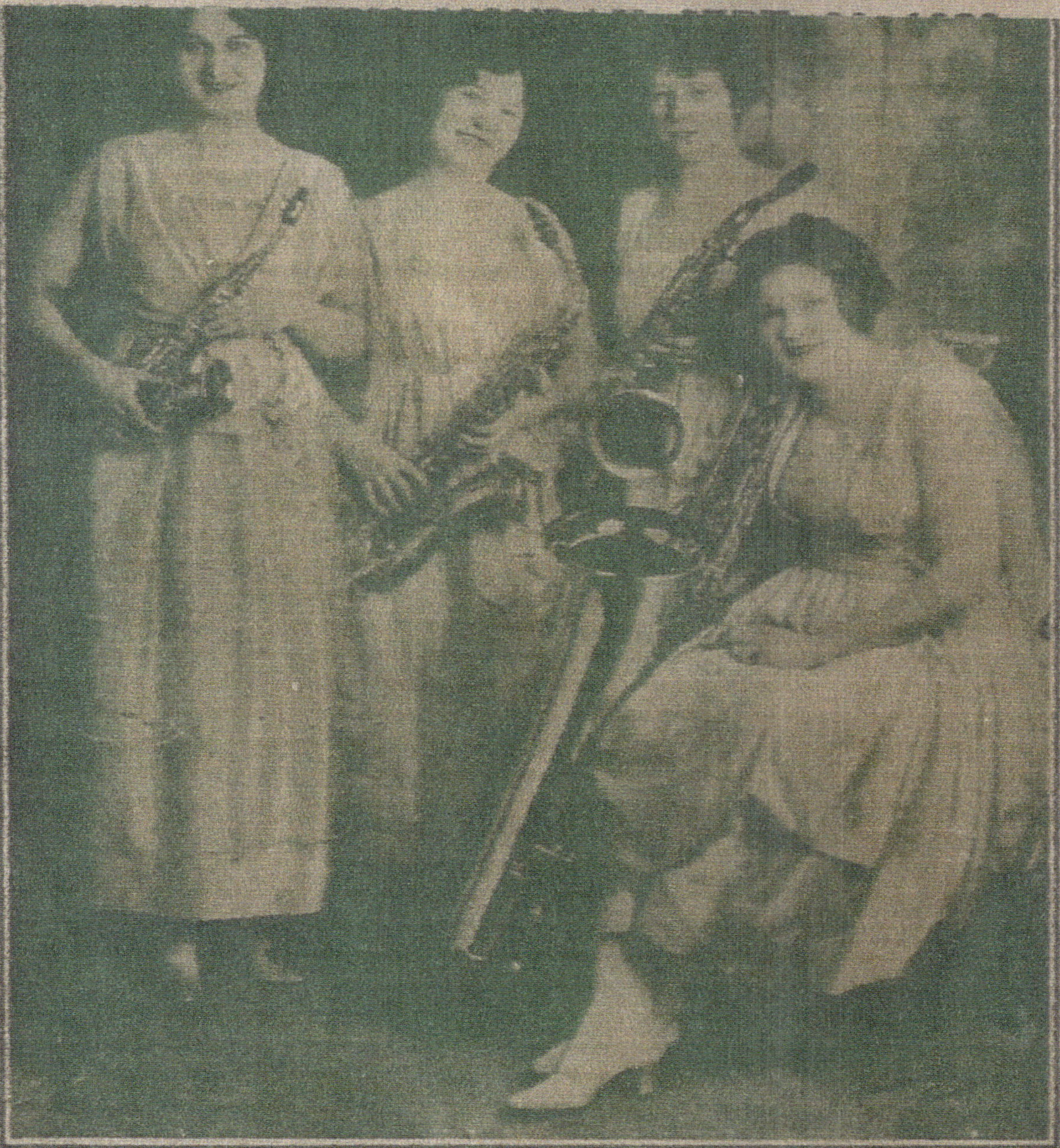

DARLING SAXAPHONE FOUR

THE ACT YOU'LL ENJOY

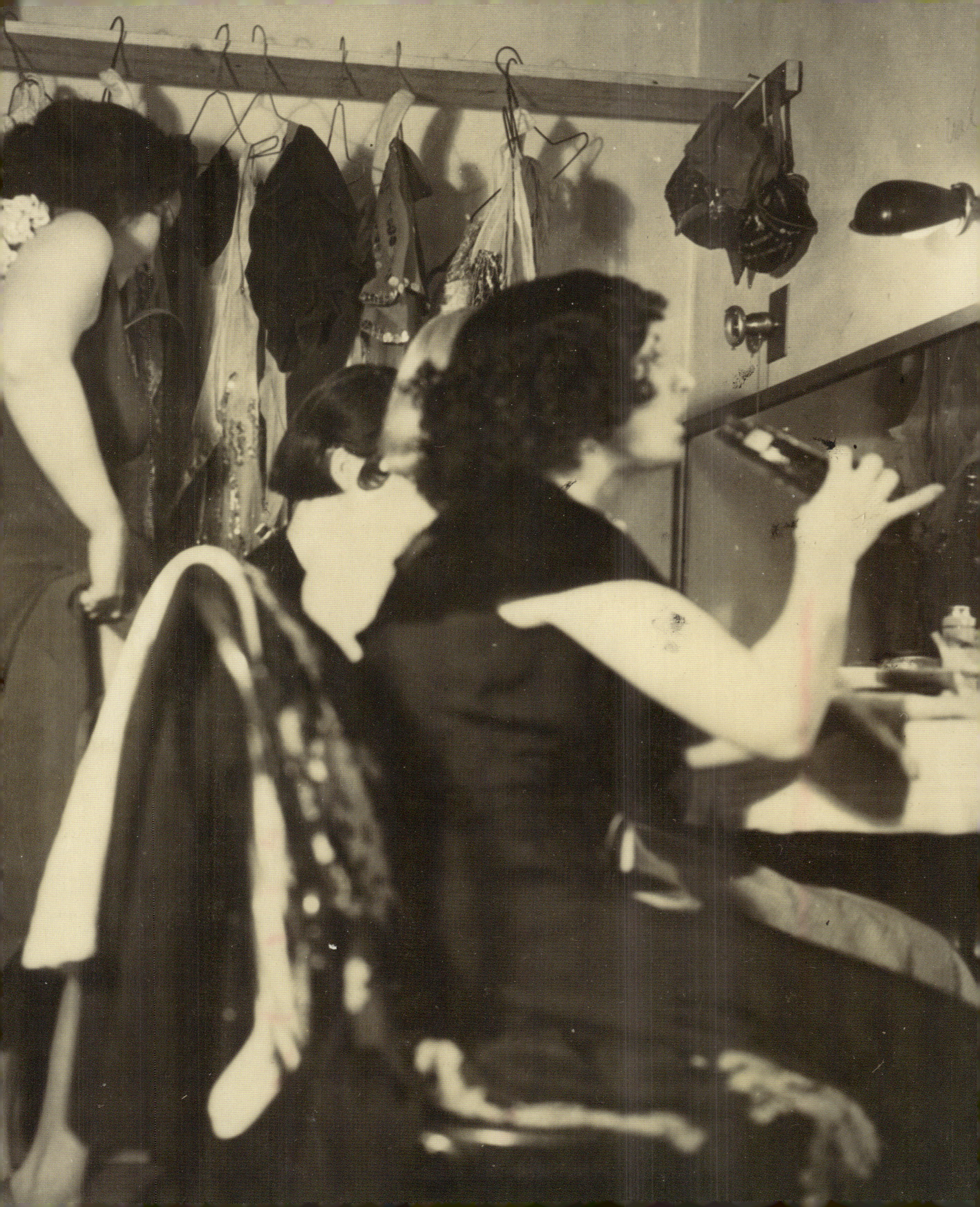

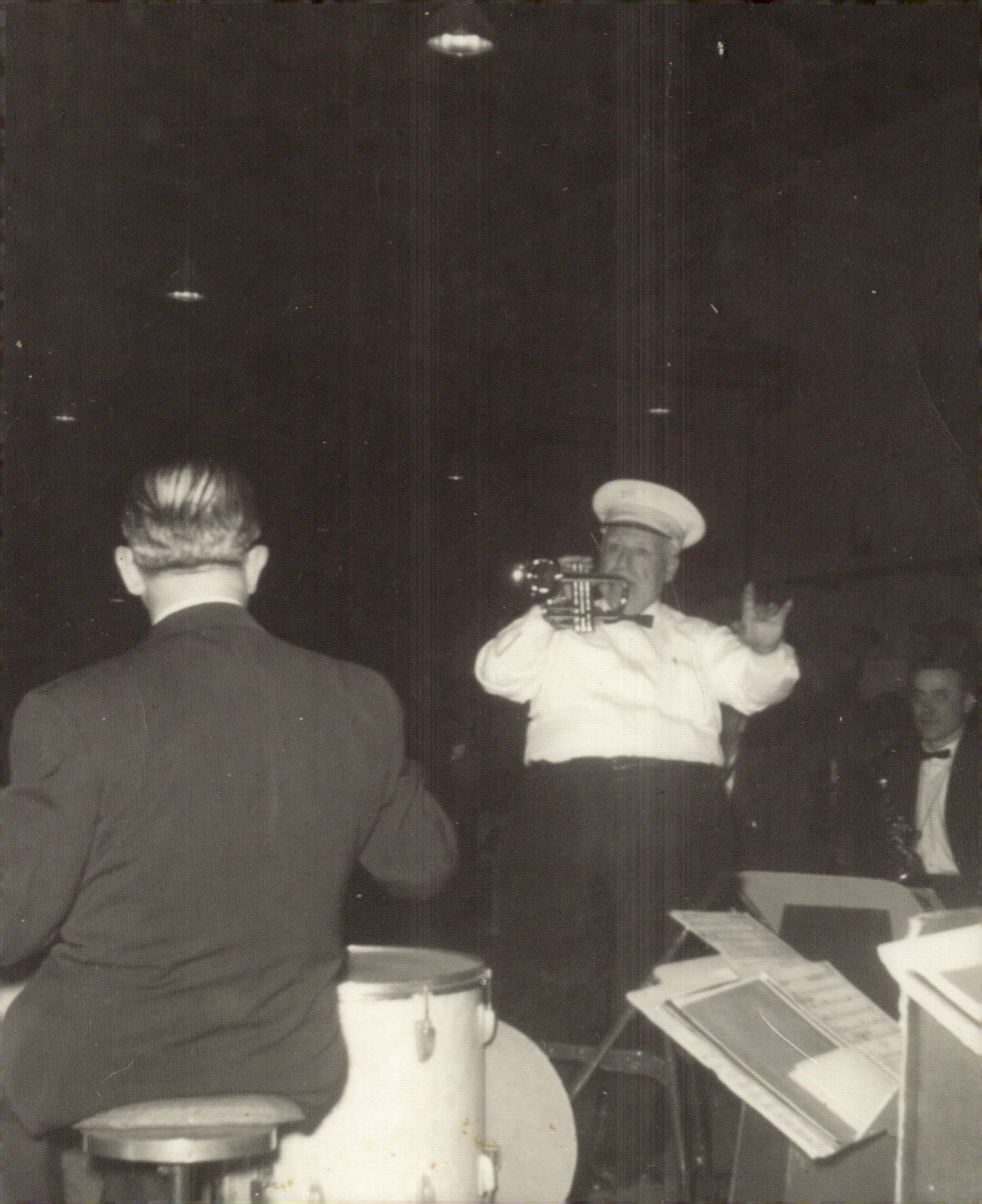

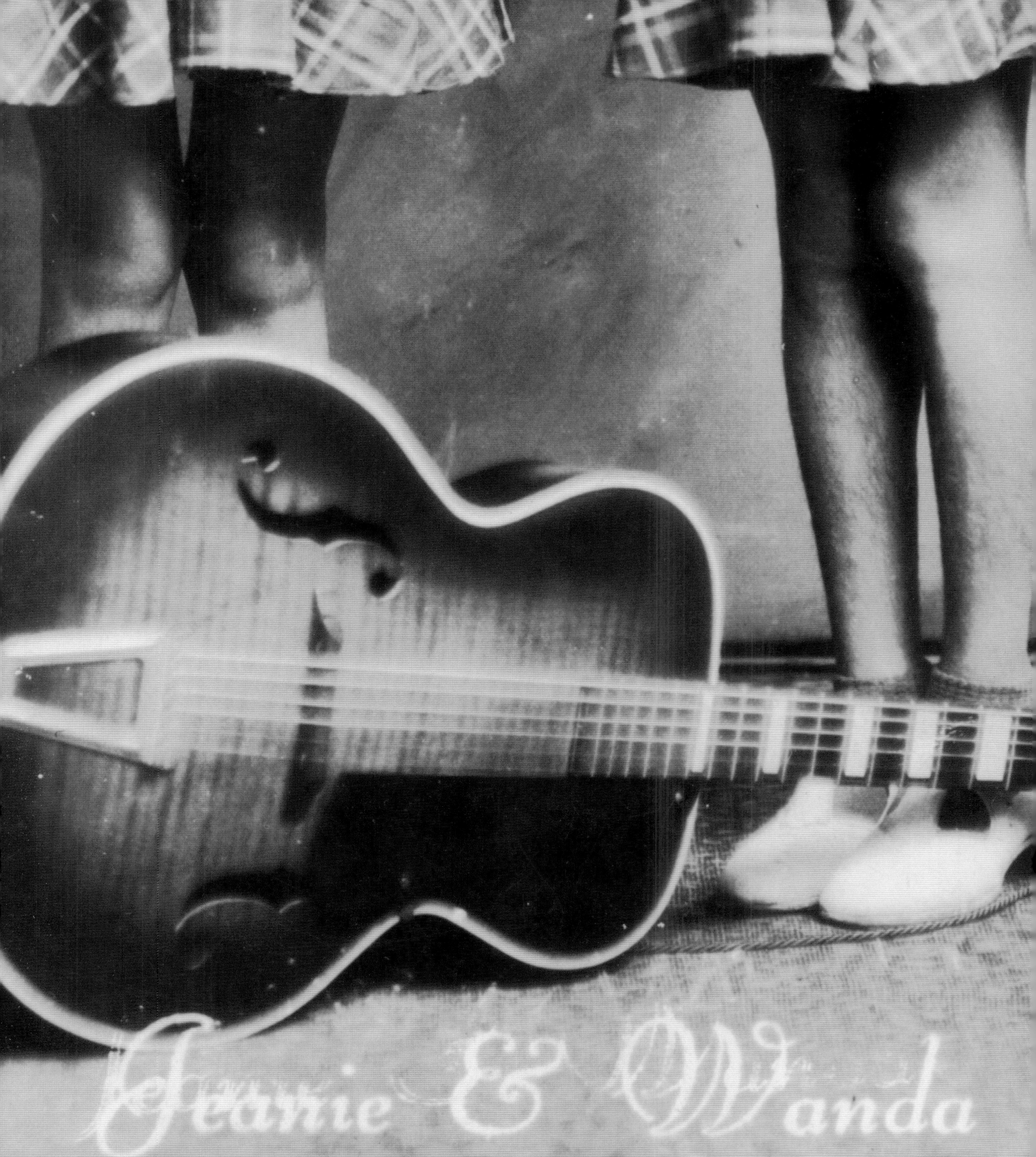
Jeannie & Wanda

Collector and Americana yay-sayer Jim Linderman is an archivist of the obscure.

A conversation with Jim Linderman by Joe Bonomo

At his wide-ranging and lively blogs *Vintage Sleaze* ("The true and untold story of smut in America"), *Old Time Religion* ("Vernacular religious detritus"), and *Dull Tool Dim Bulb* ("Surface, wear, form and authenticity in art, antiques and photography") Linderman acknowledges the little-known as he elevates it. For many years he's doggedly pursued the arcane and the forgotten––from late-19th Century religious iconography to mid-20th Century smut, from vernacular photography to vanished advertising.

His collections tell vast stories in sotto voce, allowing curios and objects shadowed by mainstream culture and ideology to converse and be heard. What we hear is an enormous American sub-culture speaking in forbidden, marginalized languages: stuff discovered boxed in the attic out of embarrassment or zealotry, smutty ash trays crowing next to religious pamphlets, each claiming a part of the complex, sometimes contradictory, always conflicted American imagination, a chaos of memories that will one day vanish. I admire Linderman's work, and the breadth of his interests: from the racy to the pious, the filthy to the redeemed. Sounds like America to me.

In *The Birth of Rock and Roll*, Linderman's arranged a storyboard of sorts that dramatizes the spirit, if not the chronology of rock and roll. Poetically, the photos evoke without naming, and have little to do with conventional iconography of the birth of rock and roll––i.e., young white men in Memphis, poodle skirts, Alan Freed, Bill Haley's Brylcream, etc. Instead they document, and celebrate, the pure but indefinable essence of rocking. Ordinary, nameless men, women, and children, some white, some black, are holding guitars and strumming while looking relaxed or frantic, but nearly always blissful. Some of the action takes place in rural fields, some in dance halls, some at civic events, some in living rooms and basements. Wherever there is an urge to make acoustic or electric music––whether to help at a rent party, busk in front of a crowd, or testify in the name of Jesus––there's an uncredited photographer there to snap an image.

There's little historical documentation. A scrawled caption might name a family in a photograph, a venue for dancing, or the spiritual calling of a subject, but the common thread among these disparate photos is music's ineffable power to inspire and unite the anonymous: as dancing groups, guffawing gangs, shaggy rural orchestras, kids entranced by a strumming grown-up, or urgent, flirtatious pairs on a make-do dance floor. (Of course there's the occasional solo star, the center of amused or nervous attention as he cuts loose.) These photos narrate 20th century's noisy pop history, from impoverished acoustic blues to middle-class square dancing, country fiddling and rural spirituals to urban R&B and twisting. There are cheap organs, and cheaper guitars, patriotic warbling and beery frat rock, denim overalls and sharp suits, long, solemn dresses and hip, fringed minis, the wide gulf between posed promotional photographs and impulsive artless dancing scored by song.

The spontaneous nature of the vast majority of the images in *The Birth of Rock and Roll* adds to the exhilaration in the moments, inspiring some of the most unlikely to get up, testify, shout, have fun. We're often in the wake of music: bottles are open, races are blending, legs are splayed, there's smiling all around. Mostly, I like the surprised looks on so many of the faces. Some can't keep joy off of their faces in the posed moments, clutching a guitar and winking at the photographer or a friend behind him; many others are startled into movement, aided by those in the frame and those outside, all, it seems, eager to get up and move to music that's strummed, broadcast, or simply playing in their heads. In *The Birth of Rock and Roll* Jim Linderman has curated a secret, raucous chronicle of obscure America.

How and why did you begin collecting?

As soon as I could walk, I probably took three rocks from the front yard, put them next to each other and someone said "That looks nice." Three of anything makes a collection. That seems simple, but the process of assembling and categorizing always made sense to me. Before long with stamps and baseball cards. Maybe I was completing a puzzle or filling in blanks. When I could read, I was always at the newsstand the day the comics came in. The drive to collect is to appear "more special" than others, and there is a psychological need just as with any human activity. It is a solitary pursuit when done well, as a good portion of collecting is study and learning. Perfect for a shy person like me. Some collecting is highly competitive, especially when one likes things no one else has. I have always collected the hard things. I find a niche, preferably one no one has thought of (as I have never had any real money) and then sacrifice a bit to obtain things I want. I always had to be first, both with the idea and in line at the flea market.

I have always collected for a particular purpose. For a book project, for a show, to prove a point, to illustrate a truth. I don't collect things willy-nilly . . . and I seldom post anything on the blogs I haven't found and purchased myself. Folks don't quote Mao much these days, but he once wrote something like "To know what an orange is, you must first taste the orange," and the truth and beauty of that has stayed with me since junior high school. Unless I have put in the work and lived with an object, I don't think I am qualified to understand it or write about it.

Among Dull Tool Dim Bulb, Old Time Religion, and Vintage Sleaze you cover a vast, perhaps conflicting, terrain of Americana and ephemera. What, in your conception, fits inside that triangle?

Authenticity and stories not told. That is the common thread running through all three. As mass culture became so prevalent, I saw how important the little things were. It is a losing game, I suppose, but there is far more value in what is done beneath the surface than what is offered to us as product for consumption. Even as a kid I didn't like the records I could buy downtown, I liked the bootlegs I had to drive miles for. To me if 60 million people see the same hit movie, that is just horrendous. It is a massive, destructive waste of precious human time and talent. Frightfully so. Outsiders and eccentrics are far more interesting, and ultimately far more real to me, so I seek out their stories and share them. What is "presented" or packaged for consumption tells virtually none of the truth. Long ago (or ideally) in our system, the cream will rise to the top. That is certainly no longer even remotely the case. I purposely avoid that which I am "supposed" to like. I don't watch TV or read best sellers. I don't need to, as millions have done it for me, and if I need to know anything I missed I can ask. I'm not being smug, I'd just rather find and learn about things not so easily available. I'd rather have salsa from my little sister's garden than spicy corn syrup in crates from Kraft.

I have also always been drawn to things forbidden. I don't know why. I think they are intellectually stimulating.

There is a clear distinction between all three blogs, but that current of authenticity is there in all, as is my own thread an artistic outsider. I've never studied art, but Dull Tool Dim Bulb is an art blog. It is intentionally diverse, but more than anything it is about the artistic inclinations of amateurs and passionate people from the past who have created beauty without being recognized for it. My aesthetics, which drive both my collecting and the material I post, come from the honest, direct and worn surface of folk art, and the blog is about surface, wear, age and form as much as it is about people.

Similarly, I don't believe in God, but Old-Time-Religion is a blog about believers and how they are manipulated by others. It is about the interesting, beautiful and often hopelessly eccentric and hilarious graphics used by preachers and personalities involved in a massive, pervasive fraud . . . but I seldom editorialize. I let the material speak for itself. The origins of the religious right are shown there every day, and I delight in digging up that which has been passed over or swept under by current practitioners. The more crooked and silly, the better. It is amazing, just amazing to me that in this day and age there are still people getting away with being "faith healers" and when I find one lining his pockets, I might point it out . . . but for the most part it is about the striking graphics and pictures. And again . . . as no one wants the things (most of them were given away after all) I don't have any competition. I usually find a pile of tracts at the end of the shelf in used bookstores and that keeps me busy for a while. Sometimes I'll spring for a particularly beautiful photograph and add that.

Vintage Sleaze might appear to be about sex, smut and boob jokes, but it is in fact about hypocrisy and untold stories. It is also just funny as hell. My entire life there have been attempts to censor smut, usually by folks with equally offensive morals as the smut producers, but everyone bought it. I don't care how upstanding someone appears to be on the surface, when they pass away you'll find a dirty book in a box in the basement. This hypocrisy meant no one ever wrote about the producers, the writers, the artists or the models who created the material, and what a group of eccentric, talented, unusual folks they were. Because you weren't supposed to acknowledge it, no one has told the stories, and I have found it an incredible rich, fertile area for study and writing. The women's movement made much of the material passé and taboo, and rightly so, but at one time it was so pervasive that to pretend it didn't exist is not only wrong, we are missing so much history and entertainment. Personally, I believe Bettie Page and proto-pornographer Lenny Burtman have had more influence on popular culture than virtually anyone you can name. I like to think of the blog as a James Ellroy novel but with every word true.

Can you talk a bit about the distinction between collecting and hoarding? Does the line ever blur?

Everything I have fits on the shelves behind me. I used to collect large things. Folk art objects, paintings, handmade furniture . . . and I have been through a dozen art forms which did take up space. But today, as I collect to tell stories and put together books, little paper ephemera and photographs fit the bill . . . and they don't take up any space. I also use collections as tools. I'm not a pristine Mylar bag kind of guy. I'd rather see the wear and the surface. It lends that all important authenticity. When I was working as a librarian, most of my colleagues seemed more concerned that the material be on the shelf in the right place, but I'd rather have it circulating and being used, even if a kid stole it.

When I'm done with a category, an object or a collection, I feel I have mastered it and pass it along. Increasingly as donations to museums, but back when I was living on a librarian's salary, I traded or sold things I had put together to afford to collect in another area which interested me. To me, stuff is a tool, and when I'm done with it someone else gets it. Plus there is always something else to study. I might add that I have learned

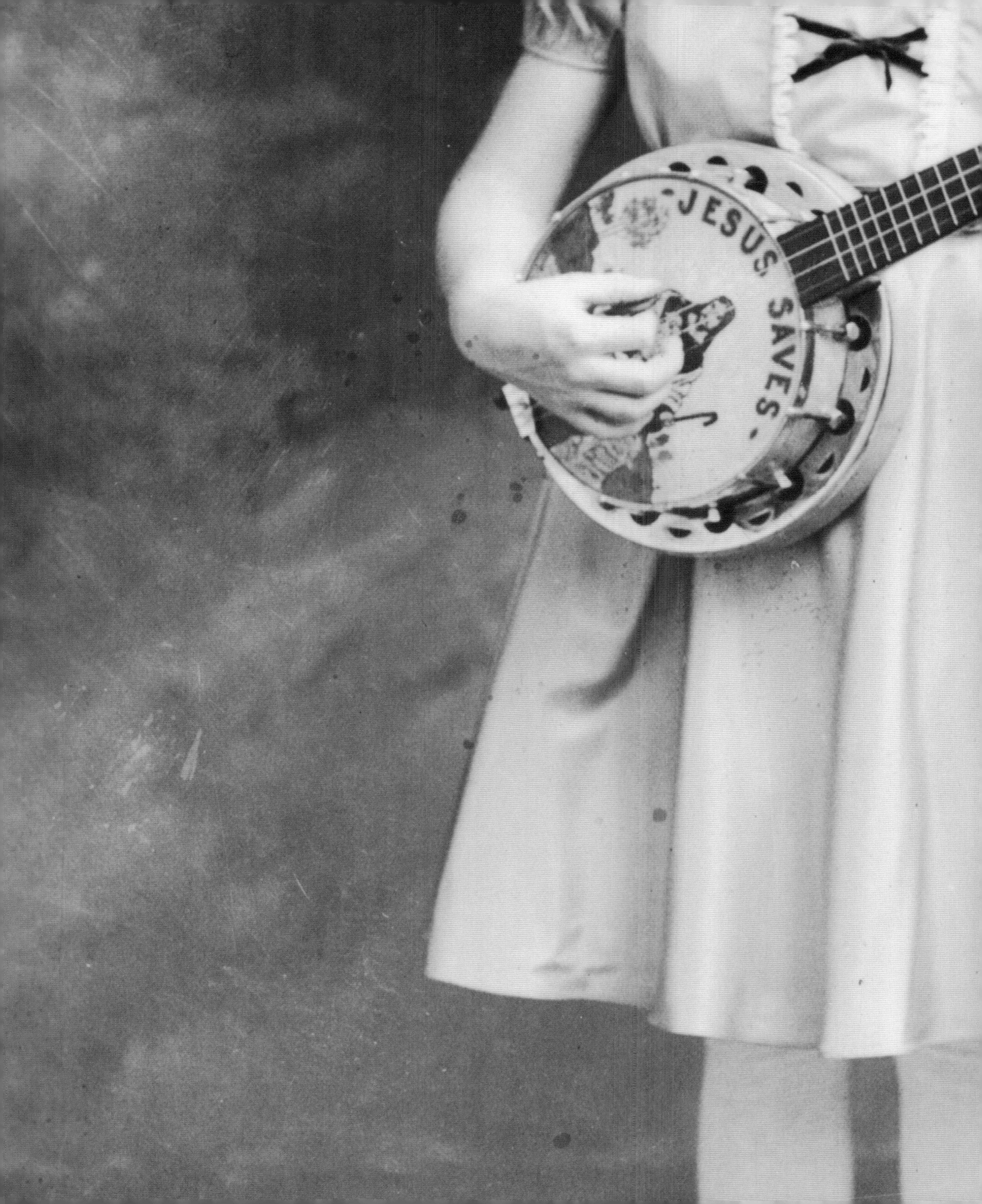
JESUS SAVES

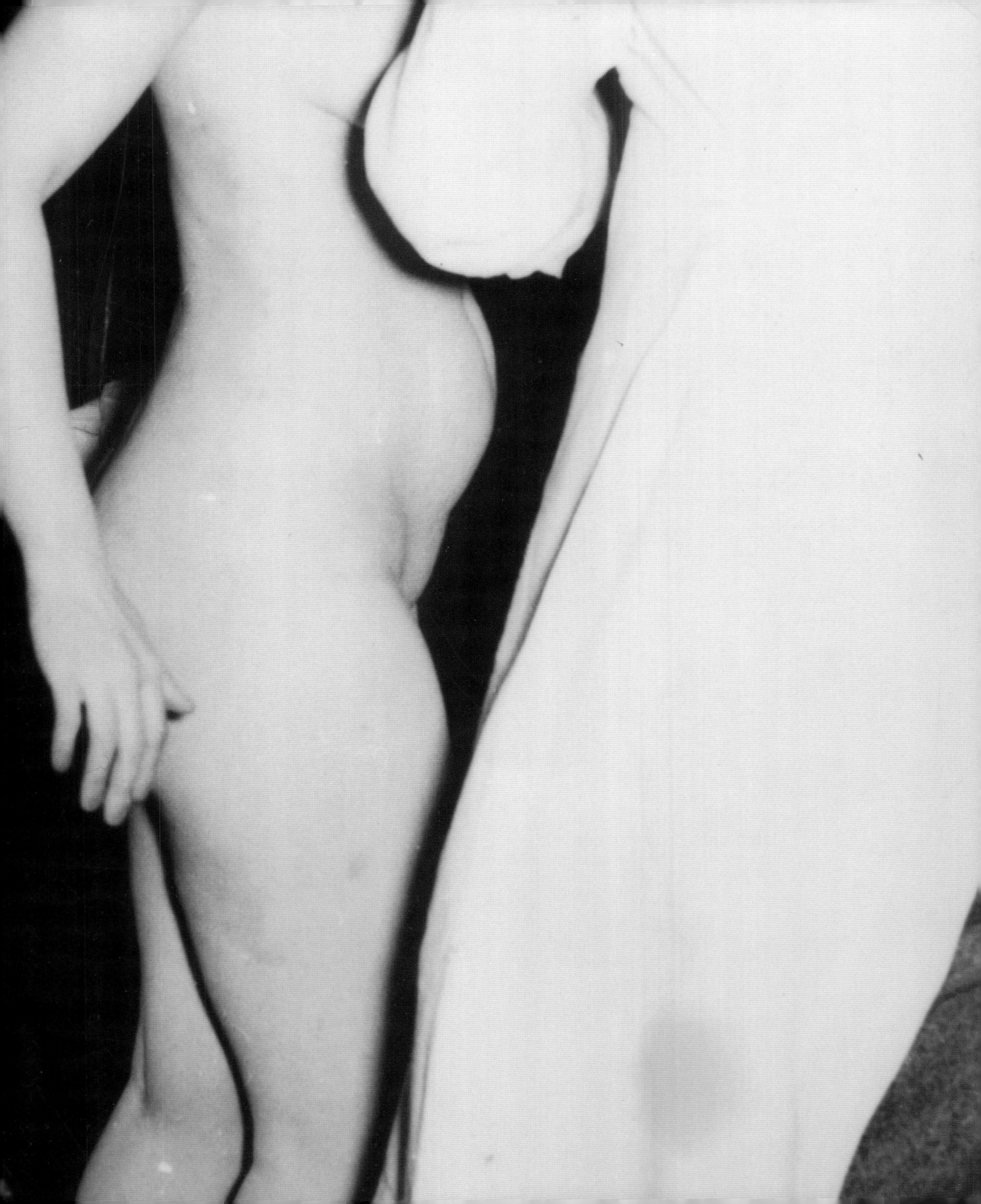

one or two splendid objects against a white wall look better than 50 objects in a pile . . . so I edit a little as I go along.

How do you define "vernacular photography"?

More than anything, to me it means amateur. I suppose it actually means "photography of the people" or "photography of the common man" or something like that. I'm not too interested in "mistakes" or "shadows" or the commonly collected categories. Photographs which mistakenly turned out approximating beautiful art are interesting, but I just like pictures taken by those who happened upon it themselves. I usually collect photographs of things . . . like my collection of folk art objects being made or where they are placed . . . and many of them just happen to have been taken by amateurs. I also love press photographs which have been virtually obliterated by cropping and "touch-ups" before publication, as they help illustrate how we have been manipulated by photographs all along.

Can you talk a bit about the distinctions between smut and pornography? Is it a question simply of relative explicitness, or is there something less quantifiable involved? Does smut still exist in the 21st Century? If so, where?

My blog only deals with smut up to around 1965, when through court rulings and such virtually anything went. The characters I profile worked at a time when they could be arrested at the whim of a local politician or authority, and living on that edge made them interesting characters. With the 1970s, porn became a much larger business with larger profits and also unfortunately became less interesting.

Pornography used to be something kids shouldn't see and still is, but because of the Internet I think it has become something kids have virtually no interest in seeing! When is the last time you saw a cartoon showing a kid trying to peek into a nudist colony? It's over. We are saturated. Hopefully we are finally on the verge of defining the real obscenities, which are poverty, hunger, war, racism, greed, violence and sexual abuse. Those are pornographic to me. Unfortunately, at the same time we seem to be living in a productive era for ignorant zealots who latch onto the most convenient religious beliefs and try to force them on others, both here and abroad . . . so maybe my optimism is misplaced. I know some kind of clash is coming. Due to backward notions and religious beliefs, a large percent of the world's population doesn't have the lax attitude towards undraped women as the Western world, though the wealthy of all cultures still reserve it for themselves. Bin Laden was watching porn in his adobe, after all. But if I happened to come from a culture where women were forced to wear veils, I'd be pretty angry at the West, I guess. Thankfully, I was raised in a country where one could find anything and women are becoming equal.

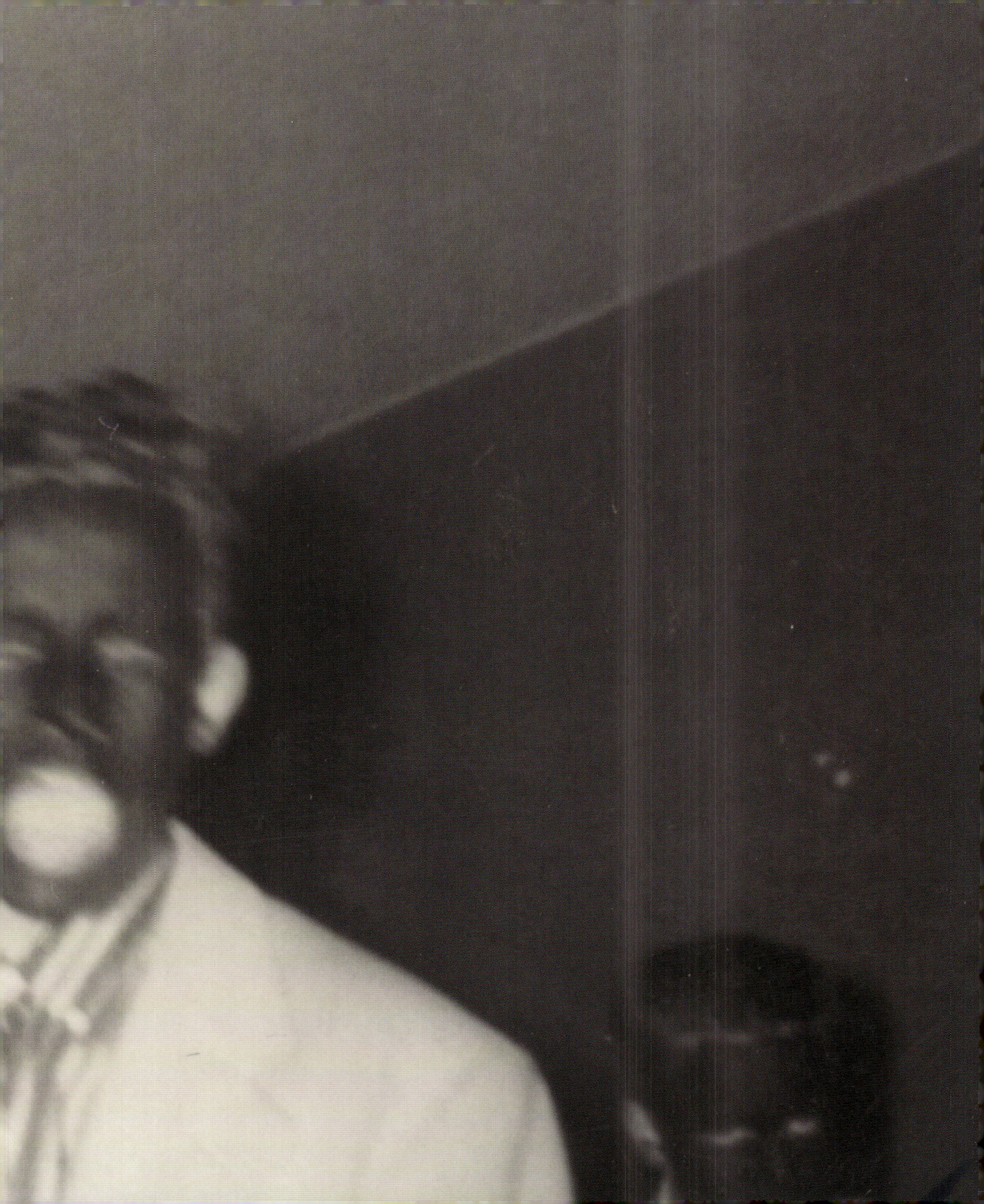

It is relative explicitness, as there are still arbitrary rules applied by censors of various forces. I never voted for them, but they still try to tell me what I can read. Today the pasties which cover nipples are blurs on the TV screen. Just like the "founding fathers of smut" I delight in getting as close as I can on the blog without crossing that arbitrary line, and just like the girly magazines of the 1950s, women have no nipples on my blog! But it appears filthy and that is the point. In the vintage sleaze paperbacks of the 1950s, folks slowly took their clothes off, over and over, but nothing ever happened. The cover of the cereal box tastes better than the kibble inside. Additionally, "pornography" today is no more real than any other mass media product. Frosted hair, breast implants, airbrushing, skin-bronzing . . . ugh. That is pornographic to me . . . the false presentation, the lies, the artificial "allure" which just looks pathetic. I'm not old fashioned in the least, but I can see phony, and phony is what we get today.

I should point out women far outnumber men as regular followers of the site. The guys pop in by mistake looking for the real thing, but I think women appreciate the irony, the history and the kitsch more. I hope everyone reads the text, as the images mean little without it . . . but we have become more visual and less word savvy.

What's the cultural value of collecting and exhibiting smut?

Americans can only handle one or two cultural figures at a time. For example, (as Harry Smith, John Fahey, Joe Bussard and others have shown) there were thousands upon thousands of folk and blues musicians, but we only know Bob Dylan, Peter Paul and Mary and B.B. King. Today Dita Von Teese represents the entire concept of the pin-up, but as I try to show there have been thousands of hard-working models doing the same thing and in very harsh conditions indeed for decades. R. Crumb draws dirty and funny cartoons . . . well, so did a thousand other cartoonists, illustrators and artists. The richness and depth of our culture comes not from celebrities, no matter how much the increasingly concentrated and interlocking media wish us to believe. By the way, I use the examples above because I love them very much, except for Peter Paul and Mary, who sucked. But then they loaned their microphones to Garth Hudson who recorded the *Basement Tapes* for Dylan . . . so I'll cut them some slack.

I am most interested in smut because this was fugitive literature. The libraries didn't collect it, the material wasn't indexed, there are no bibliographies and often not even a copyright. That makes documenting it challenging. It as such a large part of our collective nature, but in a secret way. It should be known about. The sex drive is as basic as eating and drinking, and yet we have this huge vacuum in our understanding of how it has been treated in popular culture.

Who's working in your field who you admire, or have admired, and why?

I have dozens of heroes from history and popular culture. Those who influenced me most directly in what I am doing today are friends I was fortunate enough to make some 25 years ago, Herbert Hemphill Jr. and Sterling Strauser. Hemphill was a folk art collector who helped found the American Museum of Folk Art, and Strauser was a painter who happened to collect self-taught artists. They both impacted me in ways I can hardly describe, and spending time with each in their homes were among the most meaningful times of my life. We swapped stories, discoveries and both taught me to be fearless and collect the hell out of what I found interesting, no matter what the prevailing experts were shilling. As for writers and bloggers, John Foster at *Accidental Mysteries*, Joey Lin at *Anonymous Works*, Carolina Miranda at *C-Mon* and Jim Marshall at *The Hound* are essential. Every day essential. The Bob Dylan site *Expecting Rain* is the best music site around.

Could you talk a bit about how you came in possession of *The Birth of Rock and Roll* photos? How old is your collection? Did you have guiding principle in selecting images for the book?

I am always collecting with a project in mind, and usually few projects at a time. I love vintage anonymous photographs of musicians. Originally, I had in mind an "old timey" musician book, purely rural and full of banjos, but the project broadened as it developed. I wanted to give a fuller impression as complex and alive as the story, and also to include participants and the audience. The beauty of anonymous, vernacular photographs is that they leave so much to the viewer's imagination, and yet for the most part, the collections which have been formed have not concentrated on one narrative or subject. There are specialized anonymous snapshot collections, many of them at this point . . . but for the most part the collections seem all over the place. I like to collect in a narrow area, and let the objects themselves create an expansive landscape. And make no mistake, these photographs are objects. They have shape, surface and form. Digital photography will never have that. These photographs scratch just like records, and records lasted around 100 years too.

To answer the question, all were purchased at paper and ephemera shows, antique shows, flea markets and eBay. It isn't surprising how many photographs contain musical instruments. To become adept, instruments becomes an extension to a musicians arm, in particular for guitar players. Photographs of people enjoying music are also common. I could have done an entire book of families staring at the phonograph.

Is found or vernacular photography a kindred spirit to rock and roll?

The true history of our culture is told in anonymous photographs, and whether they are kindred to rock and roll is both a good question and a good observation. I was determined to tell the story with no promotional

photos if possible. I think I included only one. Just as I would rather listen to a bootleg or a live performance, I would rather see a candid shot or an authentic image created without artifice. What is presented to us as product is today so manipulated and controlled, virtually all the reality has been airbrushed away. This applies to music, photographs . . . across the board. The real story is always found beneath the surface. It seems fewer and fewer take the time to look for the real story these days. Product need only be surface deep to sell. Amateur photographers may not have been rebels, as so many of the early musicians were, but they were documenting a life and time without pretense or an agenda.

What I especially like about the book is the way you evoke a story without naming it, the juxtaposition of strangers and eras scenes in a long, complex narrative. In the introduction you write that the book tells "a one hundred year old story." What is that story?

I came to the realization one day that Hank Williams had died the year I was born, and Elvis made his first recordings the following year. I realized I had lived through virtually the entire history of rock and roll, and how fortunate I had been to have experienced it in real time. I've seen dozens of the performers in the Rock and Roll Hall of Fame, and many of them in small, intimate venues, yet today it all seems so effortless. I began to wonder how such a diverse and rich musical form had coalesced into rock and roll at the very time I was here . . . it seemed too fortunate. I had even seen Muddy Waters perform. And yet all the books I had read about rock and roll still hadn't said how short a time the entire span of the genre was. They failed me somehow, and I thought the story could be told without words just as well.

As this is a photography book, the images really tell the story. I can only hope they provide a suitable impression in the mind of viewers, as the actual story is far too complex to explain. I wanted to create an atmosphere more than a book of non-fiction, and I think the results work well enough. History is impossible to capture. Any history is tainted with error and false memories, certain agendas and misinterpretation. The best I can do is evoke an emotional response, and I choose to do it by assembling and grouping images here.

Also in the introduction you reference racism as among the forces that created rock and roll. There are unfortunate images of blackface and minstrelsy in the book. Can you comment on them?

At the time the Caucasian rockabilly performer Warren Smith was playing "Ubangi Stomp" so what can I say? The history of rock music is filled with unsavory and inappropriate things. Hollywood, the cartoons and the dominant society as a whole were just as offensive. There have been plenty of scholars discussing the birth of rock and roll and the forces which led to it, but basically what it took was European music meeting African music here in America. There were all manner of configurations, connections and influences, and you can't deny minstrelsy was one of them. If it sold tickets, it was on a stage, be it vaudeville, the carnival or

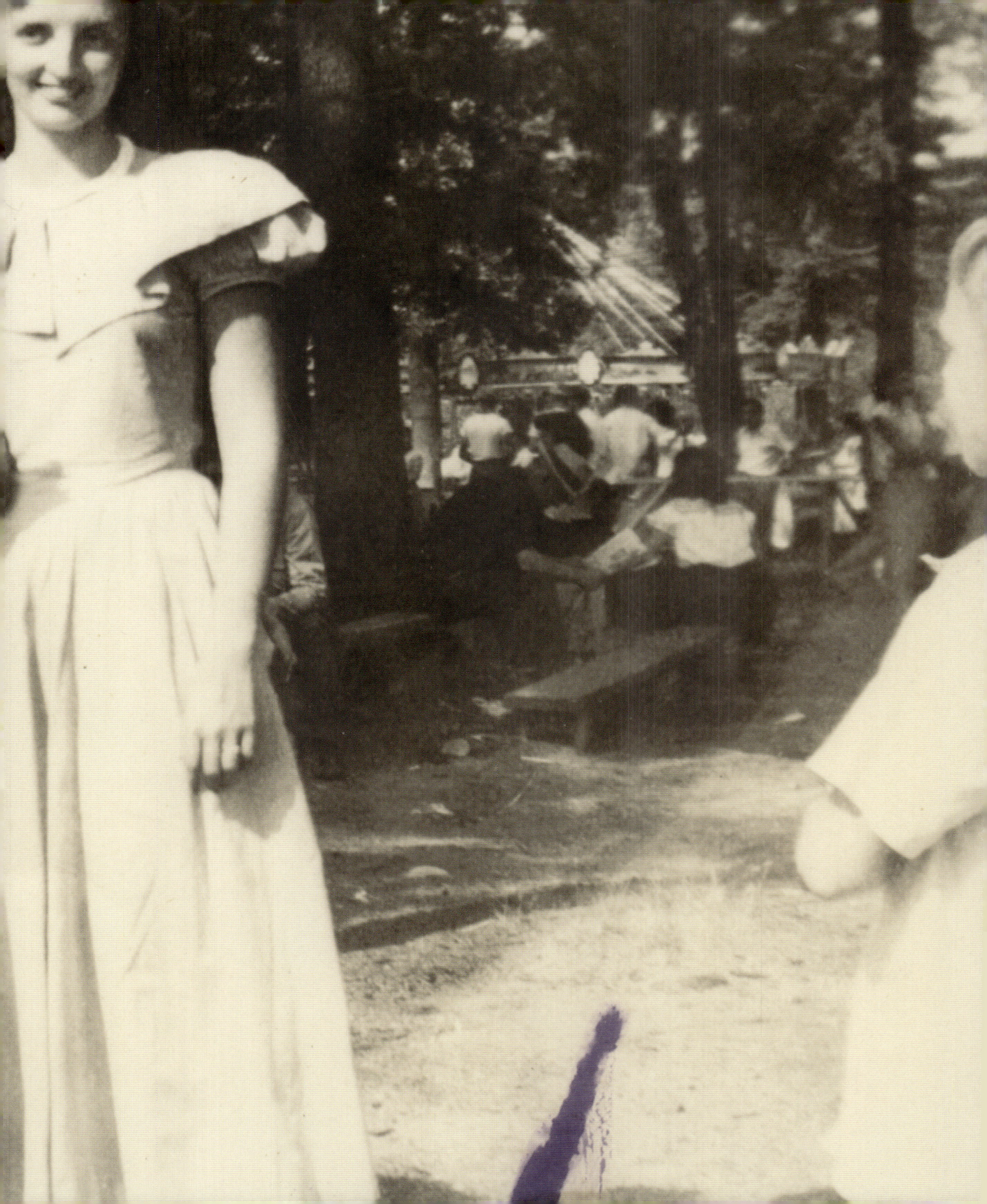

the burlesque show. All were instrumental in the forces which combined to create rock and roll, and why sugarcoat it?

Blackface is offensive, but just as offensive to some are the white covers of African-American music which happened in the 1950s and 1960s. White musicians wore "virtual" masks and repurposed the originals . . . but last I heard Little Richard was thrilled to be covered by the Beatles. One could say Pat Boone was a minstrel without a mask, but why bother. It was the relative lack of racism among musicians which contributed more than anything to what we call rock and roll. If more of us were as colorblind as musicians, it would be far better place. As I point out, once white musicians realized they could learn from black musicians and vice-versa, we got rock and roll, we got jazz and we got harmony, literally. Like it or not, minstrelsy was a part of that. No less than Nick Tosches has documented the importance of minstrelsy in his work devoted to Emmet Miller. A considerable force behind rock and roll is Caucasians trying to emulate black musicians. With a mask or not, it was appropriated. I try to be as much journalist as collector, and the photographs exist. I don't judge them anymore than I judge any photograph. The ravages of slavery contributed to blues, to gospel, to jazz, to hokum, you name it. To me, rock and roll is all about showmanship, strutting and cake walkin' babies from home. I certainly do not embrace blackface, but masks come in all colors. Bob Wills played minstrel songs. Hank Williams did as well.

The image you are likely referring to is a black and white photograph, so for all I know the witless imbeciles were wearing green masks and trying to be Martians. But few images carry that much emotion and baggage in a little 3 x 4 snapshot. This is a photography and art book, and few photographs are as thought-provoking. It is a WTF photo. Denying history is not a positive thing, and neither is censorship or revisionist interpretations of what went down. To some, the photographs here of inter-racial dancing and kissing will probably be just as offensive, but they are photographs which were taken. Same with obviously intoxicated dancers and a fellow doing the alligator. Artifacts now . . . and yet still they carry a power as strong as the music.

Do you have a favorite image in the book, one that narrates the birth of rock and roll in a particularly powerful or graphic way?

Certainly the 1949 snapshot of the Carter Family is among them. They are the only known performers in the book. It not only evokes a different time and place, but as a composition it is lovely. Even at a pie-eating contest in a county fair, they were regal. Country musicians have always been more willing than most to "meet and greet" but the picture reveals how much music evolved from "us" rather then "them." It came from the bottom up. I also favor the porch band at Olin's. It reveals the American dream, a family opening their ice cream shop, and they hired an African-American ensemble to perform for the celebration. It is hard not to appreciate that photograph as both historical and prescient.

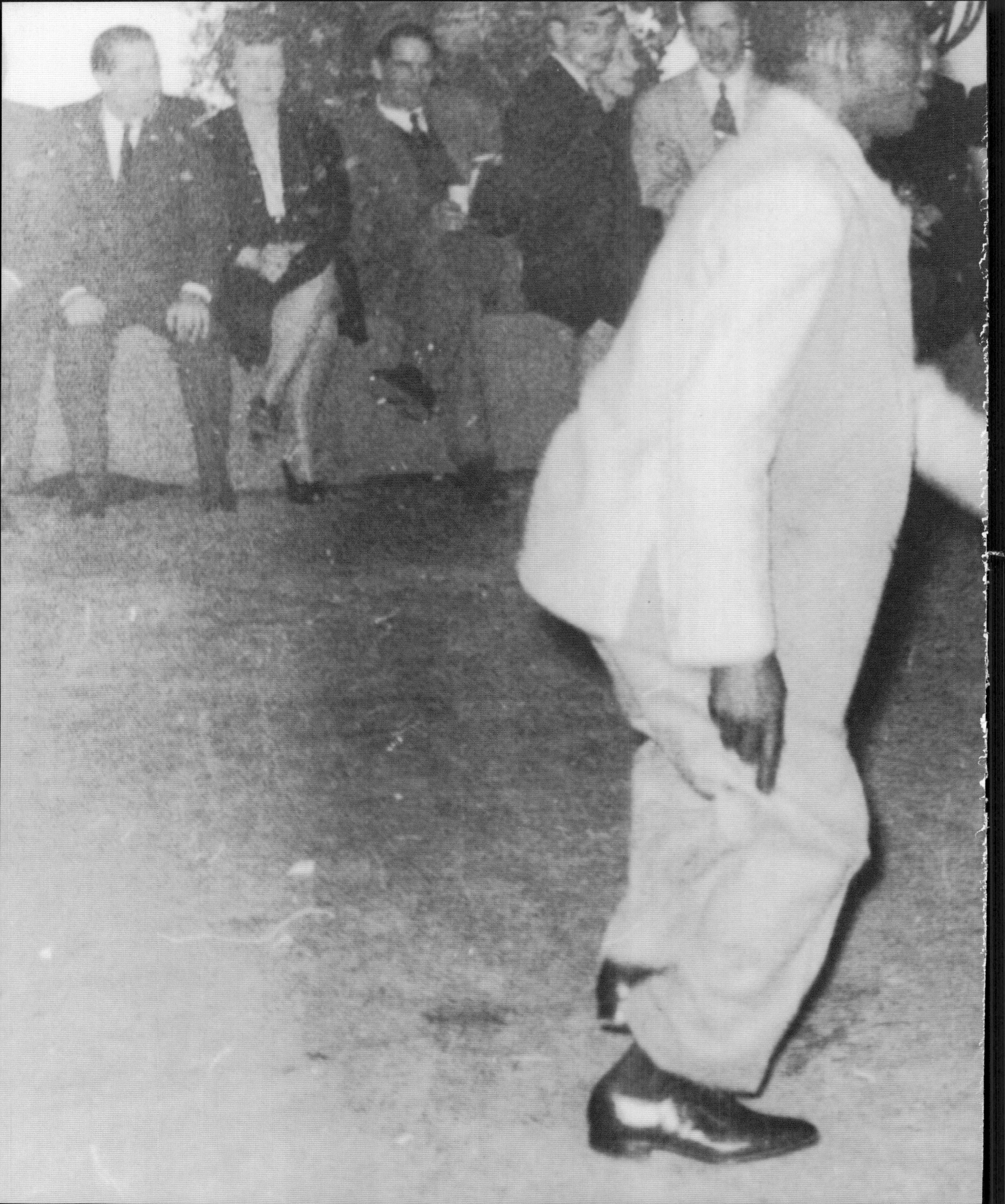

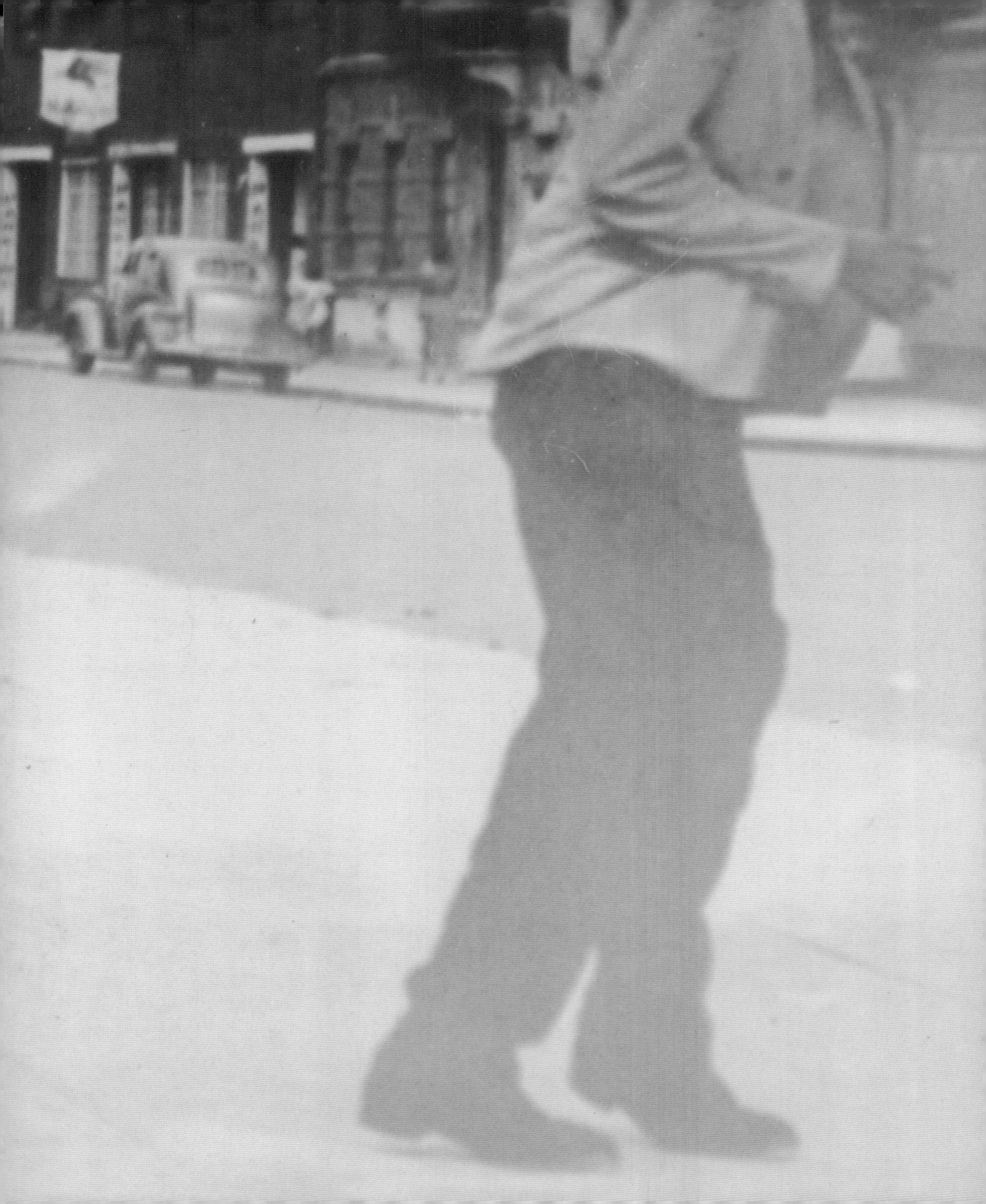

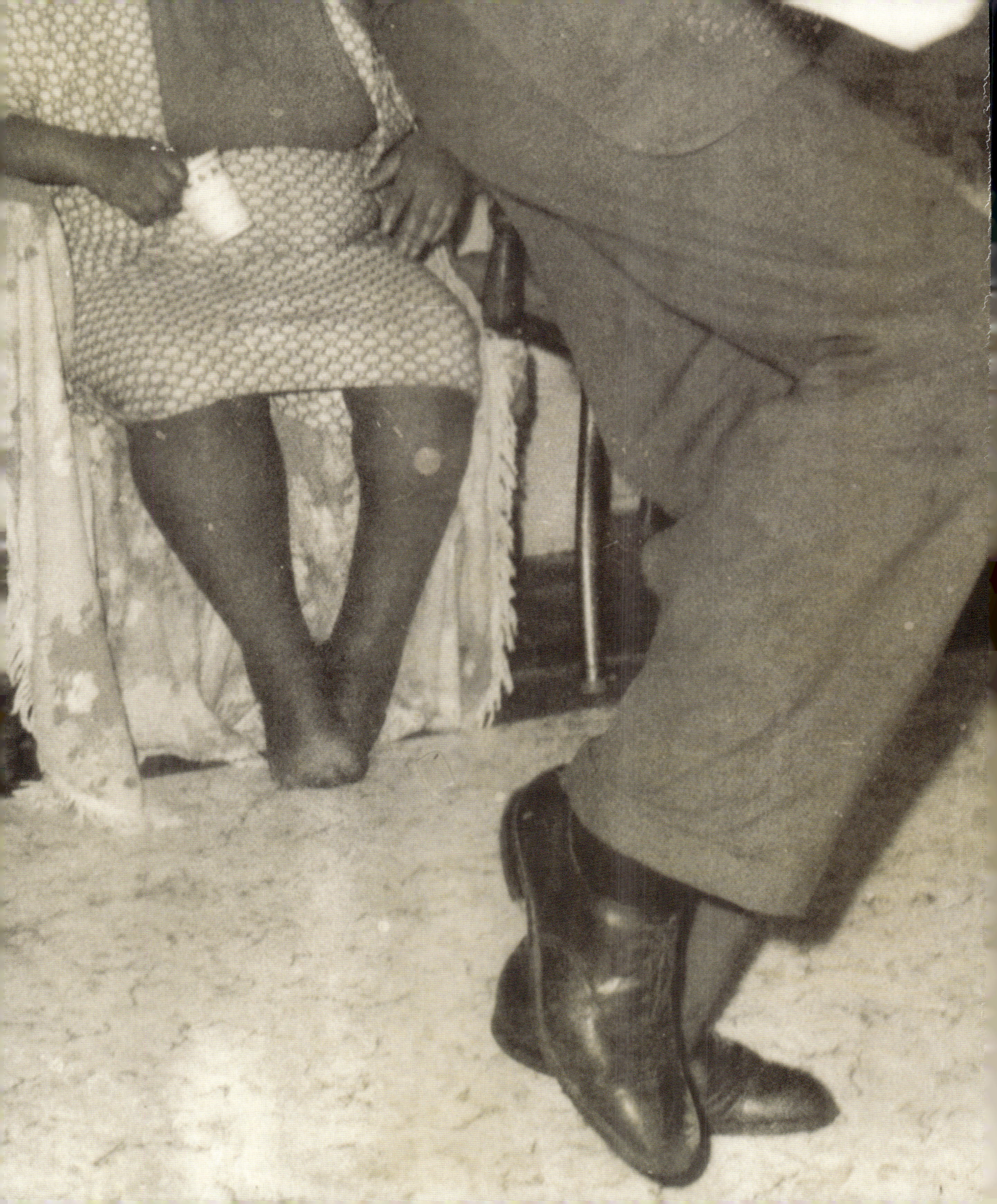

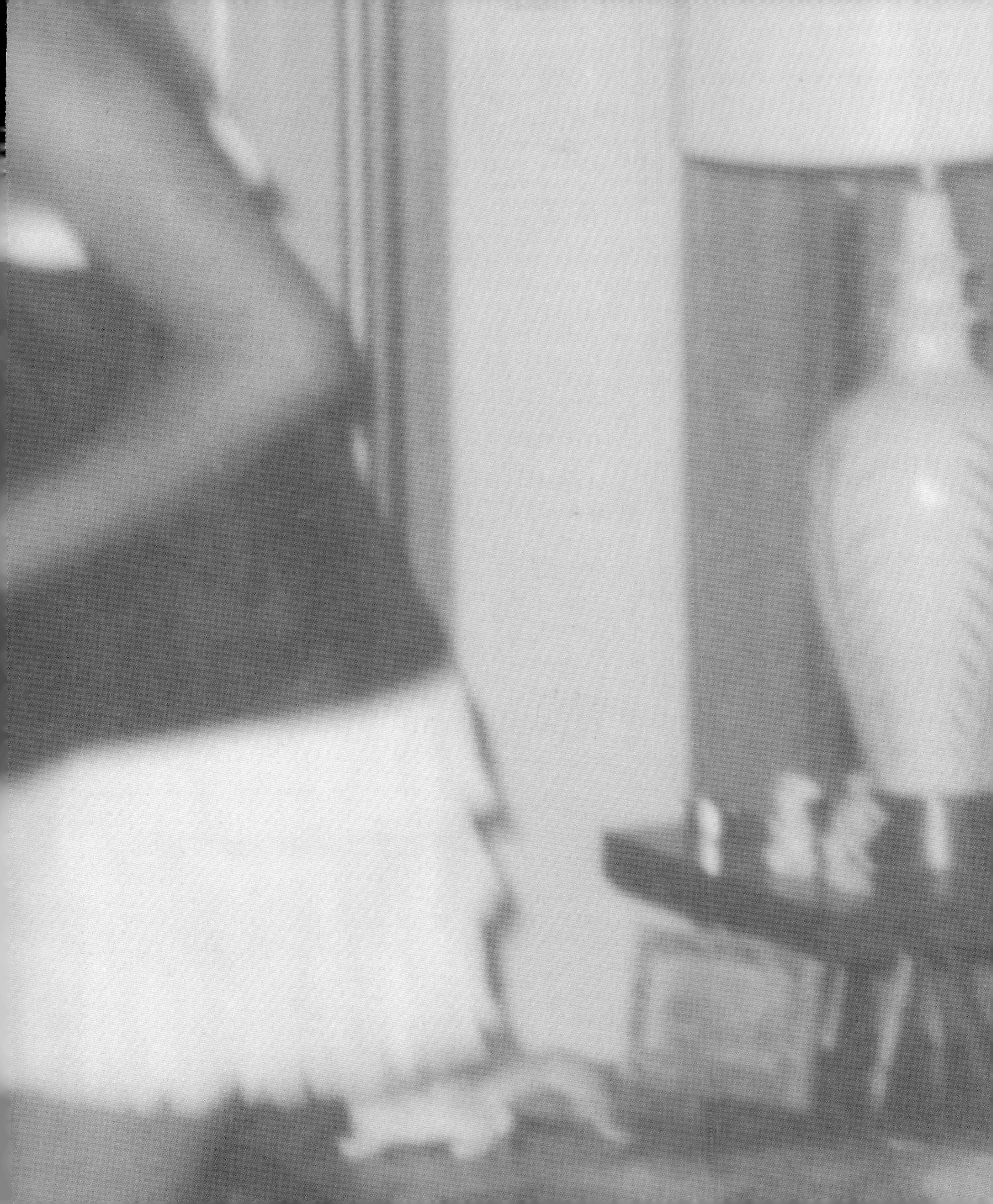

We think our lifetimes last a long time.

They do not.

Jim Linderman would like to thank Dust-to-Digital for the opportunity to share this collection with their audience. Special thanks to Joe Bonomo, a most skillful worker of words, and Martin Venezky who has similar skills with image and presentation. Thank you to the anonymous photographers, musicians and participants within. Their obvious zest allows the photographs to present joy silently, and their humanity gives these humble printed pictures an enormous collective voice. There is not a situation here I would not have enjoyed being part of. Thank you to Janna Rosenkranz and the members of the vintage and found photograph community who have welcomed me to their world of shadow and light.

FIRST EDITION 2014

DESIGN Martin Venezky's Appetite Engineers

DUST TO DIGITAL

PO BOX 54743
ATLANTA, GEORGIA 30308
www.dust-digital.com
ISBN 978-0-9817342-8-6
PRINTED IN CHINA

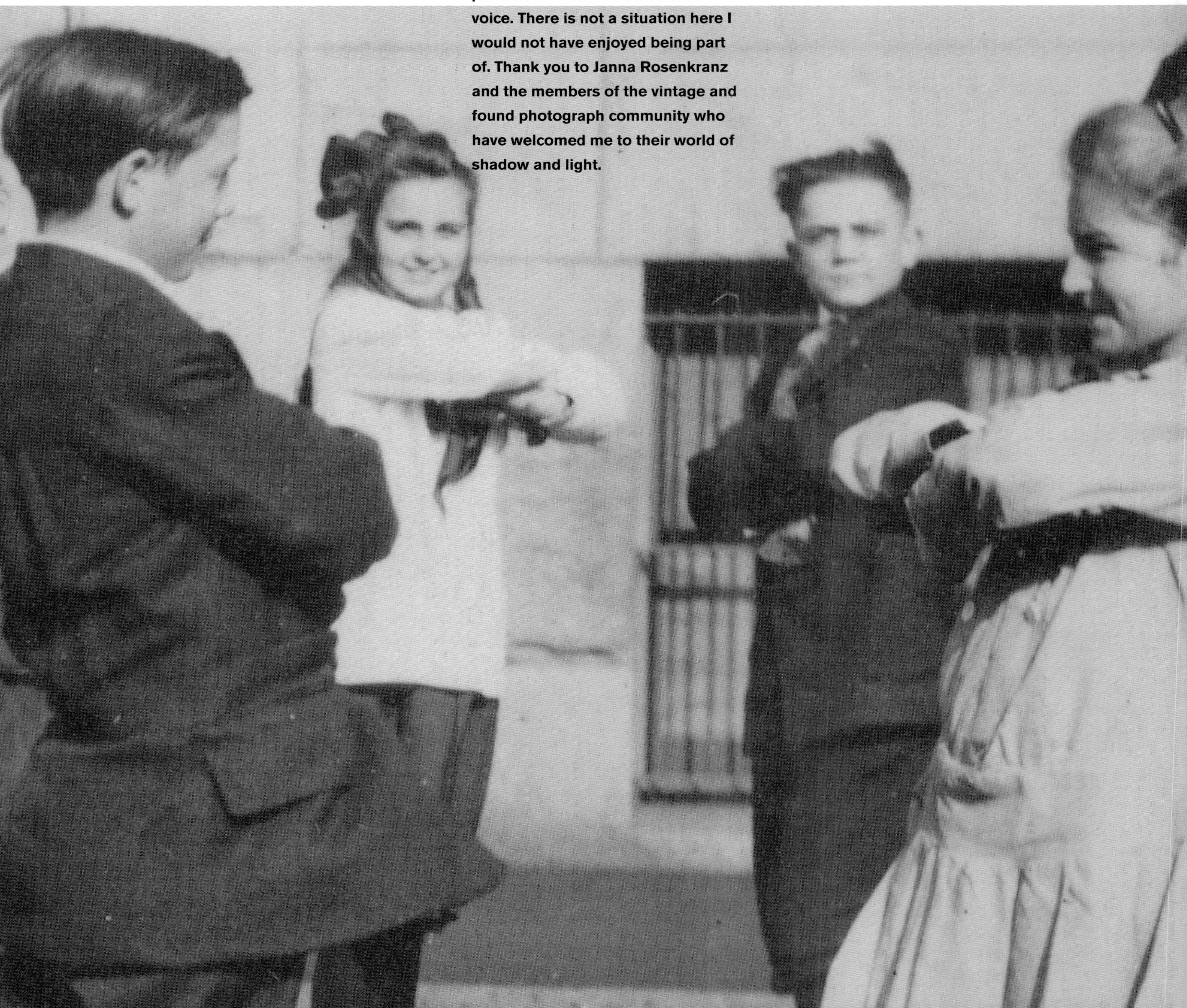

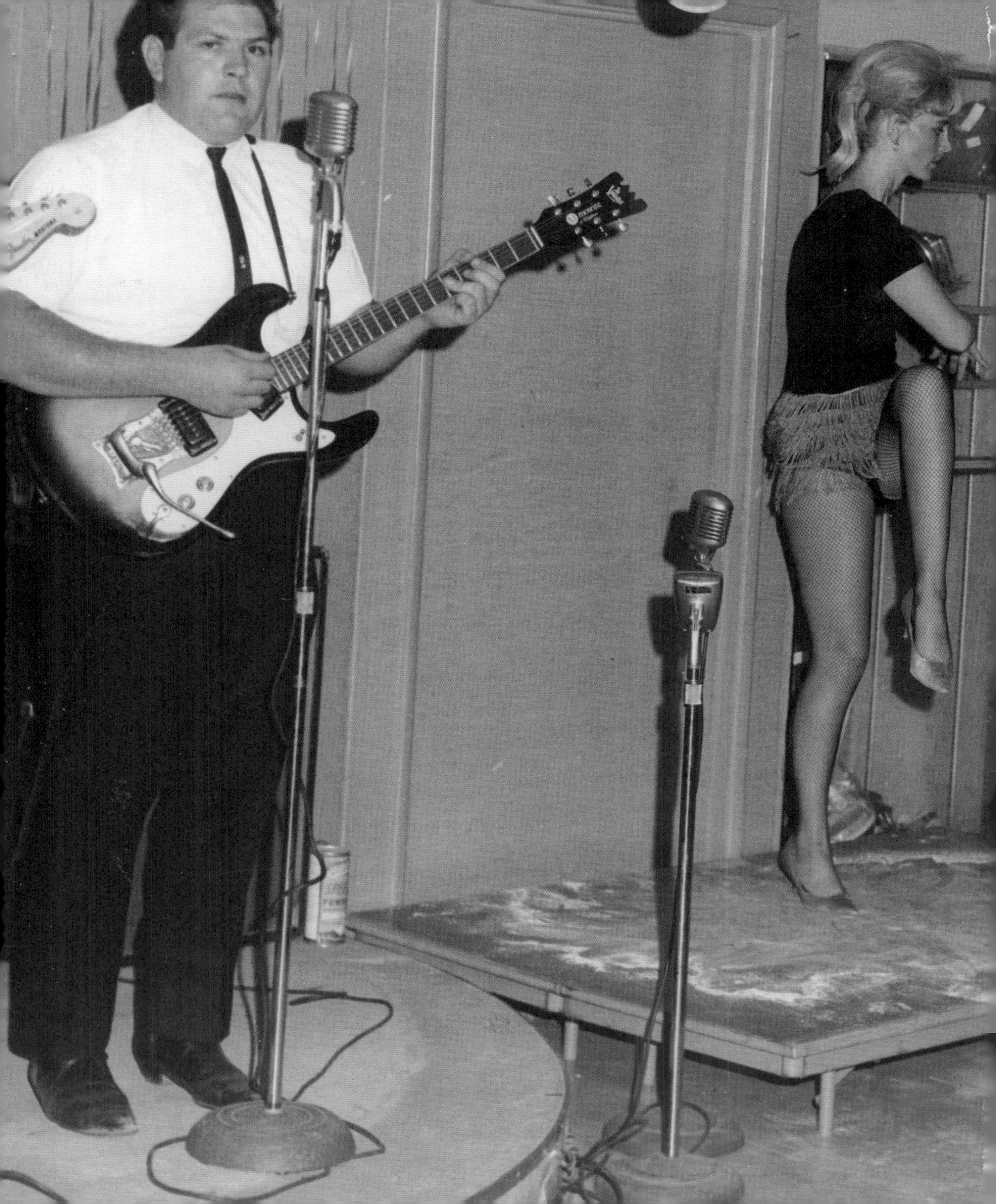